IMAGES of America

EFFINGHAM COUNTY

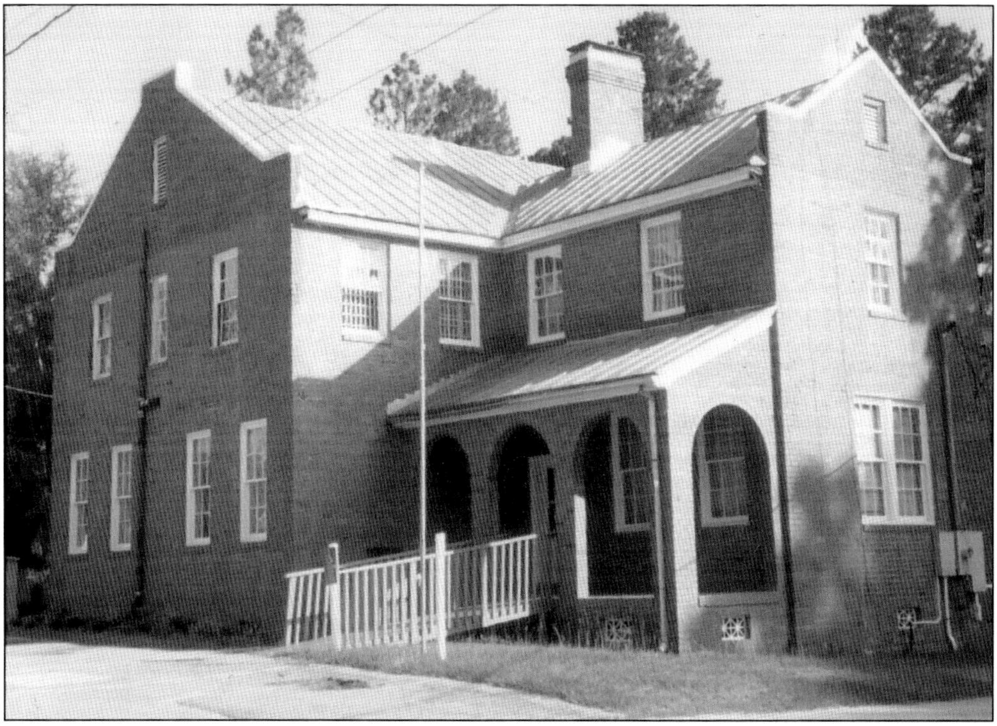

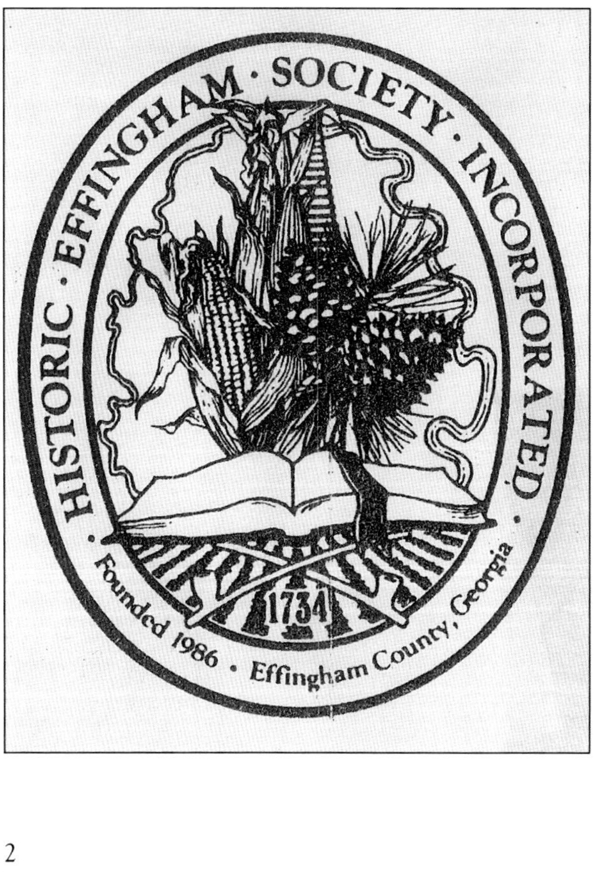

The Effingham "Old Jail Museum." This structure is the home established for the Historic Effingham Society in June of 1994. Built in 1935 by the Works Progress Administration during the presidency of Franklin D. Roosevelt, the building served as the county jail until 1993. At left is the society's seal.

IMAGES
of America

EFFINGHAM COUNTY

Historic Effingham Society

The Historic Effingham Society Committee consists of the following:
Betty R. Waller, Julia E. Rahn, Edna Q. Morgan,
Norman Turner, and Dr. E.B. Mingledorff Jr.

ARCADIA
PUBLISHING

ISBN 978-0-7385-0693-7

Published by Arcadia Publishing
Charleston, South Carolina

Printed in the United States of America

Library of Congress Catalog Card Number: 2001087303

For all general information contact Arcadia Publishing at:
Telephone 843-853-2070
Fax 843-853-0044
E-Mail sales@arcadiapublishing.com
For customer service and orders:
Toll-Free 1-888-313-2665

Visit us on the Internet at www.arcadiapublishing.com

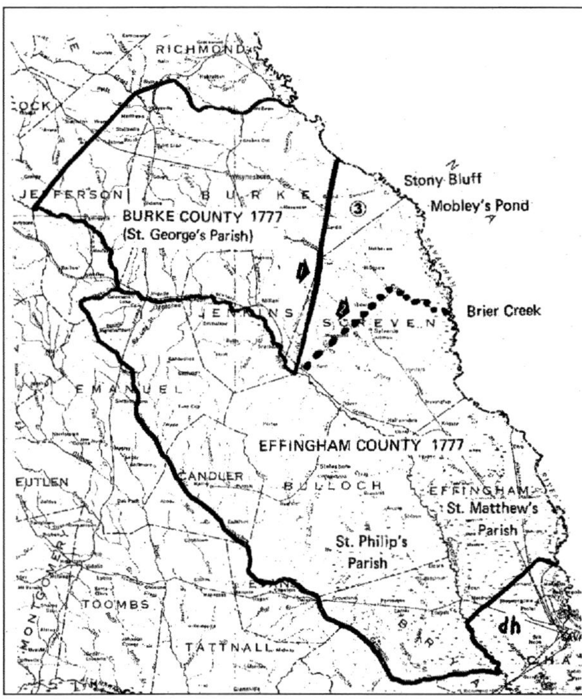

Effingham County

One of the eight original counties created by the Georgia Constitution in 1777 and named for Lord Effingham, Effingham County was originally much larger than the present geographic area.*

Effingham County covered all land lying north and east of the Canoochee River and extended to the Savannah River. The original Effingham territory now falls in parts of Chatham, Bryan, Evans, Candler, Emanuel; and all of Jenkins and Bulloch counties.

Prior to being named a county, the Effingham area was known as "St. Matthews Parish" and "St. Phillips Parish."

A MAP OF EFFINGHAM AS ST. MATTHEW'S PARISH AND ST. PHILLIP'S PARISH.

Contents

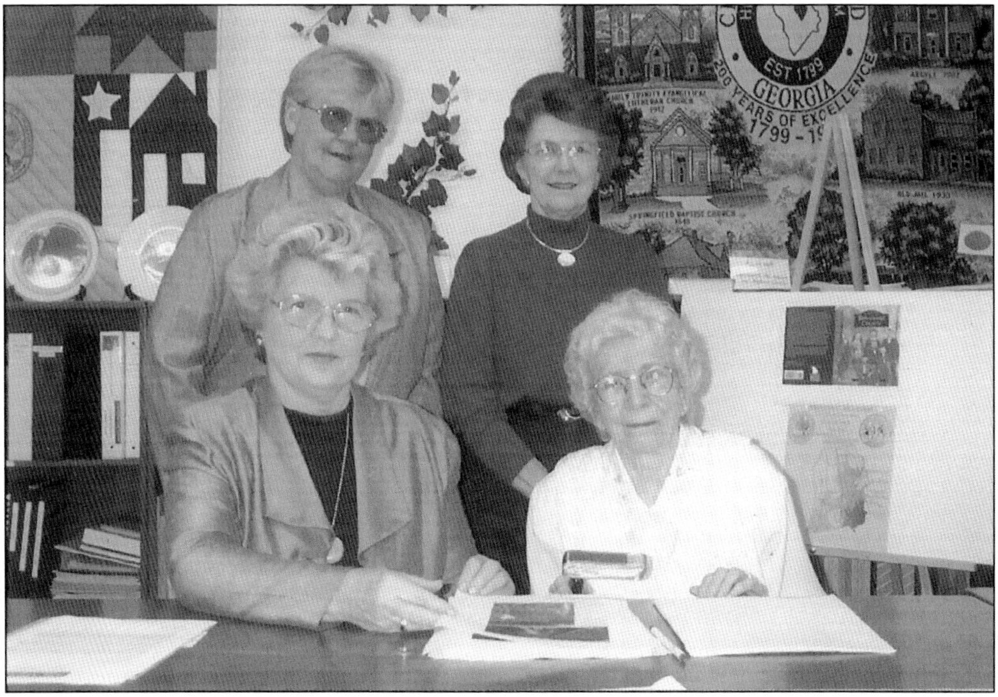

CRITIQUING *IMAGES OF AMERICA: EFFINGHAM COUNTY*. From left to right are (seated) Betty R. Waller and Edna Morgan; (standing) Betty Renfro and Julia Rahn.

ACKNOWLEDGMENTS

This volume would not exist without the assistance of a number of generous and helpful individuals. We are grateful to the many citizens who shared treasured images from their family albums, and the collections given to the Old Jail Museum were the source from which many of these photos came. The Historic Effingham Society calendar, published since 1994, also provided some images. The collections of Rebah Mallory, Dr. Charlton Tebeau, and Daisy K. Rahn were generously given by their family members. Encouragement and endless help in the pursuit of photographs were provided by past society presidents, including Milton Rahn, Gregg Arnsdorff, Herb Jones, Henry "Sonny" Zittrouer, Henry Wilkins, and Betty Renfro. Thanks also go to Susan Exley, Richard Loper, Eddie Browning, Norma Jean Morgan, Lynette Jones, Mr. and Mrs. Marion Jaudon, Toni Freeman, Harry Bird Zittrouer, and Walter Zoller. Many friends of the society have donated copies of photographs and helped us to identify those pictures; their encouragement and support have made *Images of America: Effingham County* possible.

Introduction

Effingham County was one of the eight original counties established by the state of Georgia, and its early settlers were Salzburgers and English colonists coming up from Savannah. Many of the family names you will find in this book are eighth- and ninth-generation descendants of these early inhabitants, whose lifestyle was tempered by British influence.

The folks of Effingham are industrious and faithful in their jobs and livelihoods. They are truly family oriented, as indicated by their wealth of kinfolk and family-supported homes. Many are deeply religious and devoted to their church activities, and within these pages you will see a number of churches pictured. The family farm has become a much rarer thing than it once was, and tree-planted forests are often harvested for supplemental income to industrially employed family breadwinners. Crops of corn, soybeans, and cotton are planted by a limited number of planter-farmers, who rent acreage from family-owned property. Most landowners can trace the ownership of their land over eight generations. The sawmills, once so vast in number, have dwindled to just one large private one in operation in the county. Logging and timber products are transported to the Savannah plants and shipped from the Savannah seaport.

The produce from the farms of Effingham supplies the city of Savannah at the "Old City Market" with the best of vegetables, eggs, chicken, pork, and beef. In return, country folk shopped for seafood, clothing, and housewares in the city. Shopping trips to Savannah continue to be an enjoyable outing for Effingham residents.

Children's lives center around church, school sports, social events, and activities directed by the recreation department. Educational development is the number-one priority of parents and grandparents for their children in Effingham, and schools are currently being built to meet the needs of the influx of new families to Effingham County.

Effingham is a county with a country lifestyle and family values; its residents work hard to meet the challenges of today and tomorrow for its rapidly expanding population.

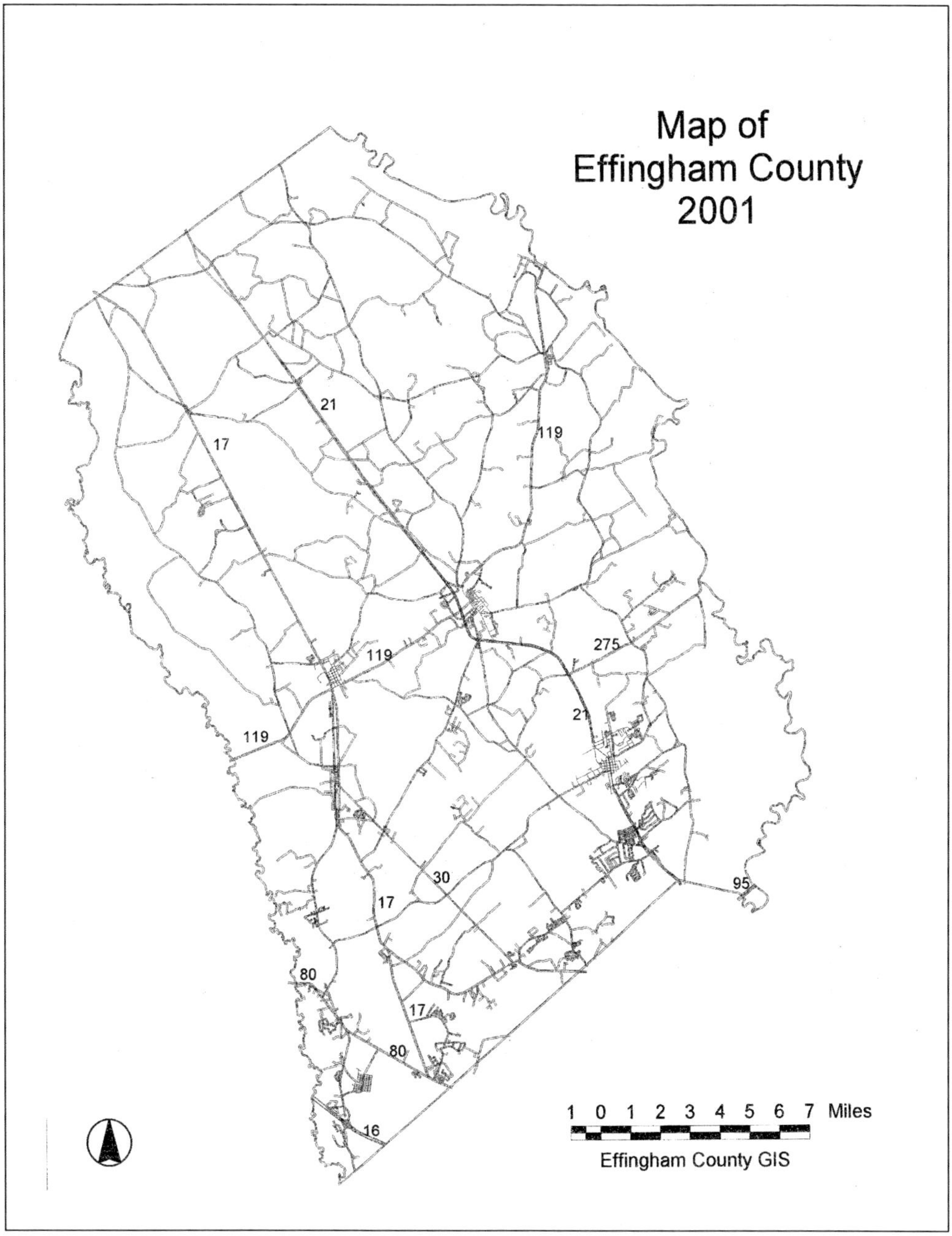

A Map of Effingham County, 2001.

One

Scenes and Historical Places

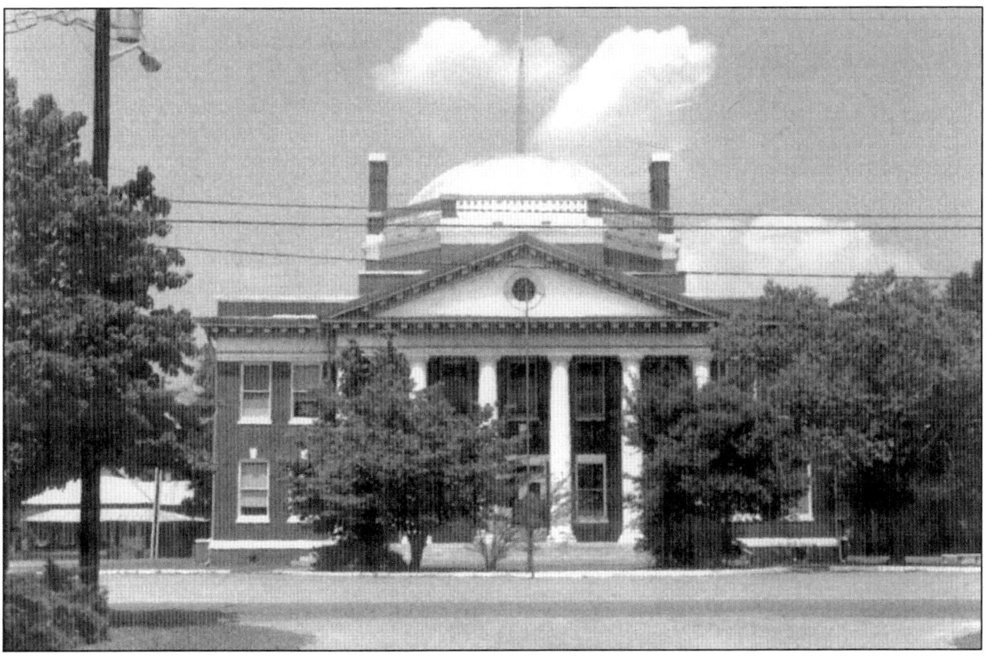

The Effingham County Courthouse. Springfield, being near the center of Effingham County, was designated the county seat in 1799. The county government was instructed by the state legislature to make a survey showing streets, lots, etc. that were to be sold. The money received from the sale of lots was to be used to build a courthouse and a jail. The present courthouse was built in 1908.

An act for laying out a town in the county of Effingham, and authorizing the commiſſi ers of the court-houſe and jail to make ſale of the lots and appropriate the amo thereof, and to diſpoſe of the former court-houſe in Ebenezer.

Preamble.

1. WHEREAS David Hall, Joſhua Loper, Samuel Ryals, Godhelf Sm and Drurias Garriſon, commiſſioners of the court-houſe and jail of county of Effingham, have purchaſed a piece of land for erecting the public bu ings in the county aforeſaid: *Be it therefore enacted by the Senate and Houſe of Rep ſentatives of the ſtate of Georgia in General Aſſembly met, and by the authority of ſame,* That the ſaid David Hall, Joſhua Loper, Samuel Ryals, Godhelf Smith a Drurias Garriſon, commiſſioners as aforeſaid, or a majority of them, or their ſ ceſſors in office, ſhall and may lay out into lots of ſuch ſize as they may think p per, the aforeſaid piece of land, and ſhall ſet up and expoſe to ſale, within ſix mon after the paſſing of this act, the ſaid lots, and make titles thereto; and the mon ariſing from ſuch ſale to be applied to the uſe of building a court-houſe and jail the ſaid county.

Commiſſioners ſhall lay out a town, ſell the lots, make titles, and apply the money to the erection of a court-houſe and jail for the county.

The town to be called Springfield.

2. *And be it further enacted,* That the ſaid town ſhall be known by the name Springfield, and hereafter be the permanent ſeat of public buildings.

Court-houſe in Ebenezer to be ſold.

3. *And be it further enacted,* That the commiſſioners aforeſaid, or a majority them, ſhall and may ſell the court-houſe in Ebenezer, and apply the money as her before directed, any law to the contrary notwithſtanding.

DAVID MERIWETHER, *Speaker of the Houſe of Repreſentatives.*
ROBERT WALTON, *Preſident of the Senate.*

Aſſented to February 7, 1799.
JAMES JACKSON, *Governor.*

THE PROCLAMATION TO ESTABLISH A COUNTY SEAT.

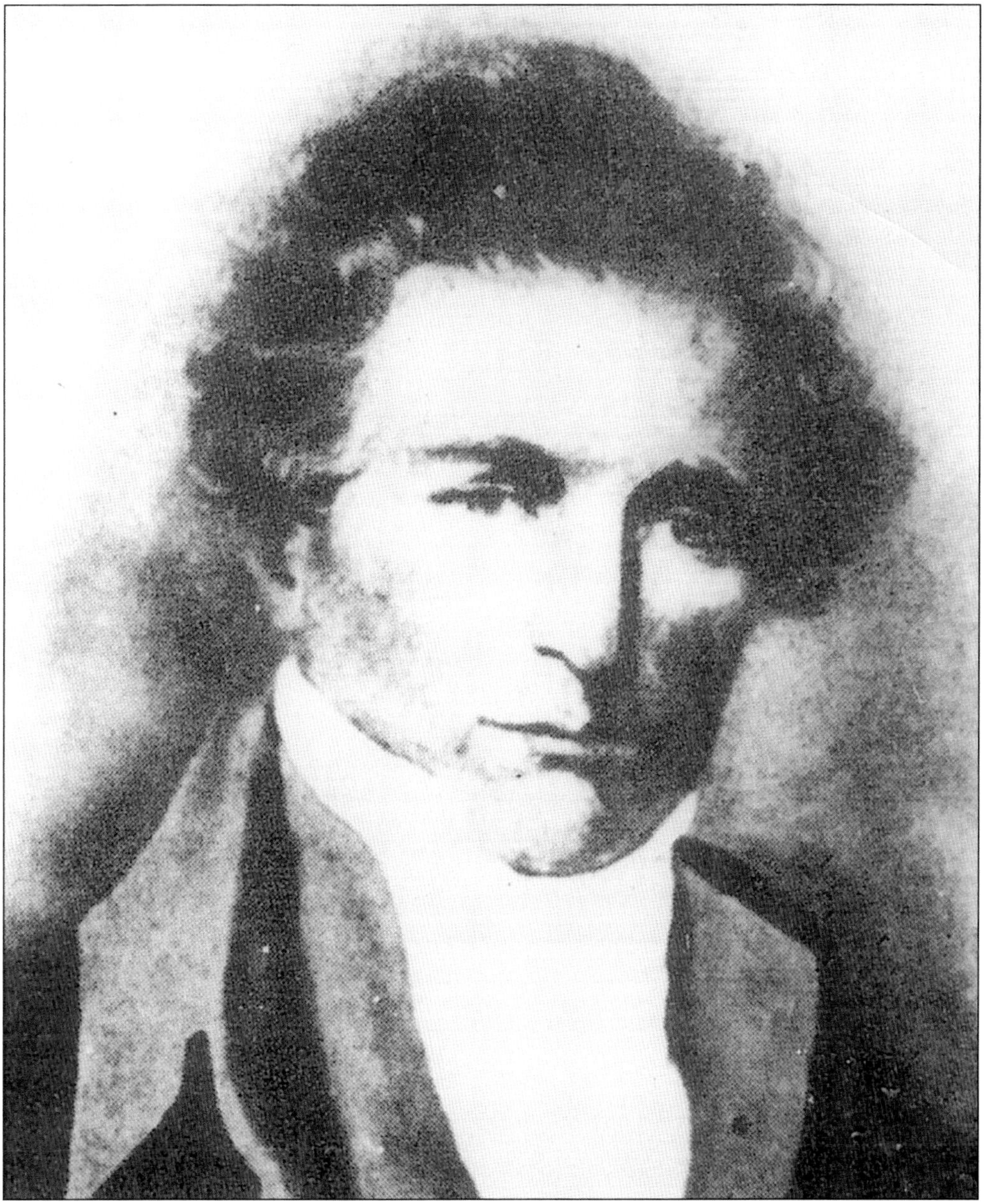

John Adam Treutlen. As a small boy, Treutlen emigrated with his family in a group of Salzburgers to the new colony. After staying with his mother at Vernonburg for a short time, he went to the settlement of Ebenezer in 1747. Like many colonists, Treutlen had a varied career and was a schoolteacher, a surveyor of roads, and a plantation owner. He acquired extensive acreage in Georgia and in South Carolina, across the Savannah River. Truetlen's most notable contributions to the colony and to his state were political. He served three terms in the Common House of the Assembly under British Governor Wright. He participated in the political debate preceding the Revolutionary War and, in 1777, was elected the first governor of the new state of Georgia under the newly approved constitution. "John Adam Treutlen, first Constitutional Governor, has been called a hero of Effingham County, staunch Salzburger, a Mystery Man, and a patriot in Oblivion."—Edna Q. Morgan.

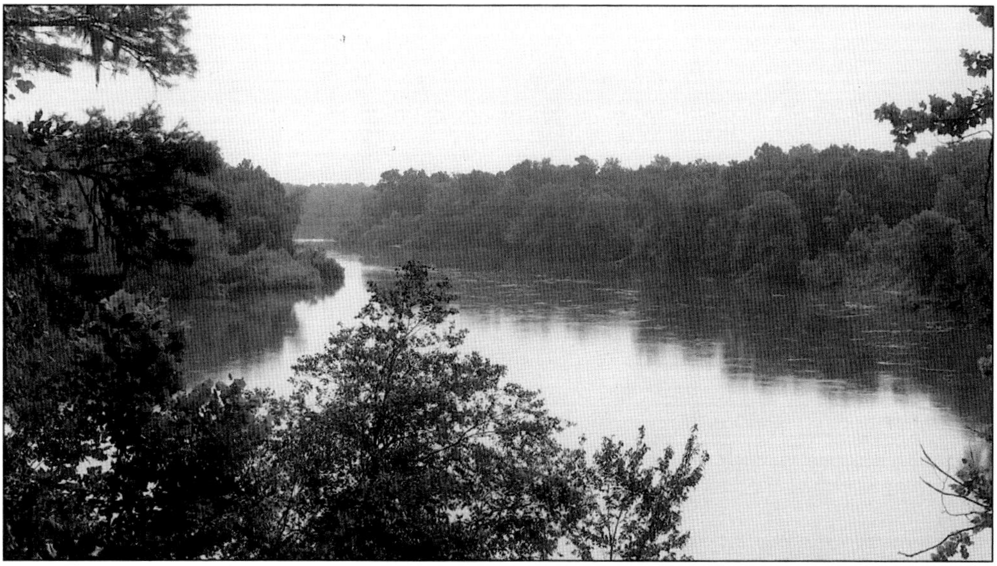

THE SAVANNAH RIVER. Serving as the boundary between Georgia and South Carolina, the Savannah River runs a swift 314-mile course through densely forested lands. The river is created by the confluence of the Tugaloo and Seneca Rivers. Recreational water sports are enjoyed here, and the river is stocked with bass, shad, bream, and catfish. This scene was captured at Frying Pan Landing, an old steamboat stop.

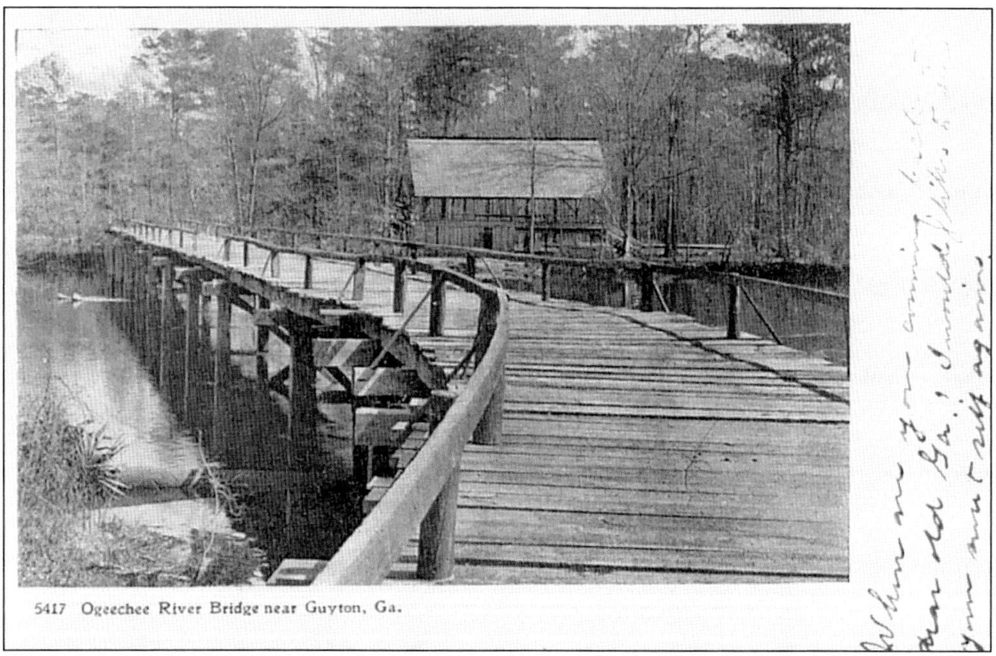

THE OGEECHEE RIVER NEAR GUYTON. The Ogeechee River flows along the western boundary of Effingham County. The 250-mile-long river extends from Greene County southwest to Ossabaw Sound, where it flows into the Atlantic Ocean between Ossabaw and Wassaw. With thickly forested banks, and its quiet charm still unspoiled, the river is extravagantly beautiful and a joy to fishermen. Its shining black waters are filled with redbreast, catfish, silver mullet, black bass, and rock fish.

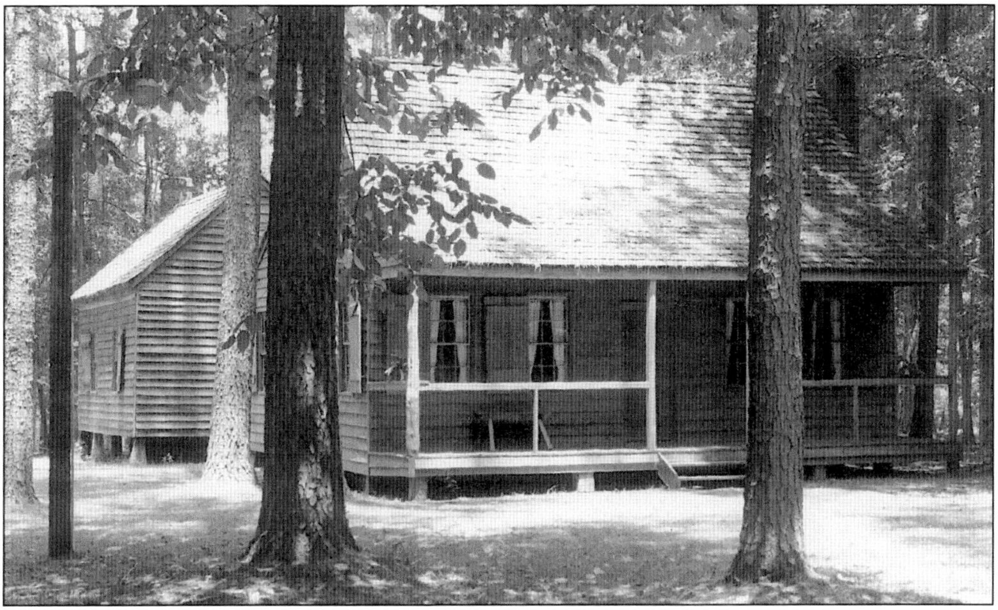

THE OLD SALZBURGER HOUSE. This is the last standing structure in the town of Ebenezer other than the church. In 1855, the pastor of Ebenezer Church wrote that there were two houses and the church still remaining in the old town. In the late 1800s, Marion Waldhouer bought the building and moved it about two miles from Ebenezer. John Fail and his wife are the last people to have lived in the house. After their death, it was given to the Salzburger Society, moved back to Ebenezer in 1973, and it now serves as a museum of early settlement days.

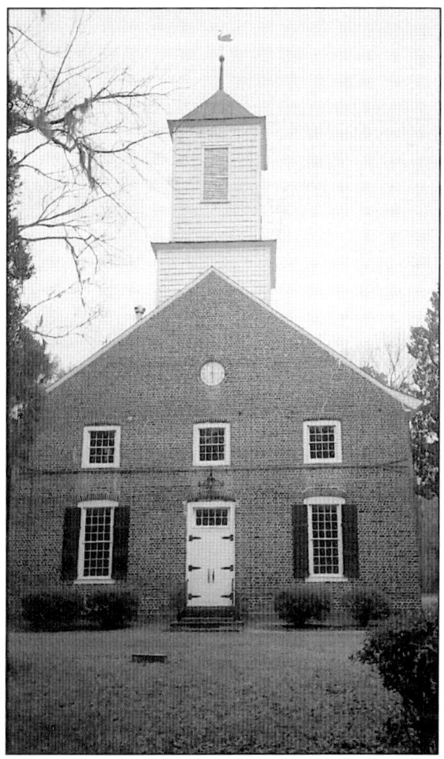

THE JERUSALEM LUTHERAN CHURCH. Located on the banks of the Savannah River some 30 miles above Savannah, this church was built between 1767 and 1769. It was constructed of materials prepared by the Salzburgers themselves—the bricks were made from clay deposits near the church site. The church is 80 feet by 60 feet with an interior balcony. The congregation was organized in Augsburg, Germany, after the group's exile from Salzburg, Austria in 1733. Rev. John Martin Bolzius and Rev. Israel Christian Gronau served as pastors at Ebenezer. The first four transports of Salzburger exiles arrived at Savannah, Georgia on March 12, 1734. They founded the first Sunday school in 1734 and the first orphanage in 1737. The church is now part of the Southeastern Synod of the Lutheran Church in America.

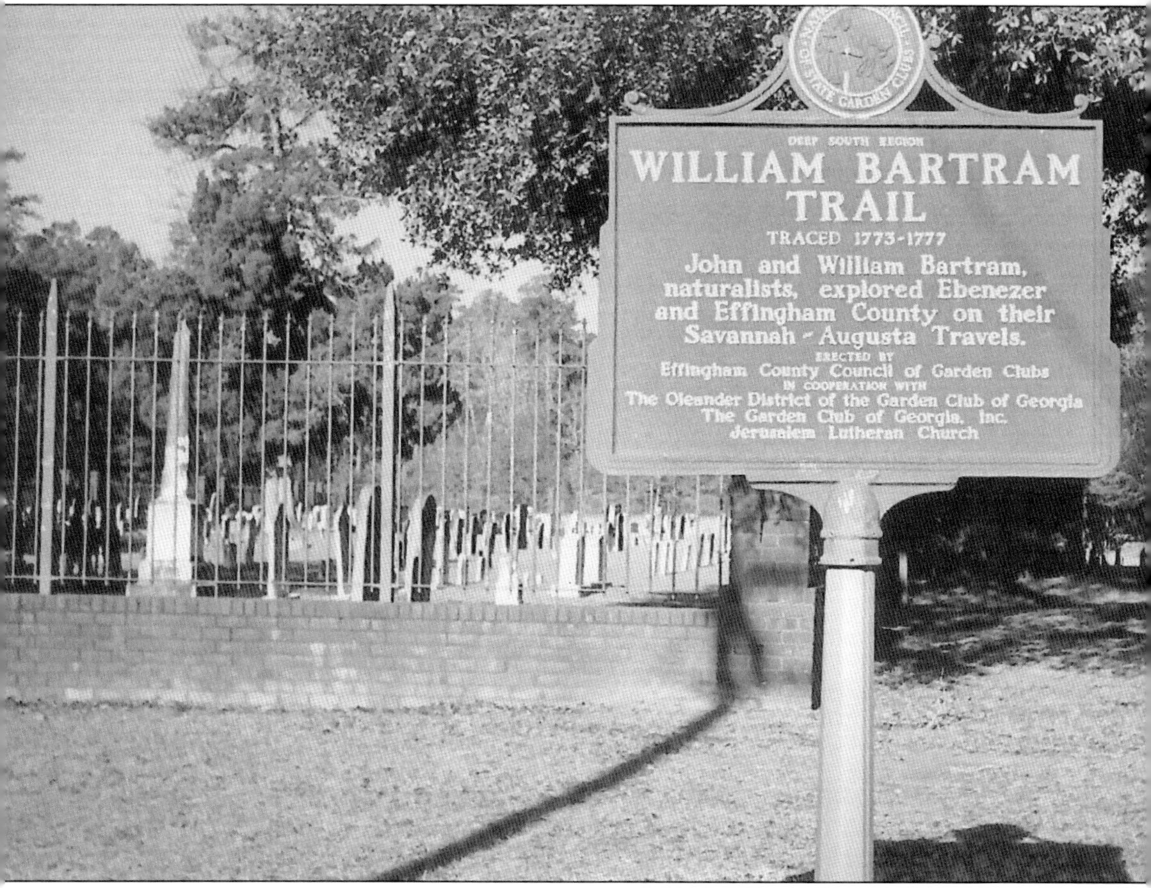

THE WILLIAM BARTRAM MARKER. John Bartram and his son William were some of America's first botanists, ornithologists, and conservationists. They made numerous drawings of plant and animal life and are credited with introducing hundreds of plants to American and European gardens. Between 1765 and 1773, the Bartrams traversed the Old Augusta Road between Savannah and Augusta along the Savannah River. The tulip tree or tulip poplar (Liriodendron tulipifera) and the flame or yellow azalea (Rhododendrum calendulaceum) were especially noted in Effingham. The Bartram Trail in Georgia follows the coast from the Florida line to Savannah, up the Savannah River to Augusta, to North Carolina, and back across the state. It was designated a National Historic Trail in July 1982.

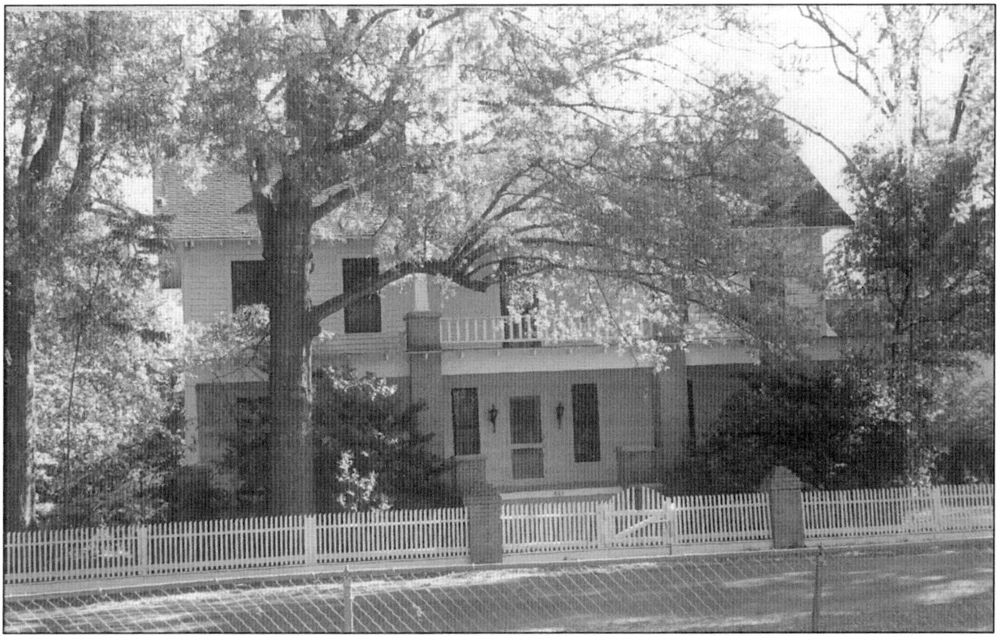

The Ramsey House. The Ramsey House in Springfield is rumored to have been a stopping off point for General Sherman's troops on the way to Savannah. It was reportedly built by Dr. Cheatam Wilson, who served Effingham as a dentist in the early 1900s. In later years, it became the home of Sen. H.N. Ramsey and Mr. and Mrs. Harry Ramsey. It is presently owned by Ed and Carolyn Ramsey McGinness, who live in Texas. The home is located on Oak Street.

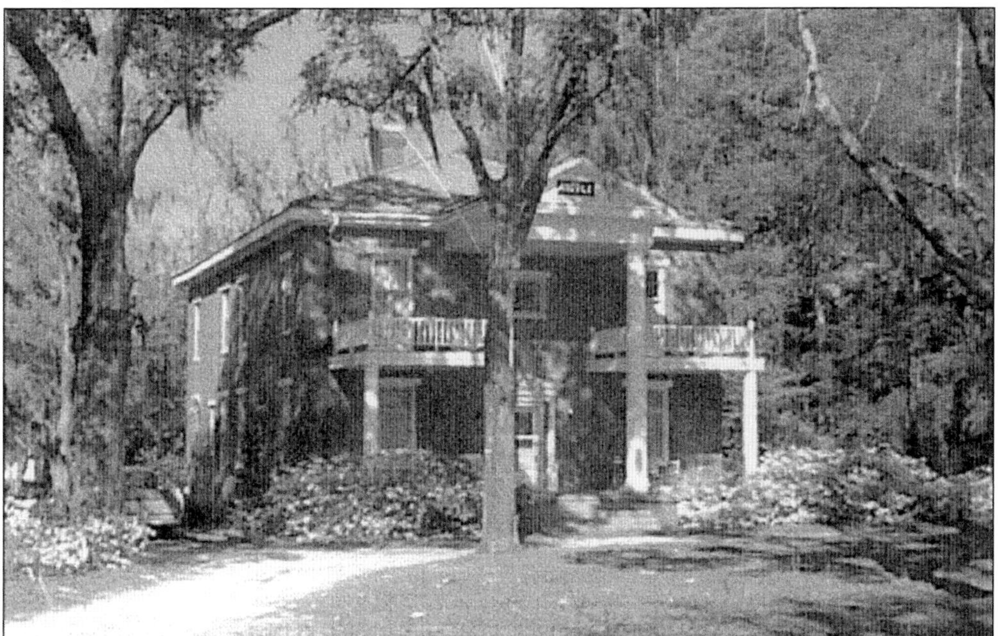

The J.W. McCareney Home. J.W. McCareney was a Virginian who came to Springfield to open a bank. Built in 1911 by Jim Tebeau, the building became the home of Dr. Walter D. Beckwith, a dentist, in 1919.

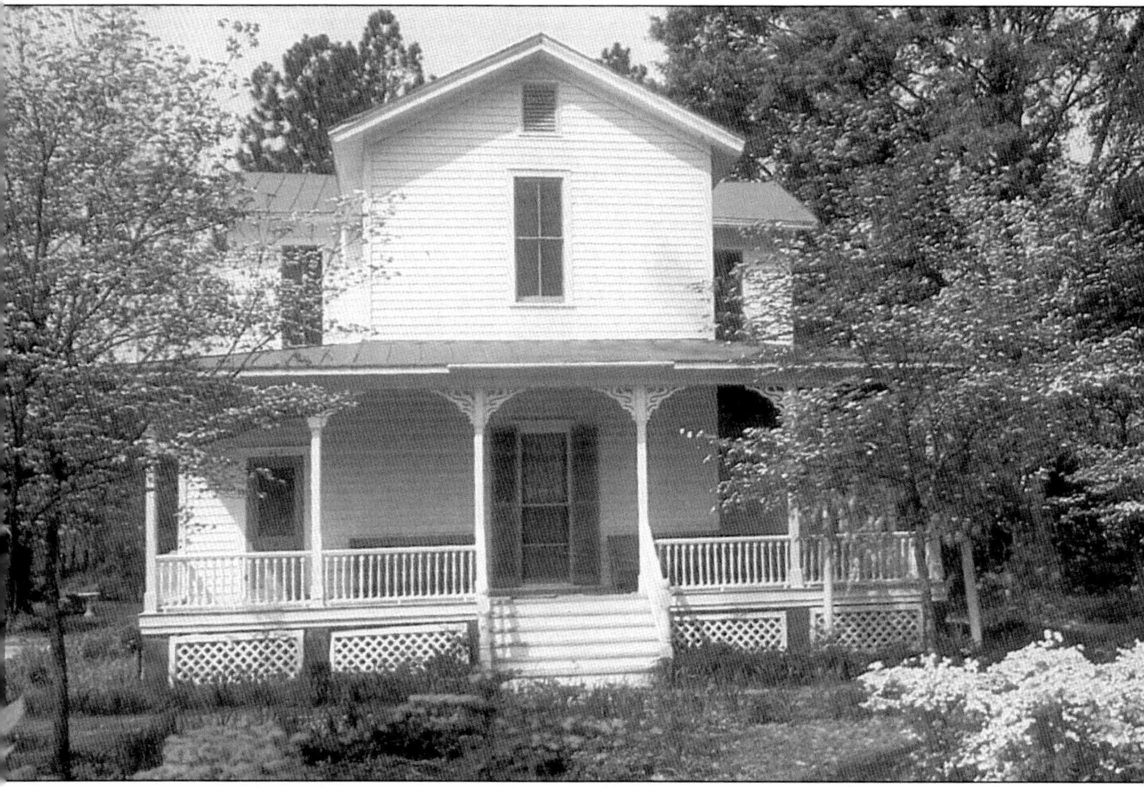

THE CARTIN-GRIER-TODD HOME, 407 CHURCH STREET, GUYTON. This home was built in 1884 by James E. Blackshear.

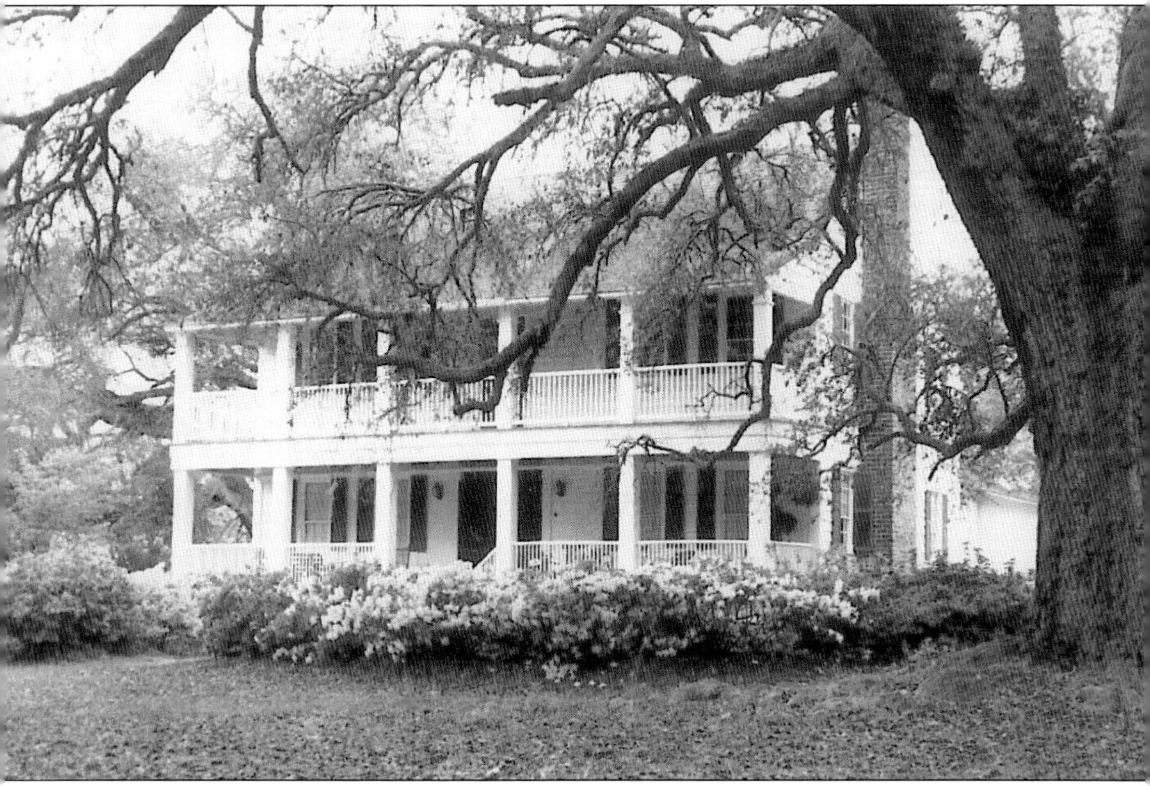

THE GNANN-SECKINGER HOME. The Gnann-Seckinger residence, located in rural Effingham County, was built in 1858 for Frederick Gnann on land acquired by his father, Benjamin Gnann, and has been lived in continuously by their descendants.

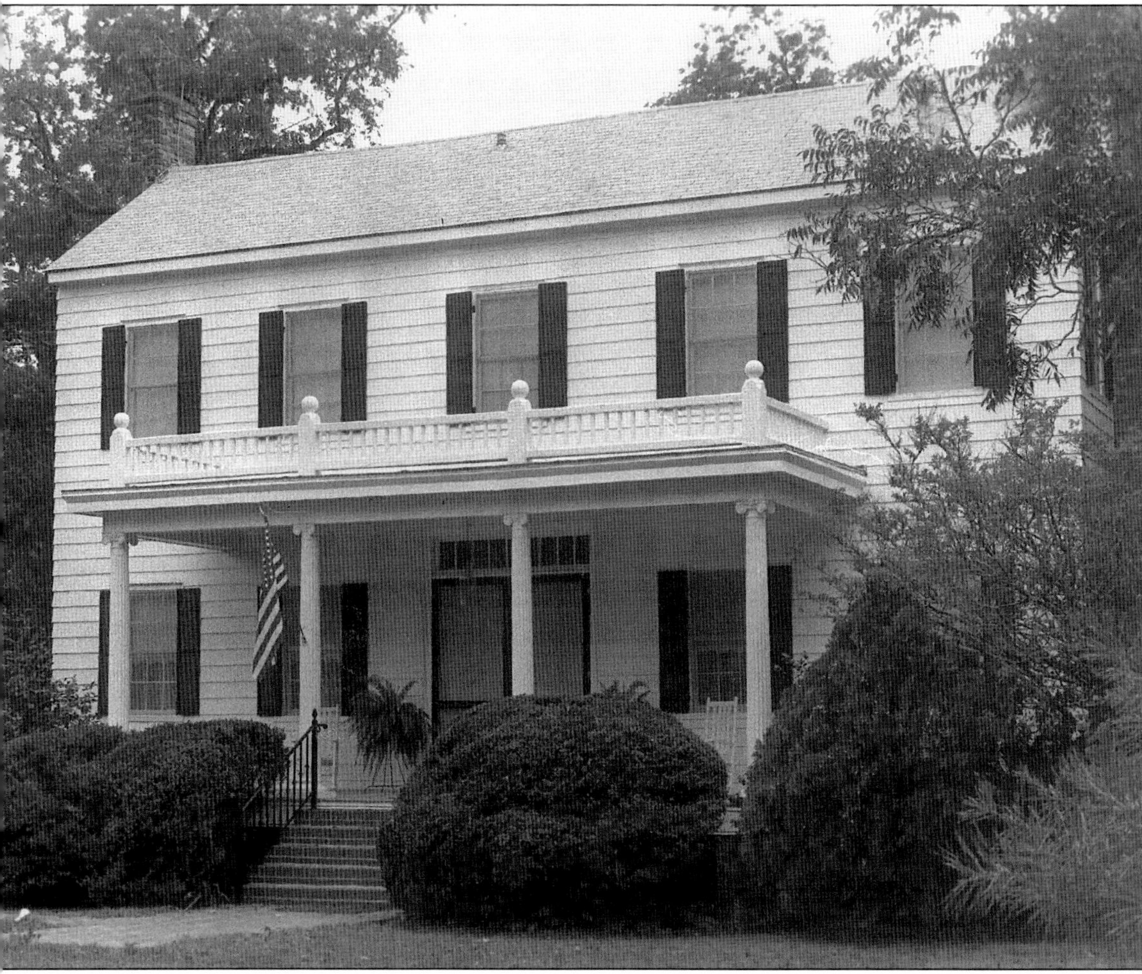

THE CLYO HOME OF ASHLEY AND NORMA JEAN MORGAN. This house was built *c.* 1830 by Judge John Gindrat Morel. Mr. Morel married a great-granddaughter of Gov. John Adam Treutlen, the first governor of Georgia. The plantation home is named Mount Pleasant.

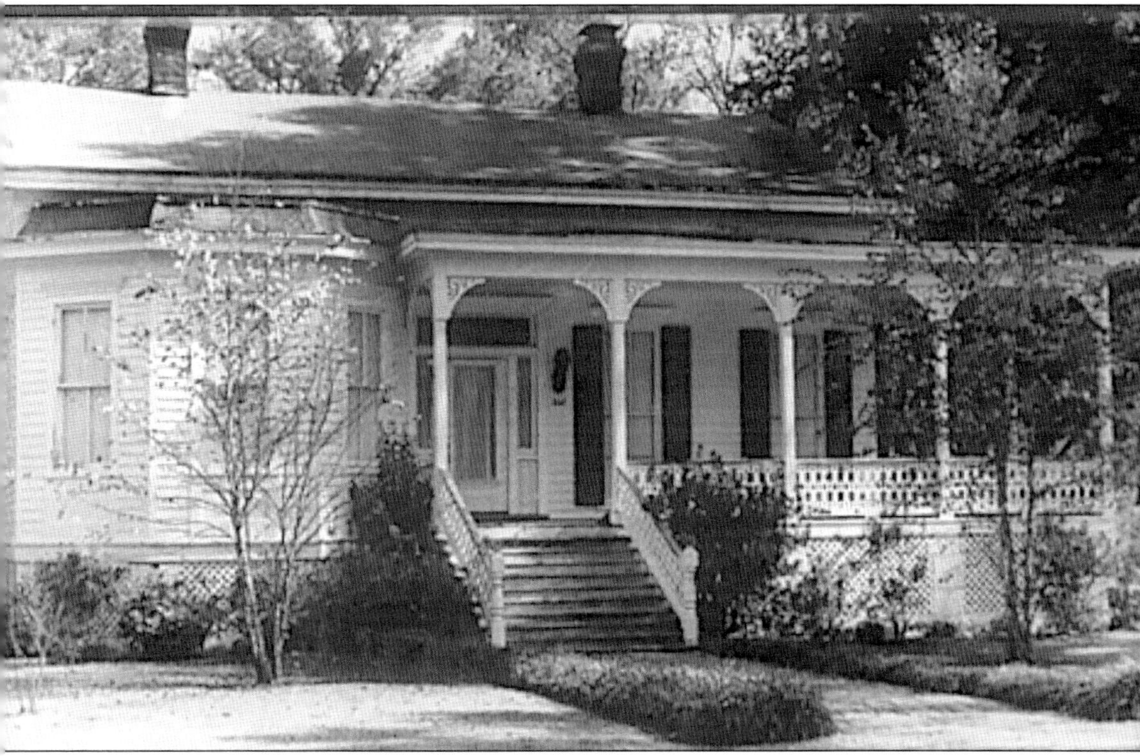

THE EDWARD BIRD-ARDEN HOME. The Edward Bird-Arden Home is one of the over 80 houses that make up the Guyton Historic District, which is listed on the National Register of Historic Places. The town of Guyton became a summer home for many Savannah residents during the late 1800s. Each December, the Guyton Historical Society sponsors the Guyton Historical Tour at Christmastime.

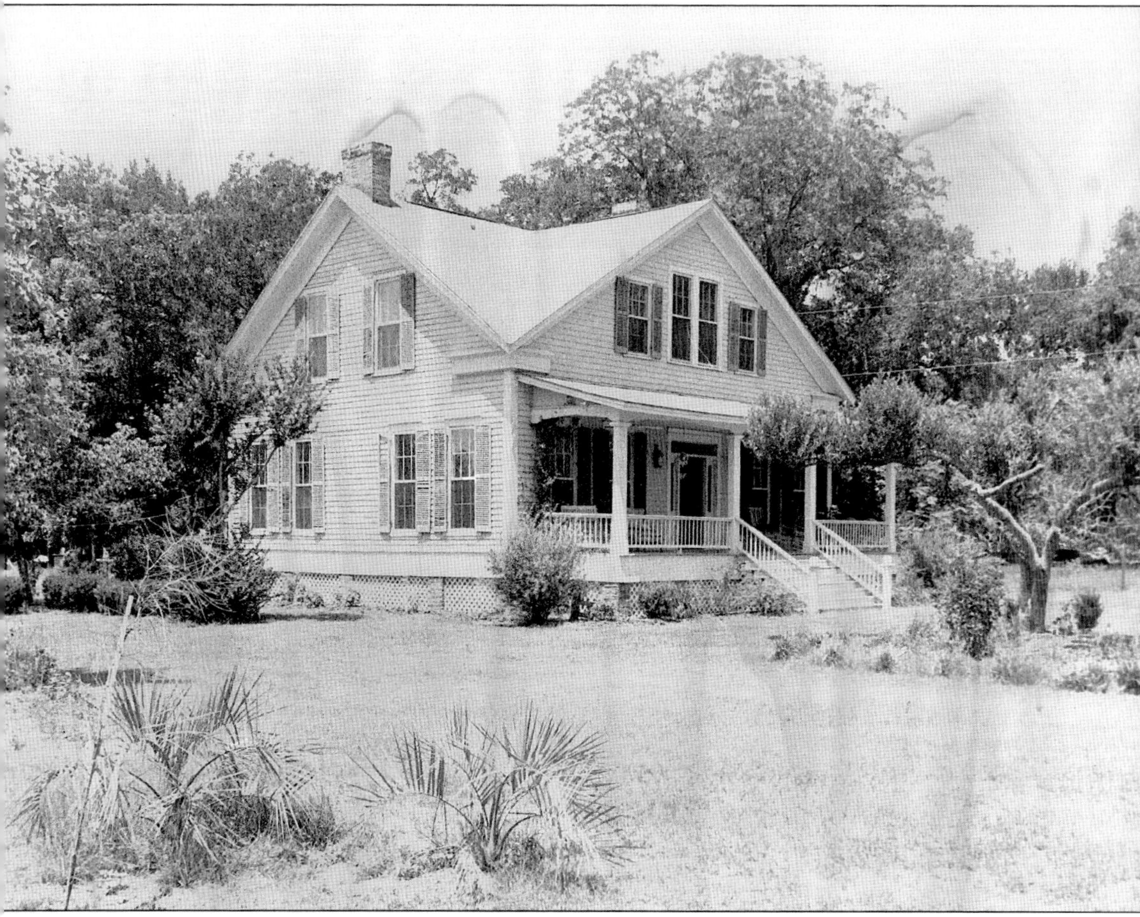

Woodlawn Planation. One of the oldest homes in Effingham County was built west of Historic Guyton in the 1830s. This house, located at Woodlawn Plantation, is a former home to Effingham's first state senator. During the Civil War, the house and surrounding lands were known as Camp Davis, an important training camp for the Confederacy. The house was completely remodeled with the addition of Victorian features and a second story in the late 1890s. Currently, the house has been fully restored with the original hand-planed woodwork and styling indicative of the lower South carefully preserved.

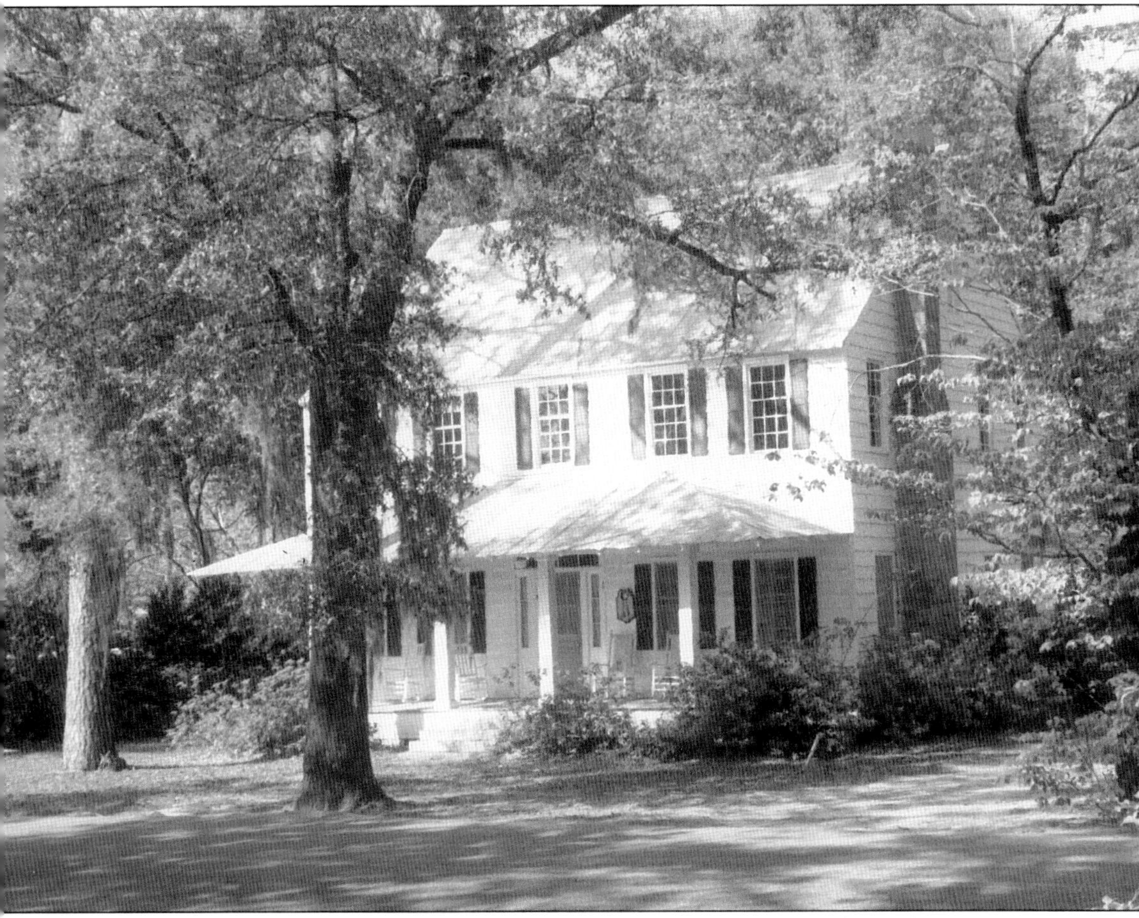

THE JONES-SMITH HOUSE IN SPRINGFIELD. The Jones-Smith House, built in the early 1800s near the courthouse, was owned by the Jones family in early Springfield. It was said that Brad Jones was hung for being sympathetic to the Northern cause in the 1860s. The house was operated as a "public house" during the 1830s. Later, Mrs. Ethelyn Mock bought the home and passed ownership to her daughter Monteen.

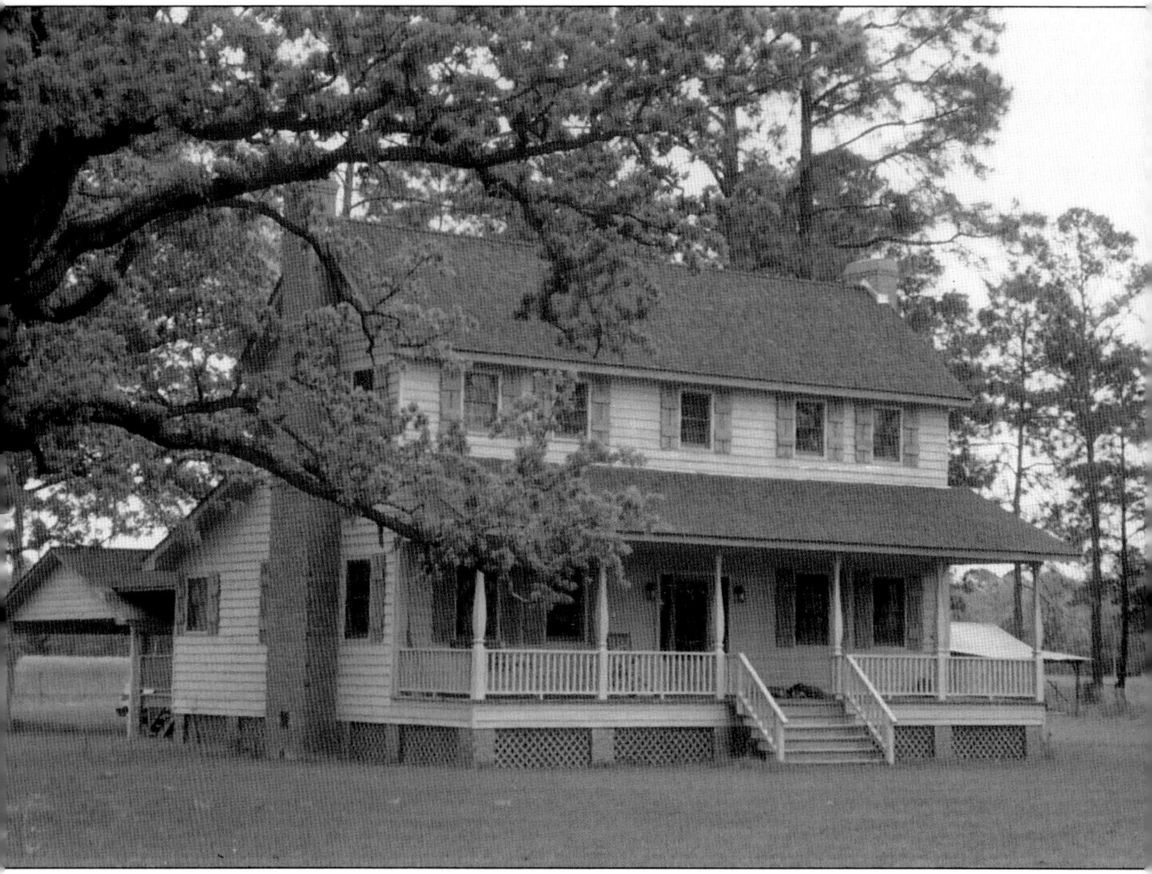

ROSE HILL. The home of Charles W. "Bucky" Morel Jr., located on Old Augusta Road in north Effingham, near the Screven County line, was once the home of Rev. Joseph C. Edwards. Known as "Rose Hill," it was built in 1812, just north of Shawnee. It had been a beautiful old homestead to many people through the years and was also known as the George Thompson Family Home. In 1991, Bucky moved it to its present location and began a restoration that took about two years to complete. The structures is a fine example of 1800s carpentry, as most of it is held together by pegs.

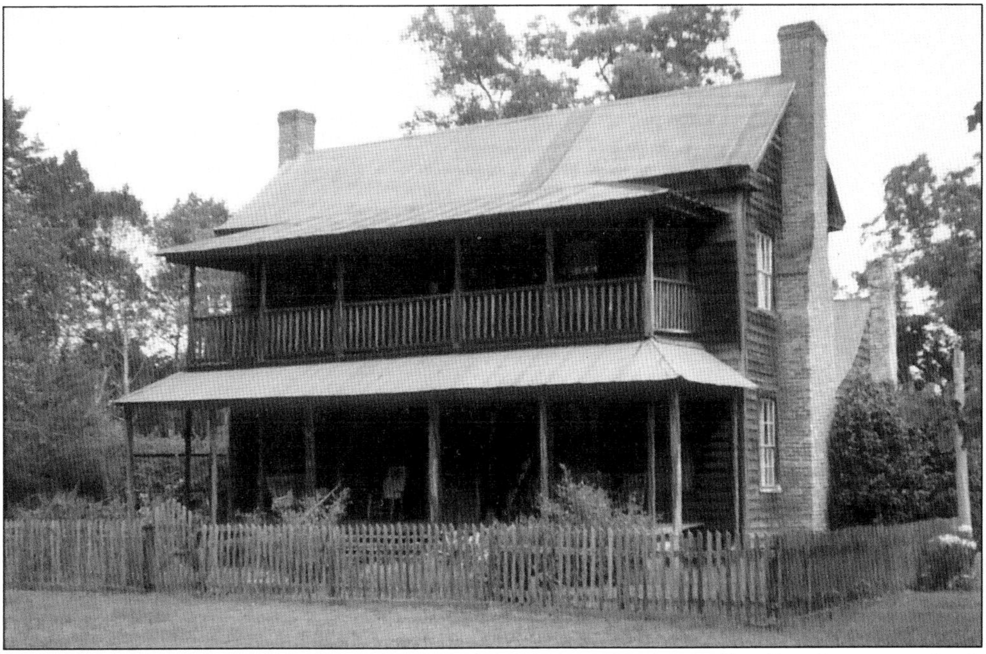

THE REISSER-ZOLLER FARM. The rear part of the present Reisser-Zoller Farmhouse was built in 1875 by Virgil Herbert Reisser, who married Ella V. Gnann in 1879. Between 1880 and 1897 the couple had five children. Around 1900 they built the second part of the farmhouse and connected it to the orginal house. The Reisser-Zoller Farm is the only farm in the county that is on the National Historical Register. In 1993 this farm received the Centennial Heritage Farm Award for its listing on the National Historical Register and farmed continuously for over 100 years by the same family. Walter M. Zoller, the owner of the farm, has lived on the farm since 1926.

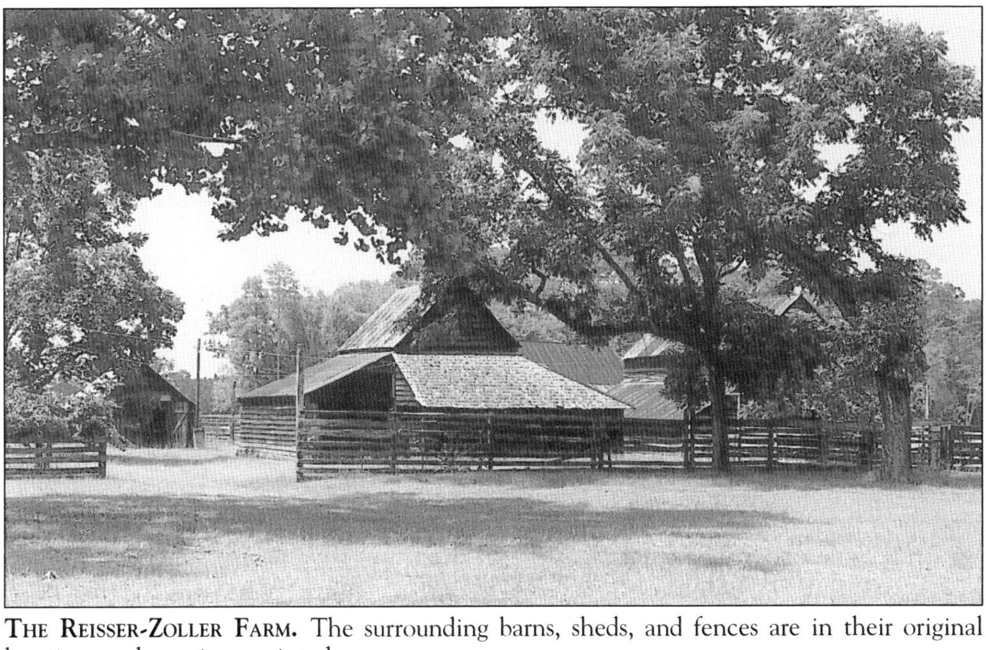

THE REISSER-ZOLLER FARM. The surrounding barns, sheds, and fences are in their original locations and remain unpainted.

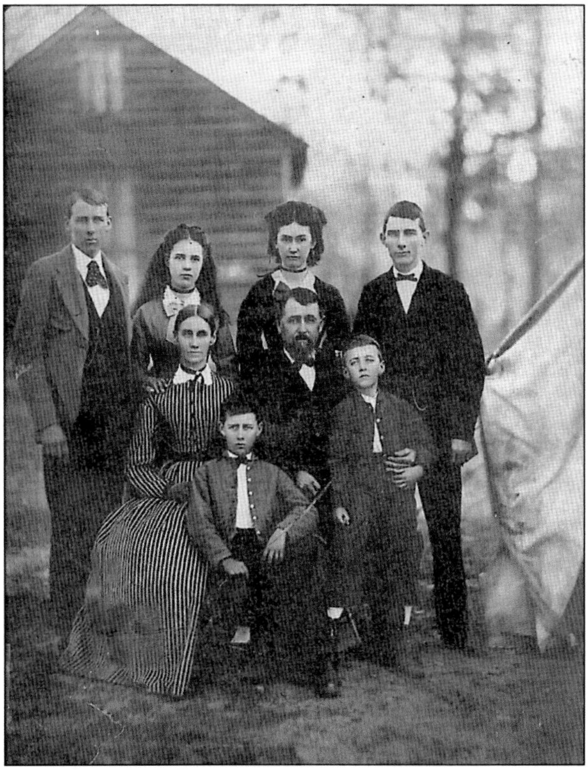

The Original Reisser-Zoller Farmhouse. The two-room house at left was the starter house for the Reissers, Virgil and Ella. Later, the family grew with the additions of Janie, Berta, Elice Herbert, and Annie Mae and this part served as the kitchen and dinning room after the front section was added to the two-story structure. The building was placed on the National Register of Historic Places in 1989.

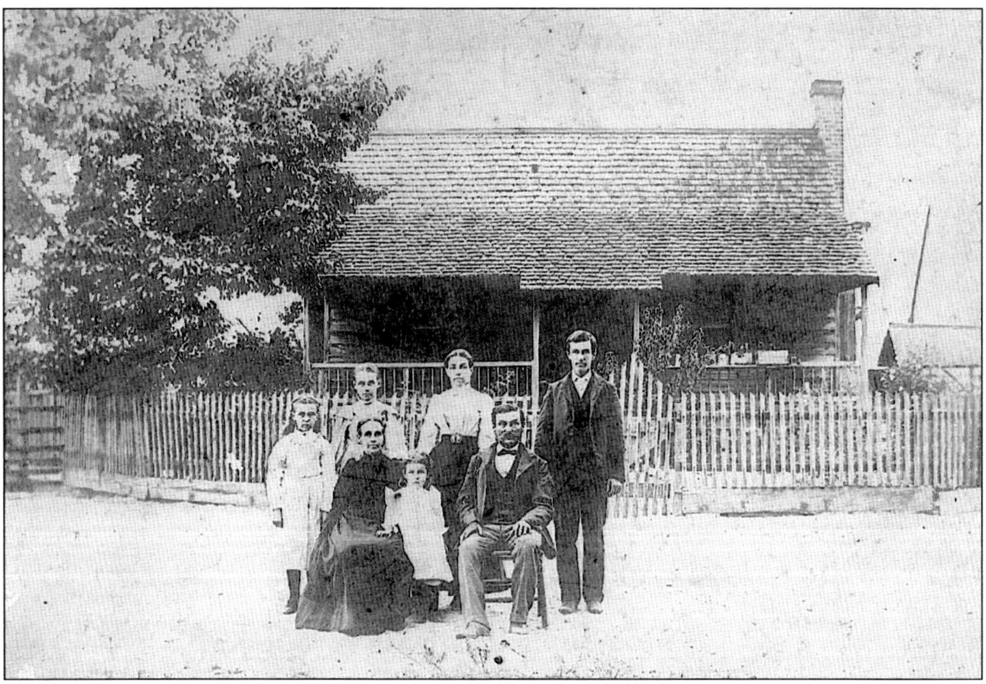

Ella Gnann Reisser's Family. From left to right are as follows: (front row) Johnny, Rebecca Dasher Gnann (mother), Annie Mae, George Bergman Gnann (father); (standing) Albert, Ella, cousin Bell, and Martin.

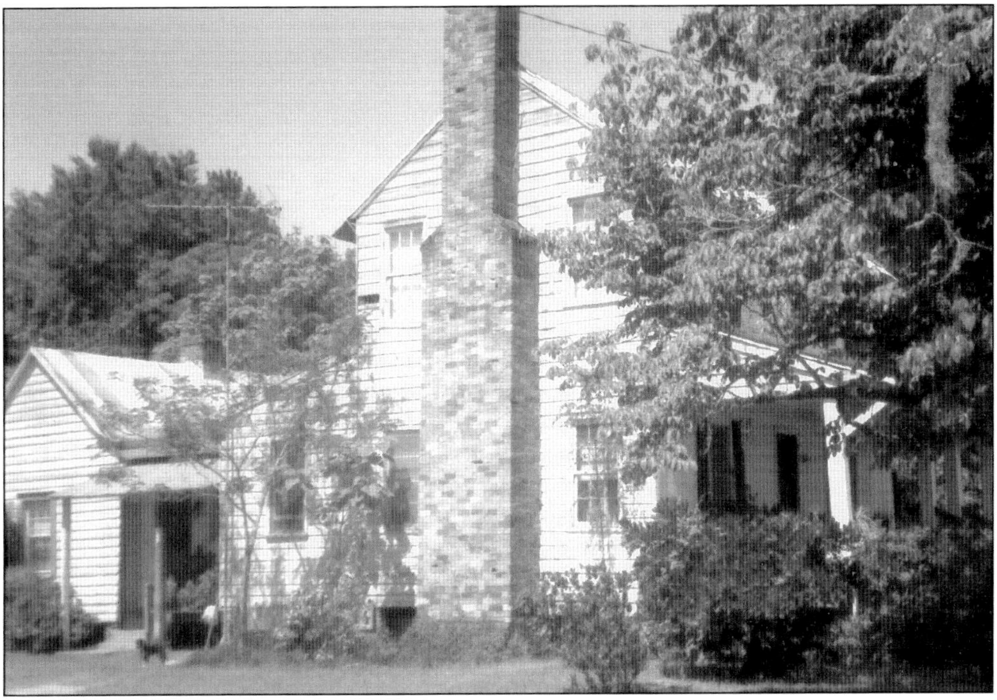

THE MINGLEDORFF FARM. This home was built in 1855 and is located on the Clyo-Kildare Road. Norman Mingledorff married Georgia A. Dasher, and they moved into this house when it was new, about six years before the War between the States. It has always remained in the Mingledorff family. When Sherman's troops marched through this area, the family's cattle, mules, and hogs were hidden in the swamp, and their meat was stored in the attic. The photograph below shows the home's orginal interior.

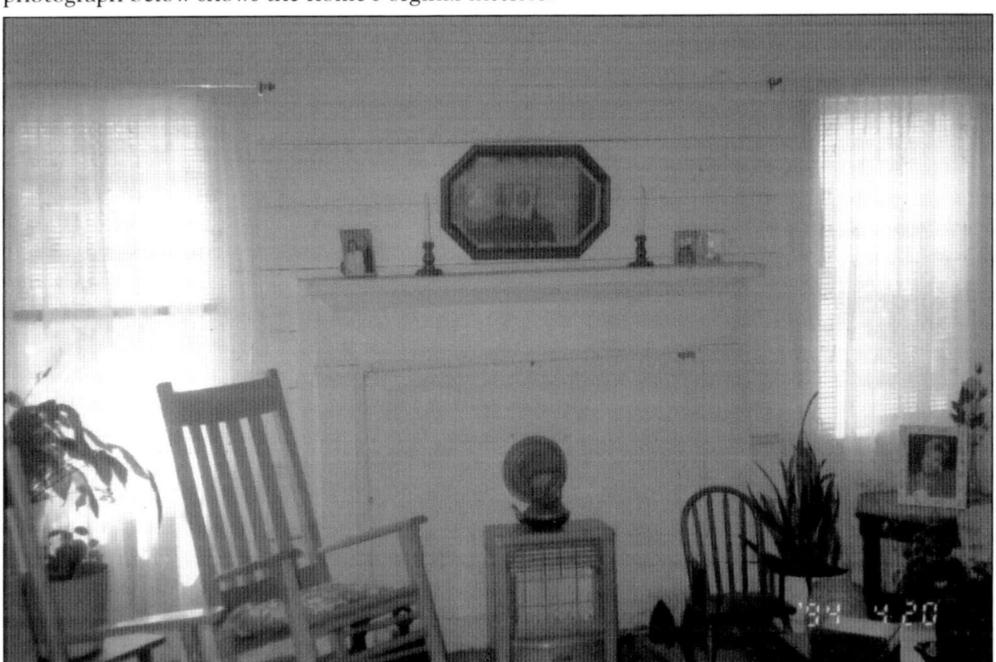

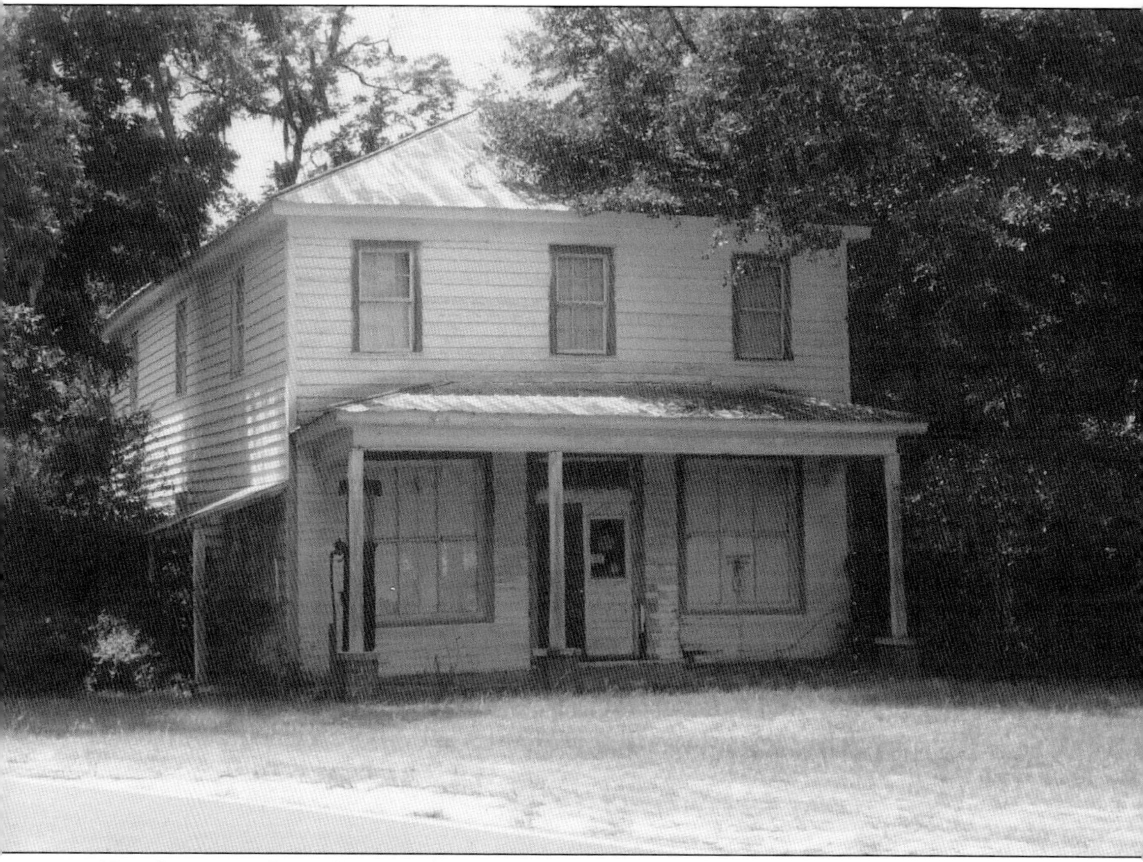

The Stillwell Post Office. The Stillwell Post Office was established in 1892, and Cletus B. Gnann served as its postmaster from that point until 1940. The above building was built around 1920 and served briefly as a home, then a general store, and lastly, a post office. Mrs. Frances H. Gnann served as postmistress from 1960 until 1986, when the Stillwell Post Office was closed.

Two

LIFE ON THE FARM

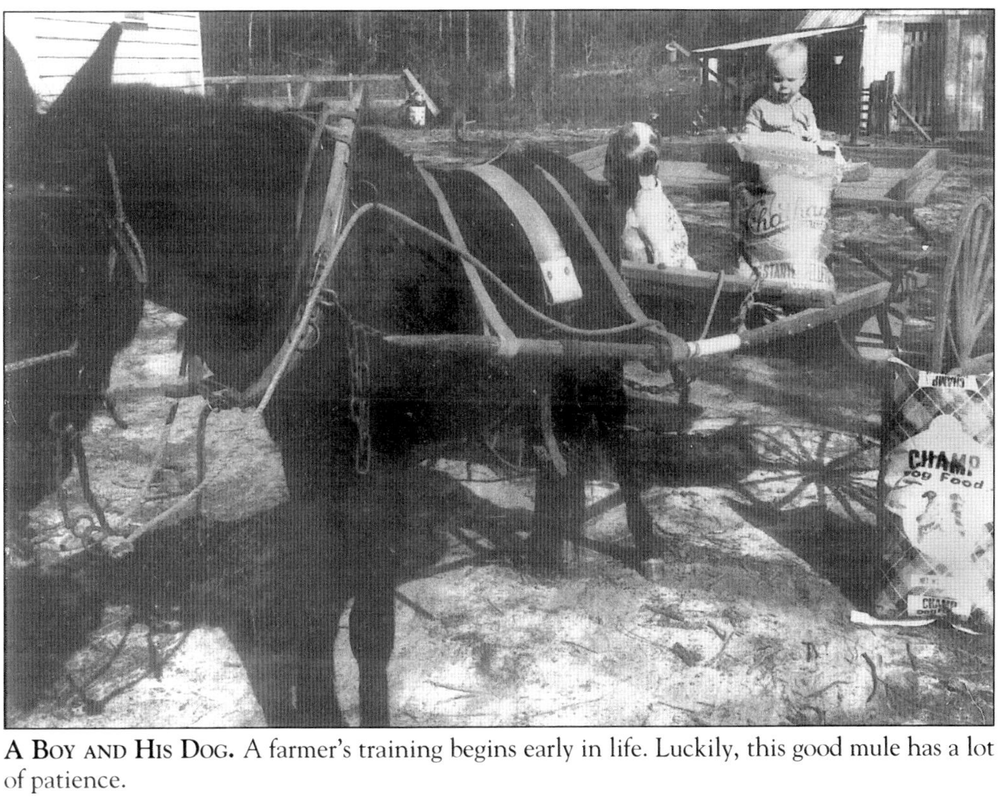

A BOY AND HIS DOG. A farmer's training begins early in life. Luckily, this good mule has a lot of patience.

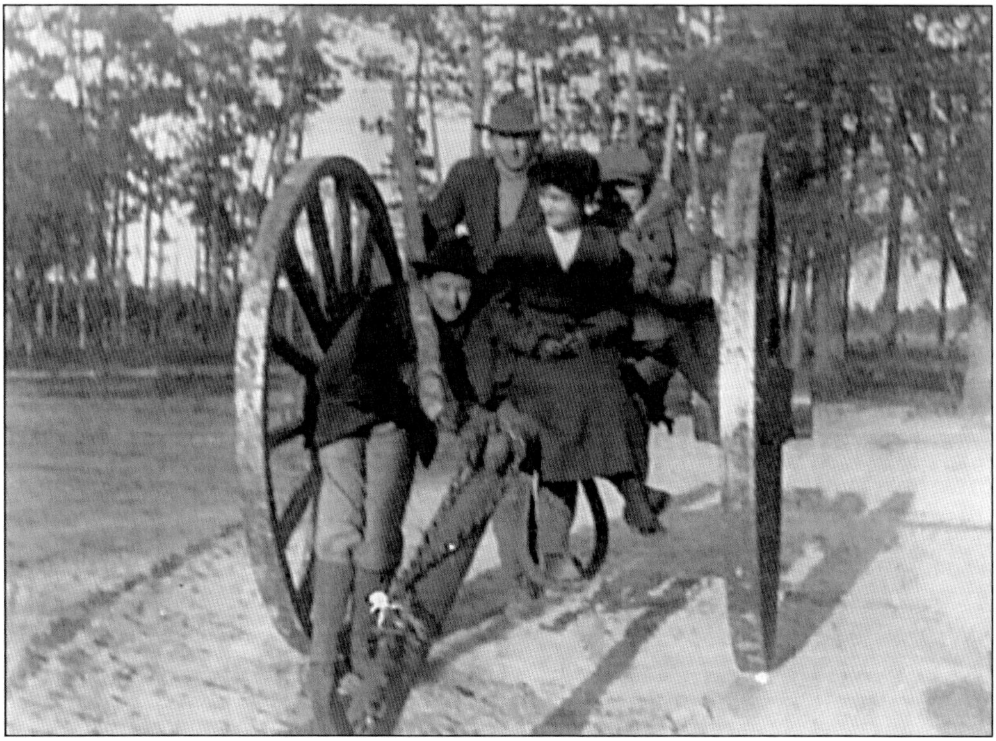

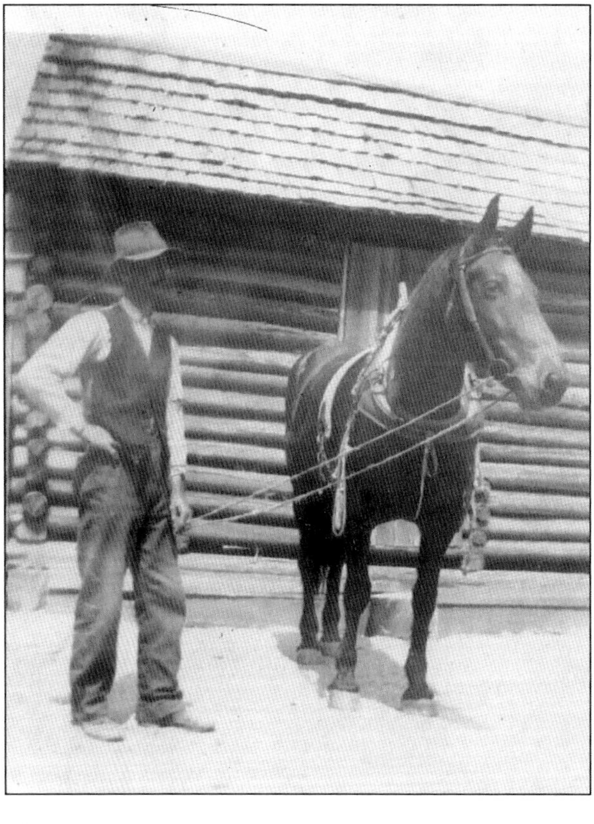

A Timbercart. Mr. and Mrs. Bowers Gnann Sr. pose with Fred Gnann and Susie Gnann for this family photo.

A Farmer and His Mule. Bobbie Kieffer and his favorite mule, Dolly, are pictured at left. This was an often-seen sight during the days of the Great Depression. The Southern farmer worked long days in corn, cotton, and tobacco fields to provide for his family.

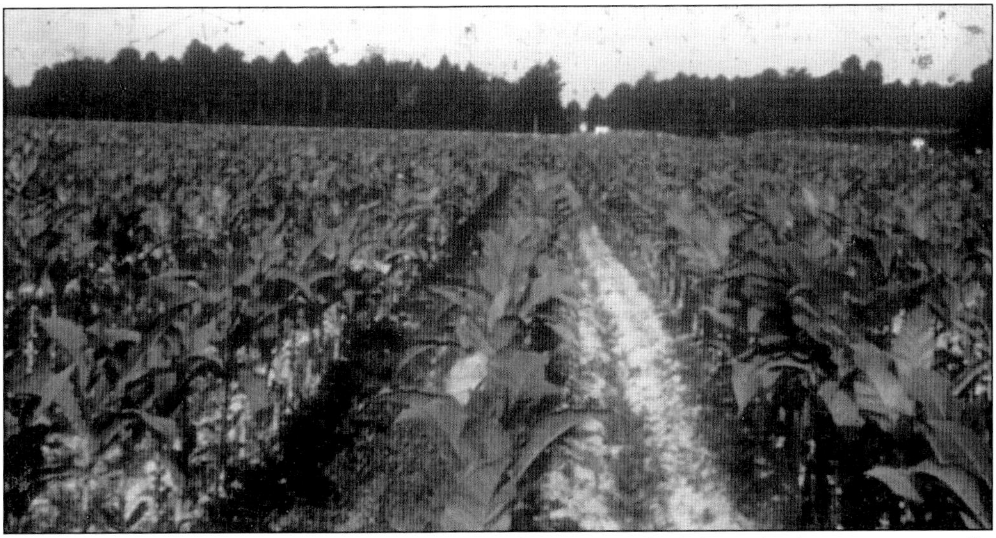

A Field of Ripening Tobacco. The tobacco plant was picked from the bottom up, usually once a week, and the rows were laid out in a way that allowed for mules and sledges to be pulled between them.

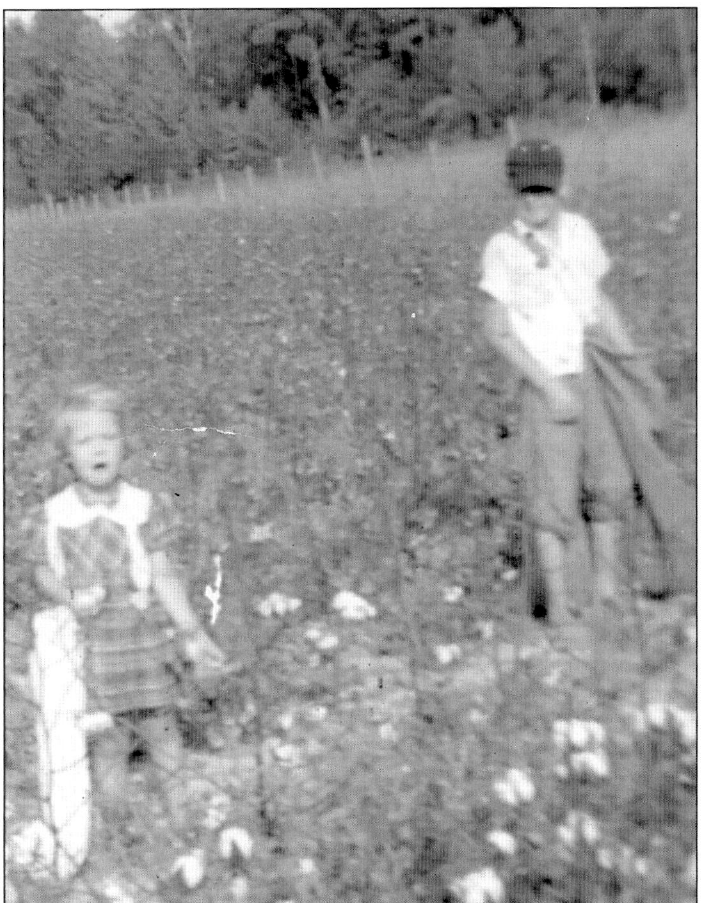

Children Picking Cotton on the Farm. Ashley Morgan and his sister Sylvia help to pick cotton in the family's fields.

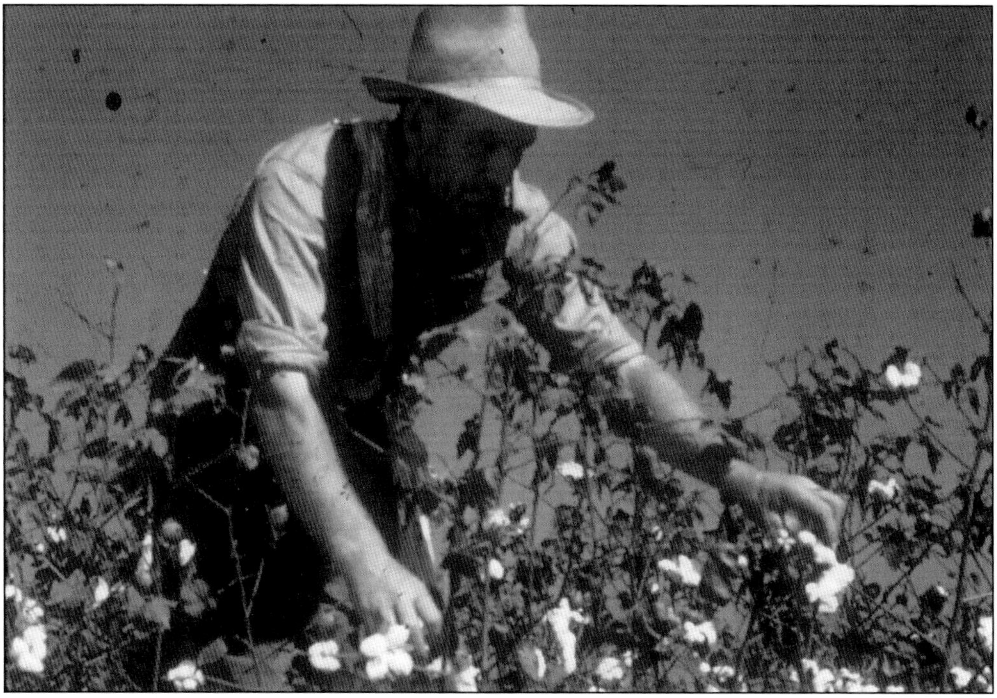

A FARMER CHECKING THE COTTON. A farmer's experience was important in producing a good yield.

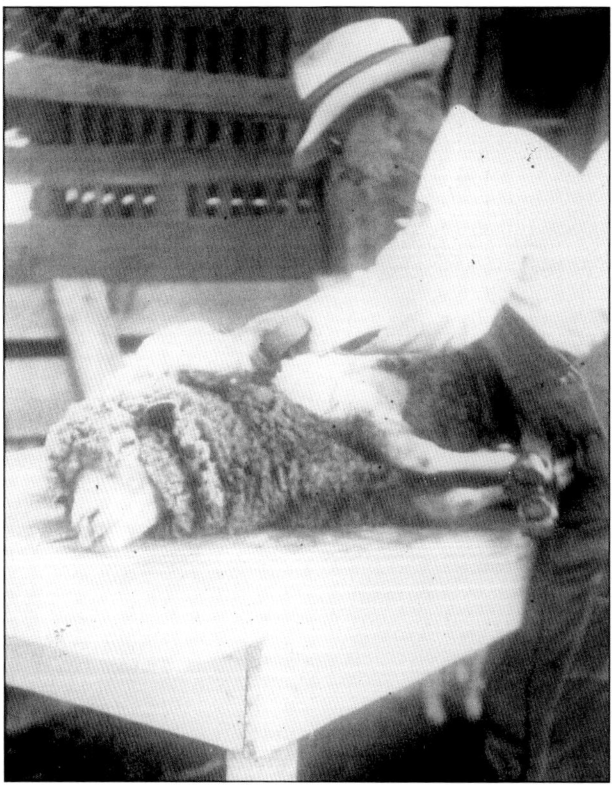

FARMER SHEARING SHEEP. One of the many tasks and skills the farmer performed was shearing sheep and marketing the wool. Herman Dugger appears in this photograph.

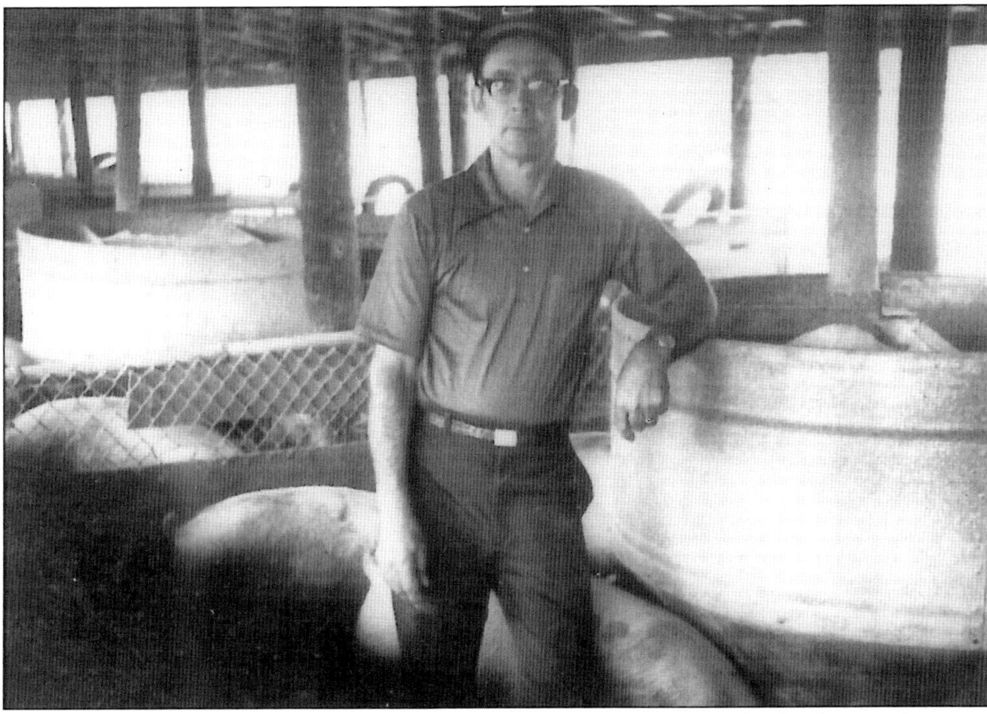

In the Hog Barn. Here, Albert Allen displays some of the newer methods of raising hogs.

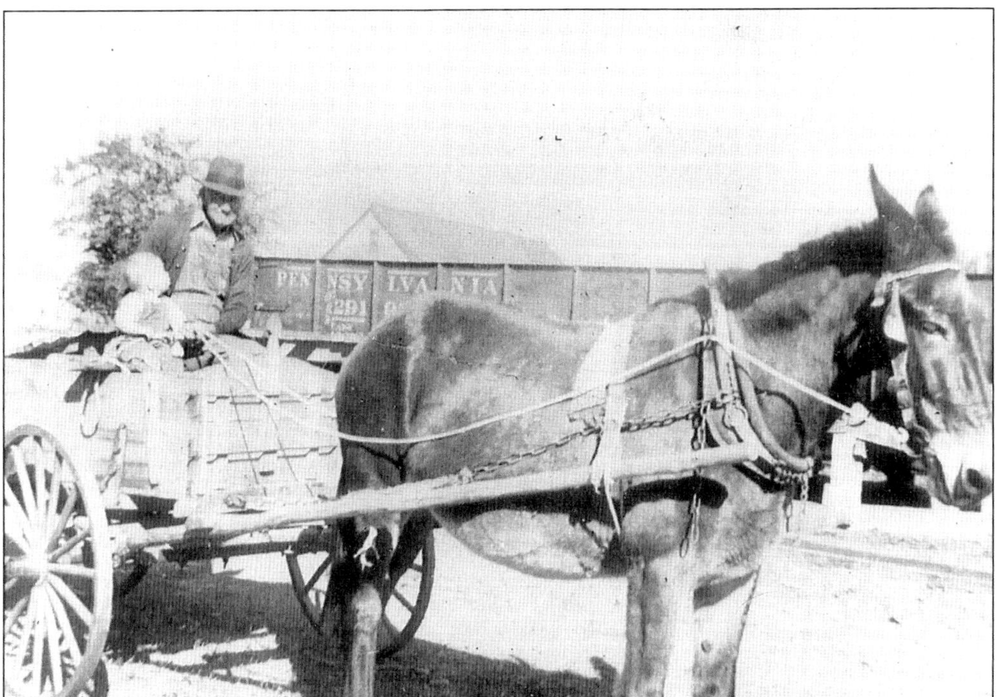

Riding with Grandaddy. Joseph Elliott Williams Jr. rides with his grandfather Oswald "Ozzie" Eve Smith.

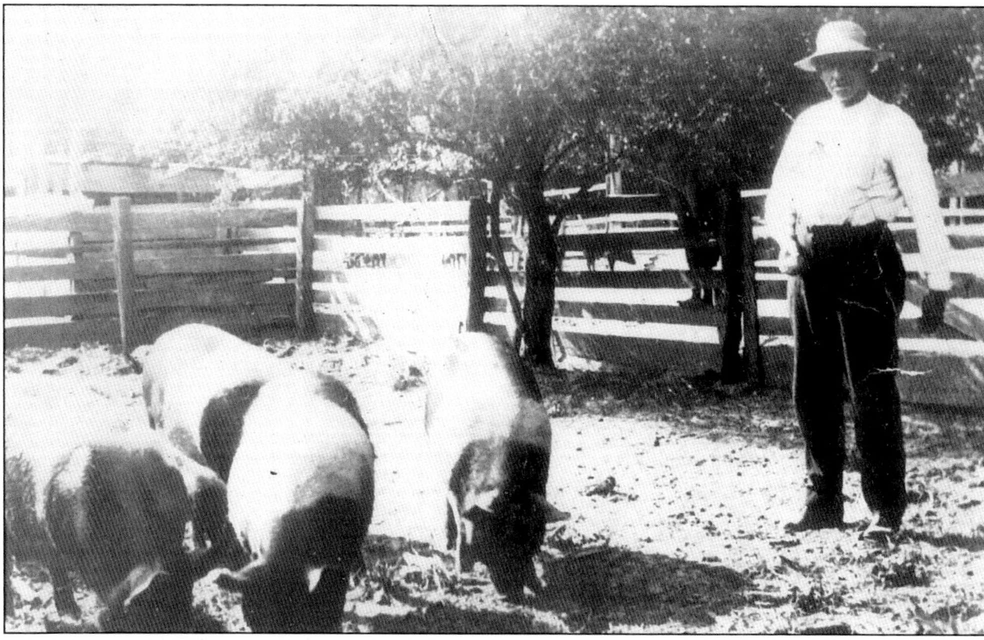

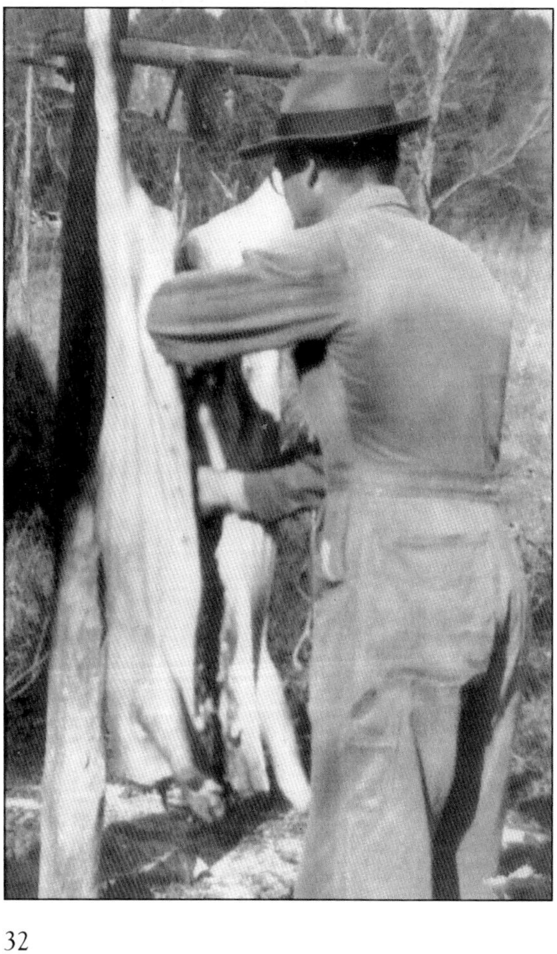

A Farmer and Hogs. Bunyan Kessler looks over his Hamshires for marketing.

Butchering a Pork. In the fall of the year and with the arrival of the first cool weather, a family could begin to enjoy pork chops and grits with biscuits. Warren Jaudon finds the task easy to do.

BERRY PICKING. Blackberry picking was an everyday pleasure, and jellies and jams were everyday sweets.

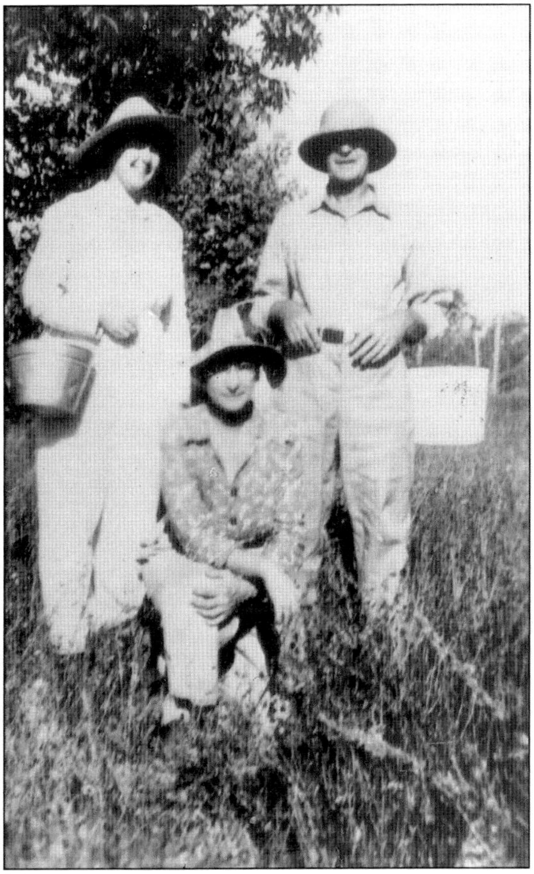

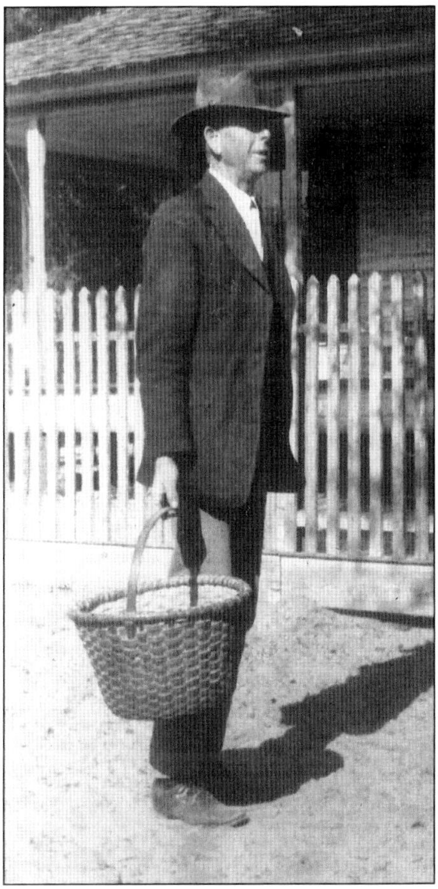

A MAN AND AN EGG BASKET. Barton Kee Shearouse has a homemade basket woven just for the gathering of eggs.

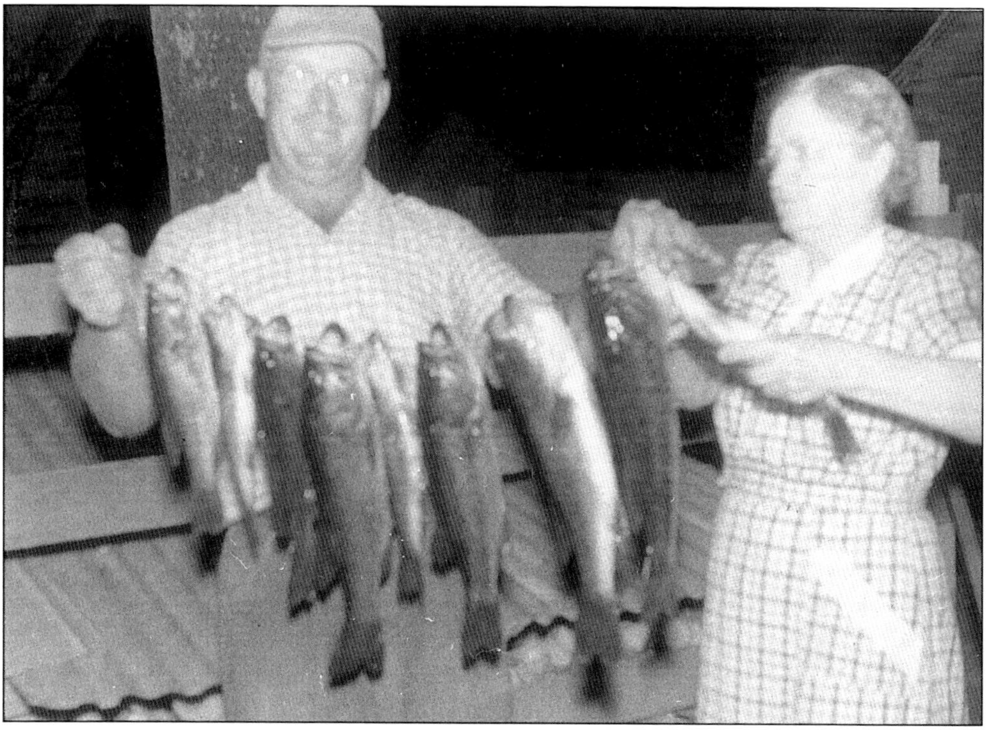

A String of Pond Bass. Mrs. Lulie and her son James Zittrouer prepare for the fish fry.

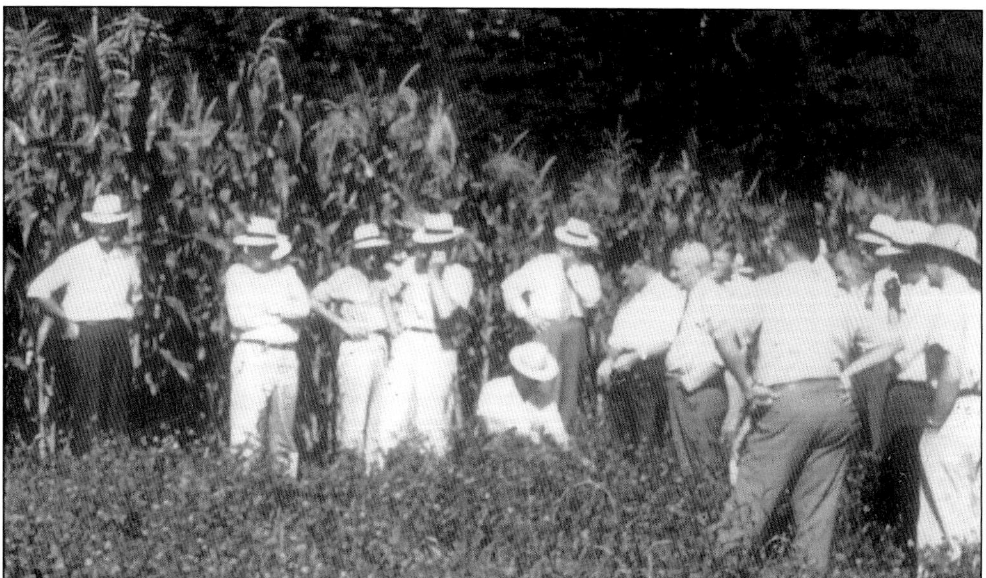

Men in a Cornfield. A group of farmers admires the crops on a farm tour. The tractor greatly increased farm productivity.

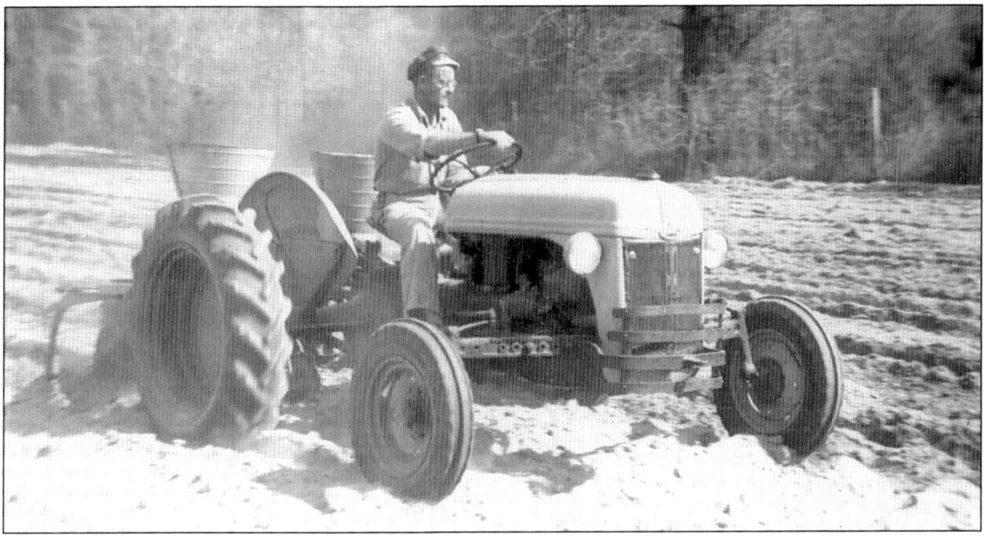

WARREN JAUDON ON HIS NEW FORD TRACTOR.

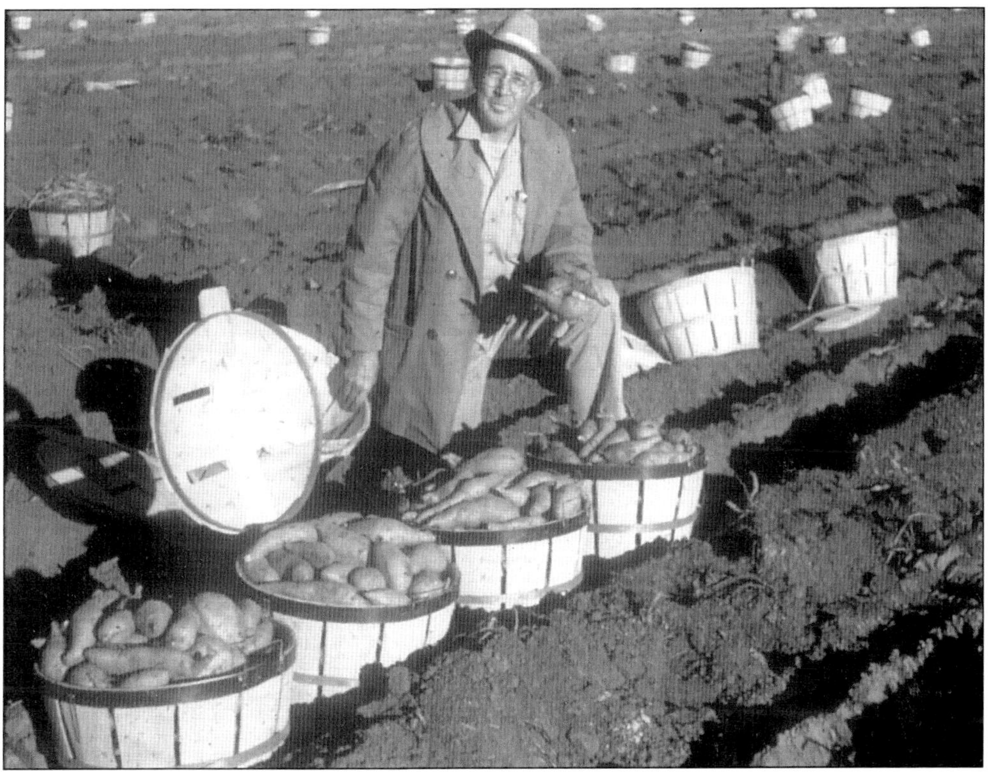

A SWEET POTATO FIELD. Sweet potatoes were a cash crop in Effingham. Farm helpers crated them in the fields.

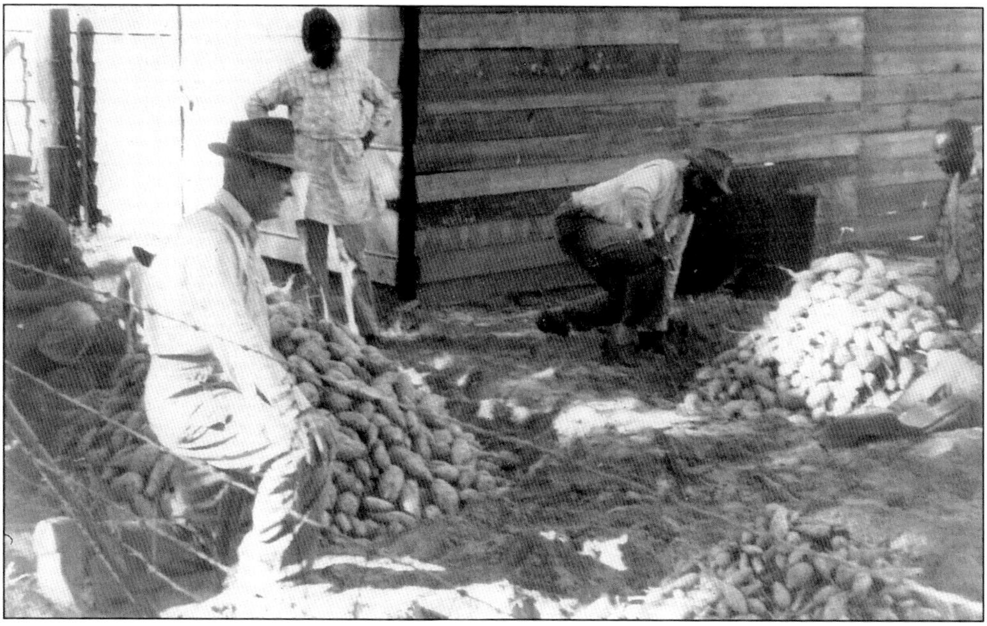

Sweet Potato Banking. Nute Pevey directs the work of Lula Williams, Paul Lee, and Earnest Johnson.

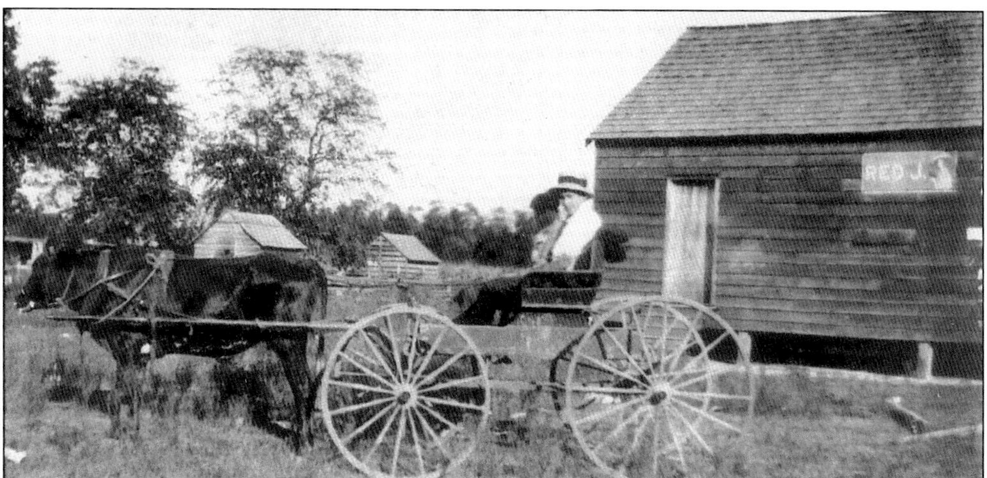

An Ox and Buggy. Frank and Ralph Rahn are hitched and ready to ride.

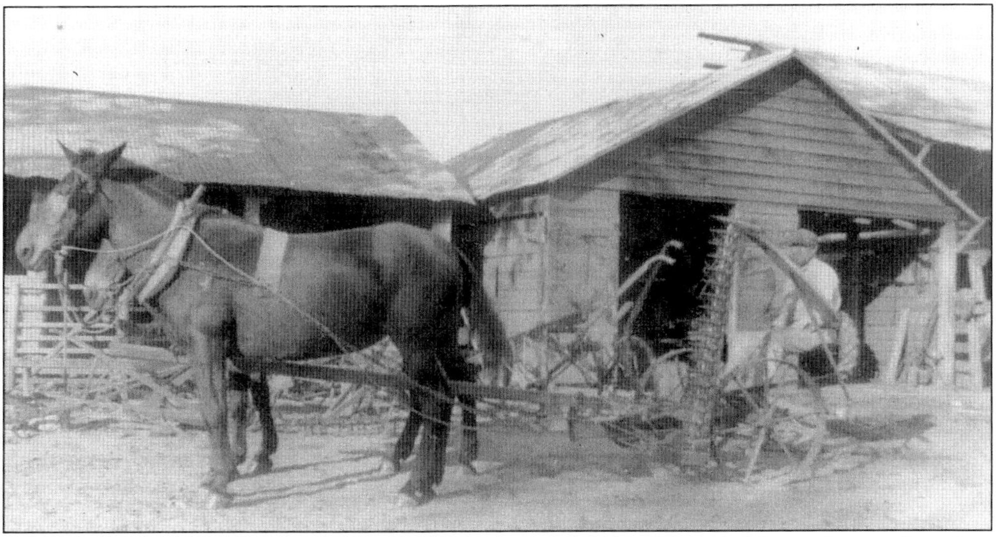

A Hay Mowing Machine. Ceasar Metzger is shown here with mules and a hay mowing machine.

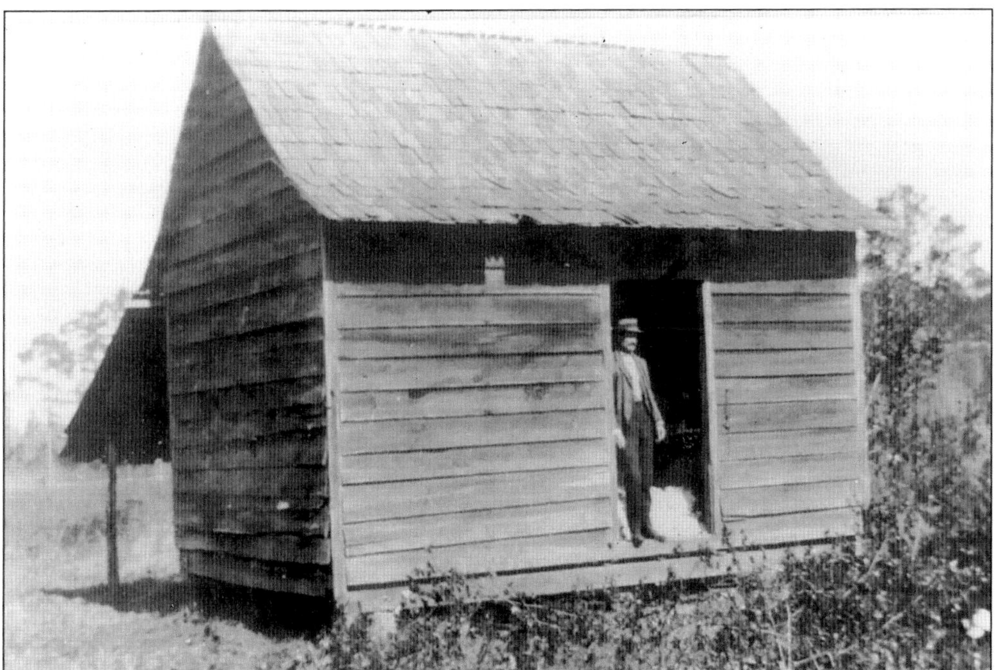

A Cotton Shed. J.A. "Gus" Exley was photographed in the doorway of a cotton shed.

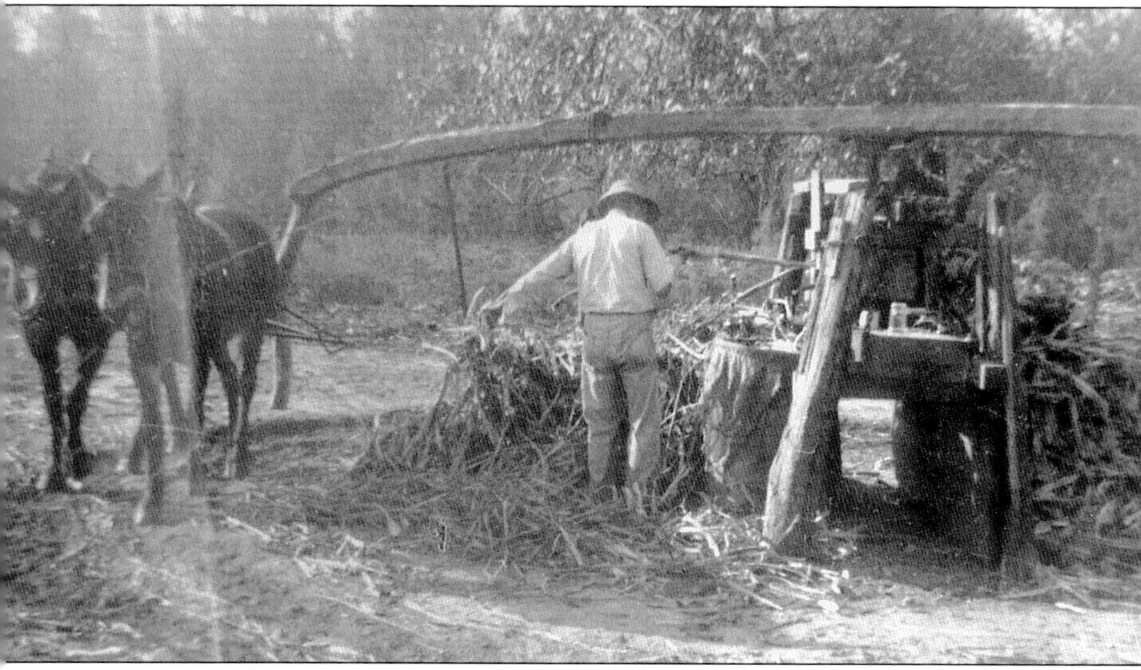

SUGAR CANE GRINDING. One of the principal crops in the early 1900s was sugar cane, and many families planted several acres, some to sell and the remainder for personal use. What a treat to sit down to country sausage, mama's homemade biscuits, and syrup. At harvest time, the cane was stripped, loaded on a wagon, and hauled to a sugar cane mill. The cane was hand fed (see Lawson Exley at work in the picture above) to squeeze the juice out, which was then cooked in a huge pot in a furnace until it was the right consistency for syrup. It was poured into gallon cans or bottled for later use.

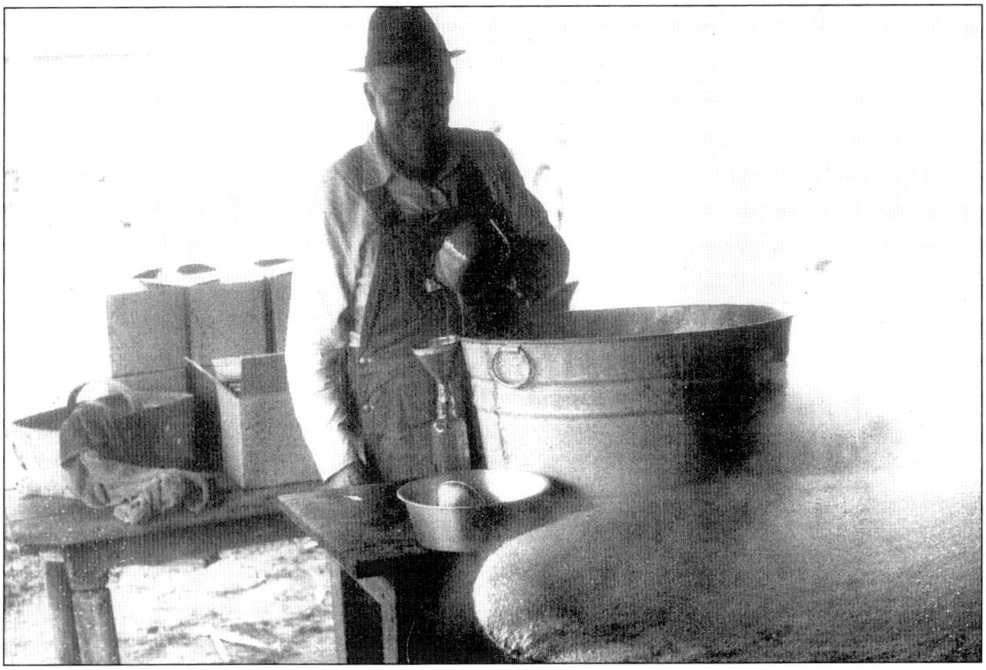

A Man Dipping Syrup. Alton Exley dips syrup and pours it into bottles for marketing.

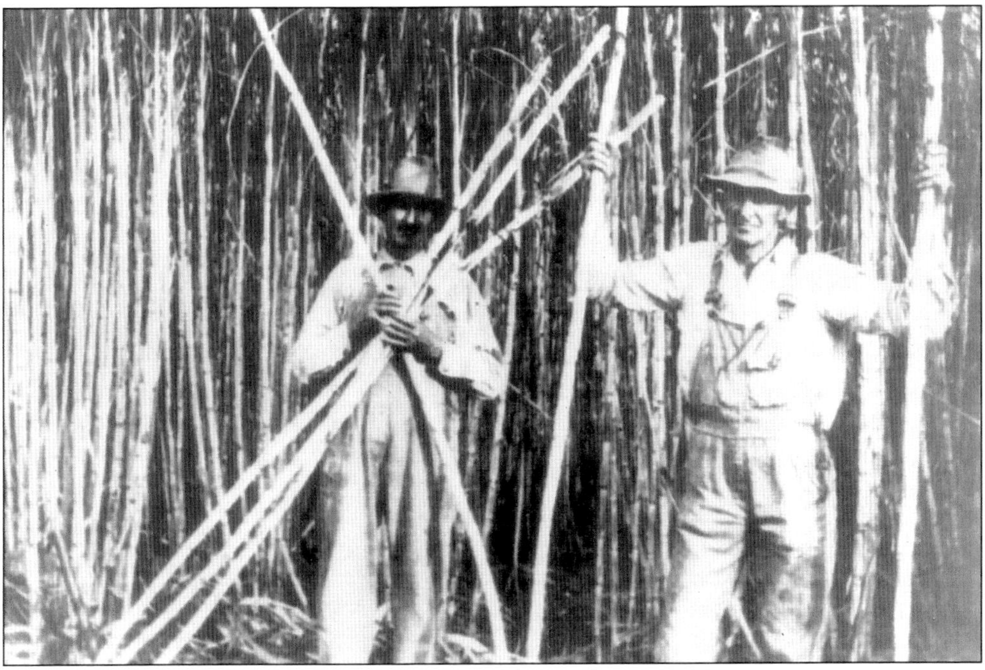

A Cane Patch. Here, Buck and John Everett gather stalks of cane.

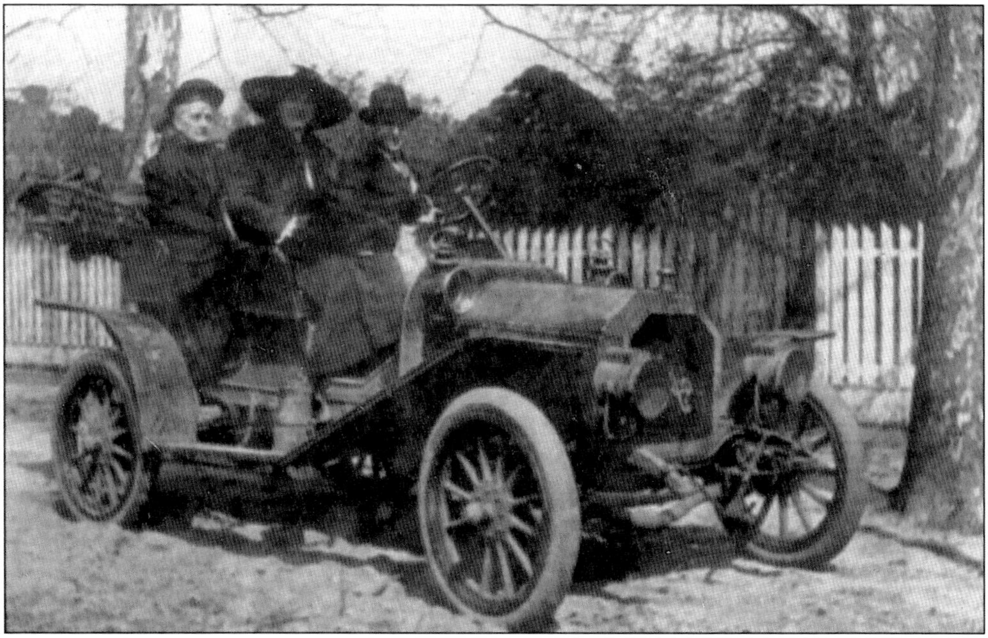

A Model T Ford.

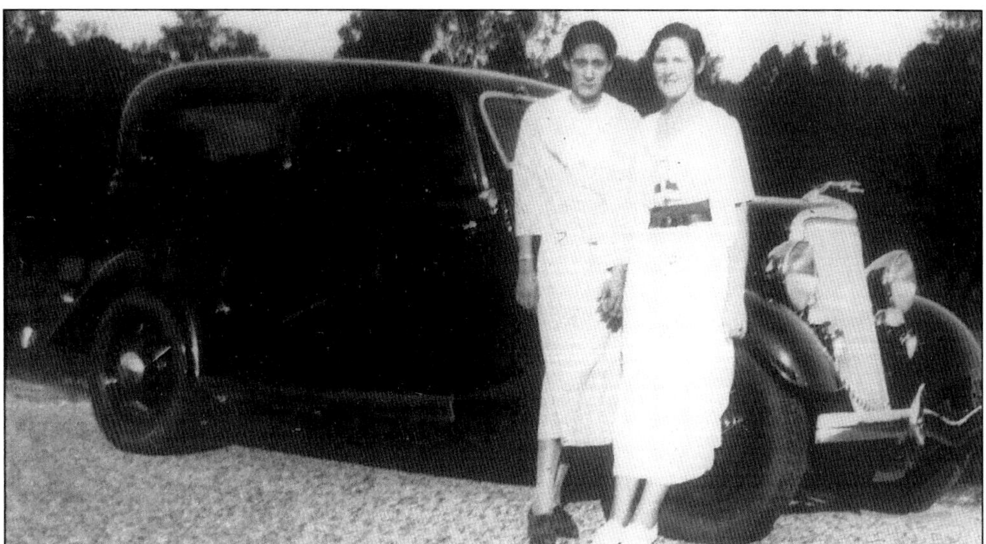

A 1934 Ford. The ladies in this picture are Dorothy Collum and Ruby Brown Kessler.

A Model A, Two-door Ford.

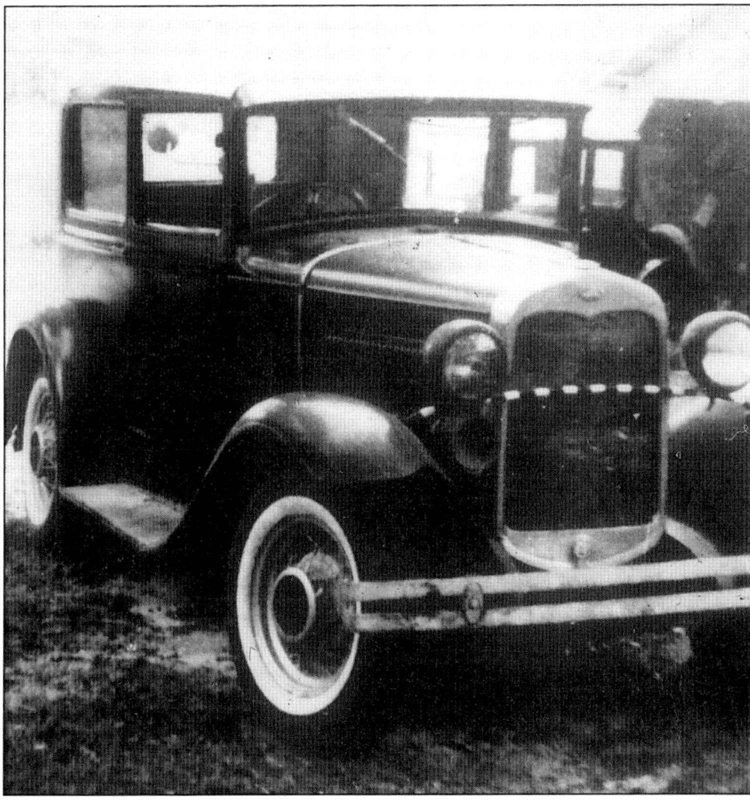

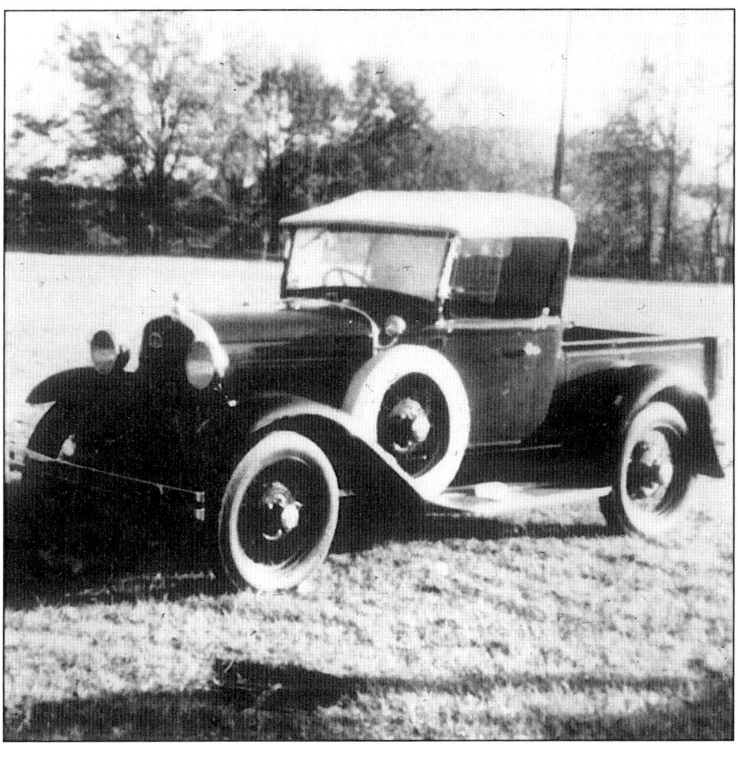

A 1930 Model A Truck.

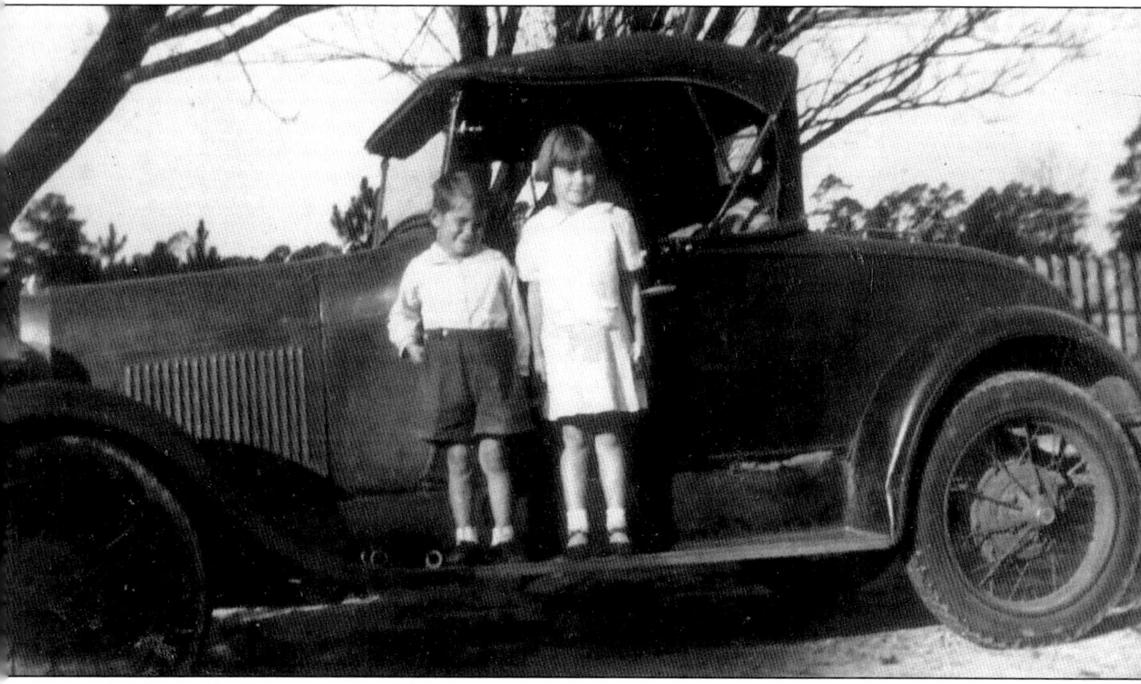

A Model A Coupe, 1933. This was Earnest Boaen Sr.'s first car, and the children posing with it are Dora and Earnest Jr.

Three

MARKETPLACE

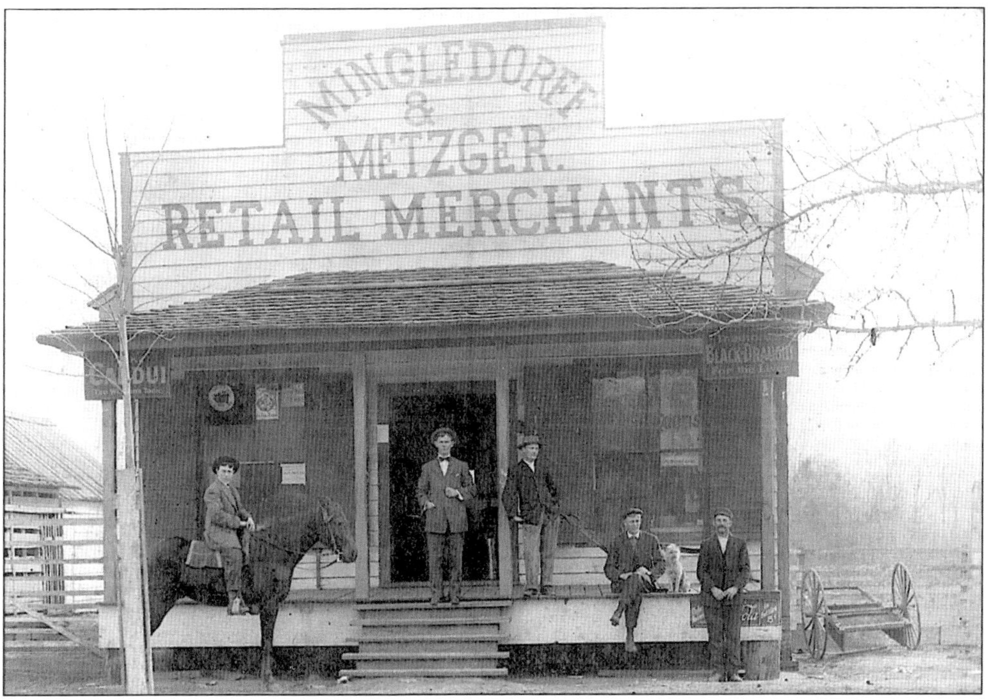

THE MINGLEDORFF AND METZGER STORE IN CLYO, C. 1910. This building, which served for many years as the Clyo Post Office, had an addition made to it in its last years. Shown here, from left to right, are Howard Metzger astride "Parker," E.M. Mingledorff, L.L. DeLoach, Paul Mallory, and Samuel T. Rector. The dog's name is unknown.

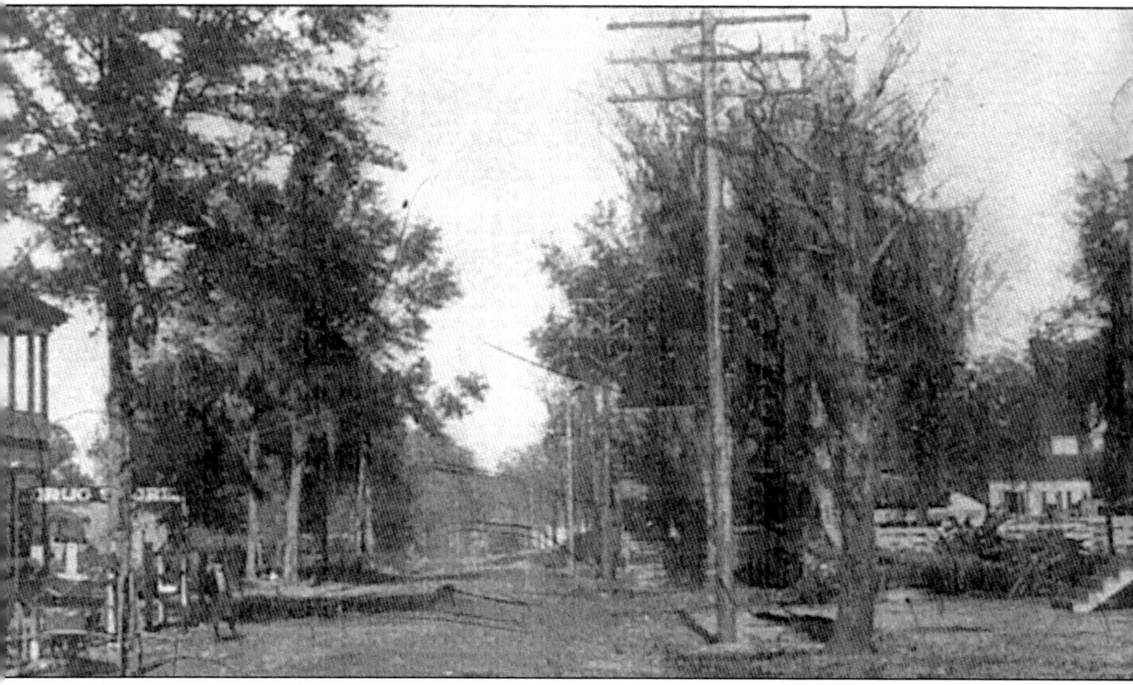

SPRINGFIELD IN A VIEW LOOKING NORTH, 1908. J.B. Simmons Sale and Retail Groceries is next to the drug store and across the street is the Baptist church.

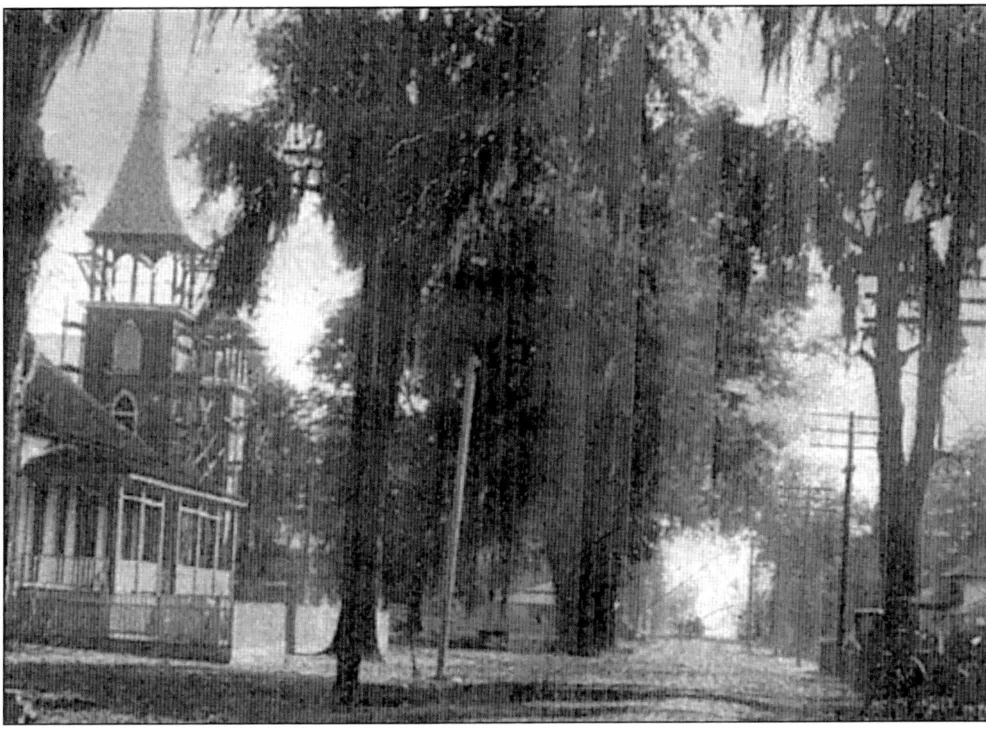

Springfield in 1917. In this view of Laurel Street looking south, the residence of R.T. and Penny Davis is visible next to Holy Trinity Lutheran Church. Across the street is a meat market and the Bird and Mingledorff hat and clothing store.

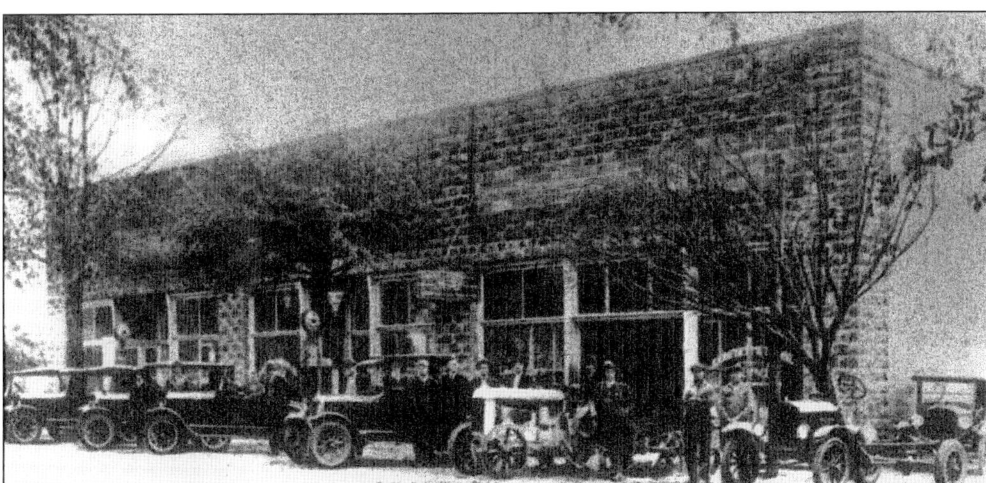

The Office of the Brinson Railroad. Built in 1907 as the office of the Brinson Railroad, this building was later occupied by the Ramsey Motor Company and Springfield Ford. It now serves as Springfield's city hall and houses the Springfield Police Department. Lewis Calhoun is sitting on the tractor.

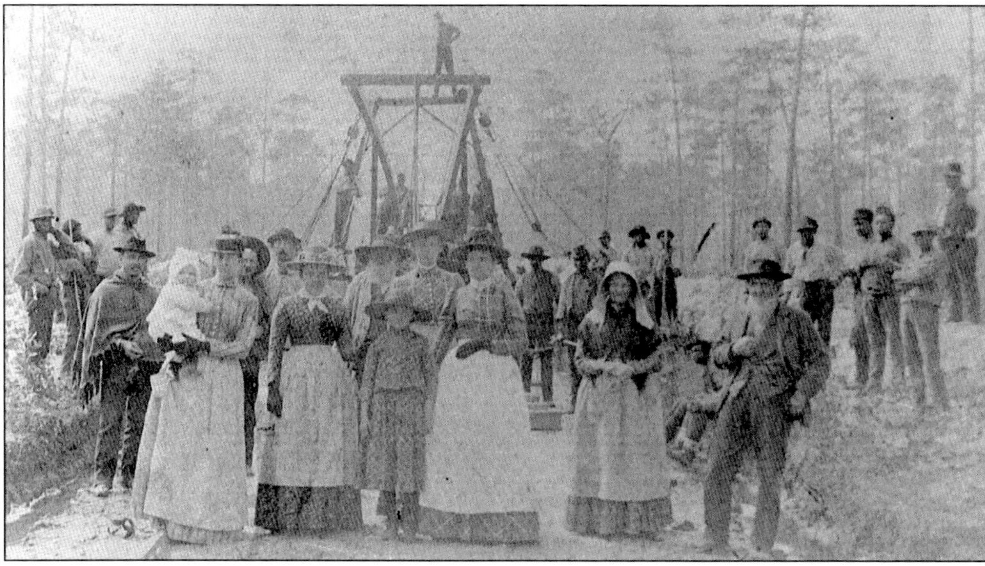

STILLWELL, 1890. Here, railroad ties are being put in place through Stillwell. Pictured, from left to right, are (front row) Alice Gnann, holding baby Susie; Aunt Julia Gnann; Margaret Ethlyn (Maggie) Dasher, Alice's niece; Matilda Reiser Rahn, Alice's sister; Mary Gugel Weitman (Mrs. Cletus Gnann), the twin to Ann Solome; and grandfather Cletus Gnann; (second row) Bertody (Bertie) Gnann; Bertie Dasher (behind Alice); Charles Frederick; Capt. Feddy Gnann; and Miss Lily Gnann (the tall woman).

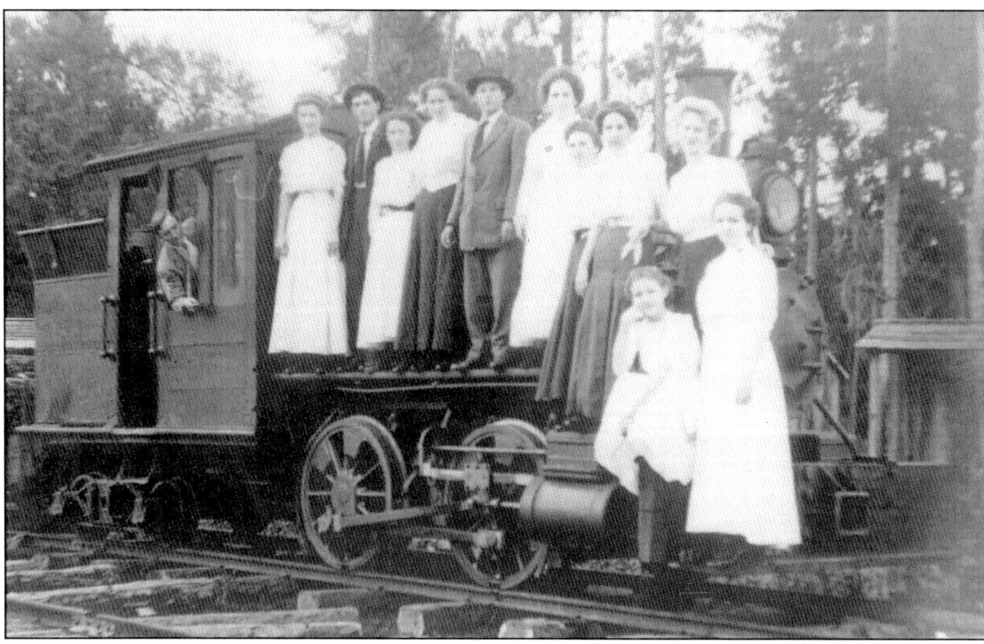

THE FIRST TRAIN IN CLYO.

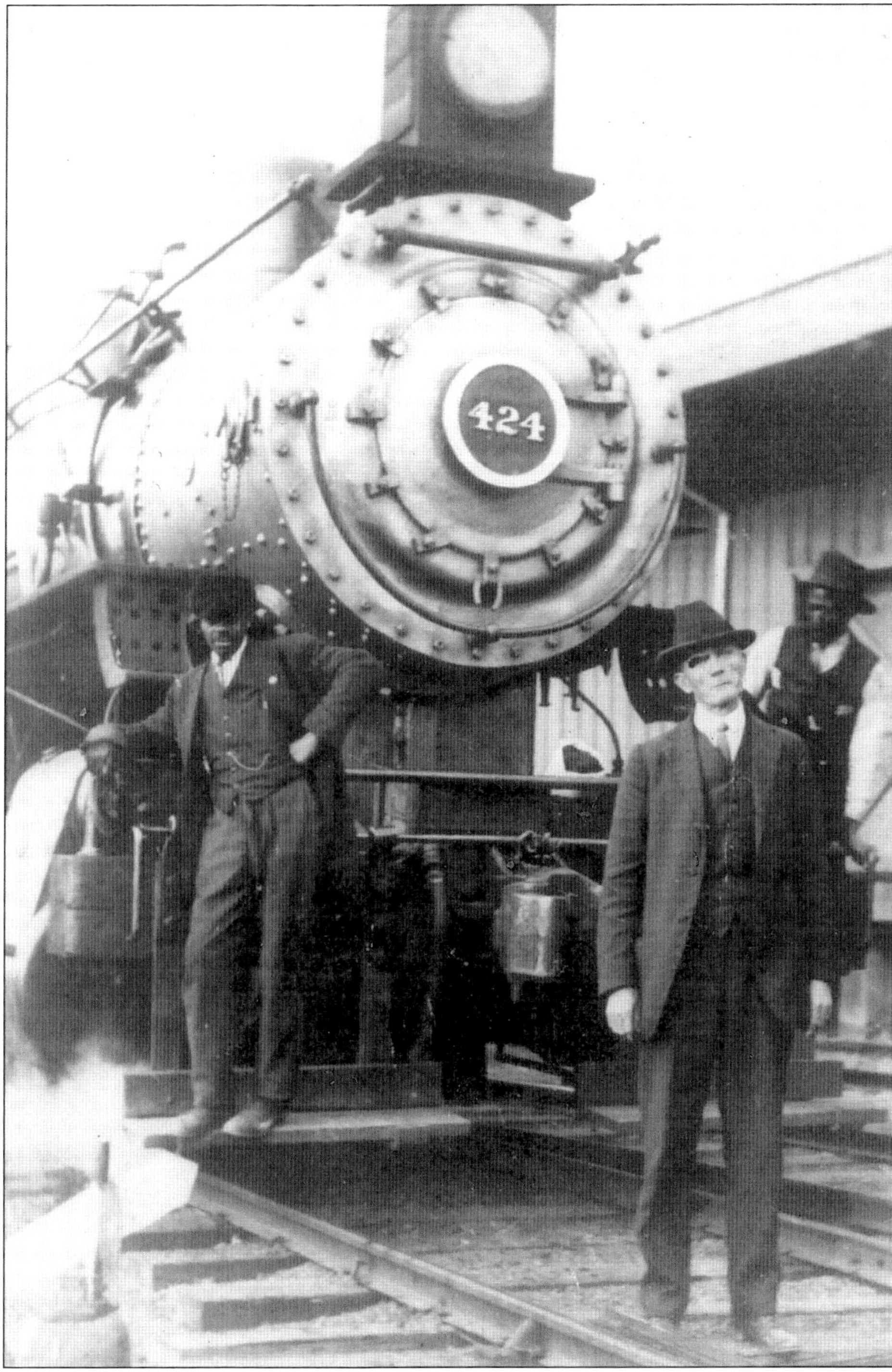

A Steam Locomotive. Ed Griffin stands on Central of Georgia rails in Guyton.

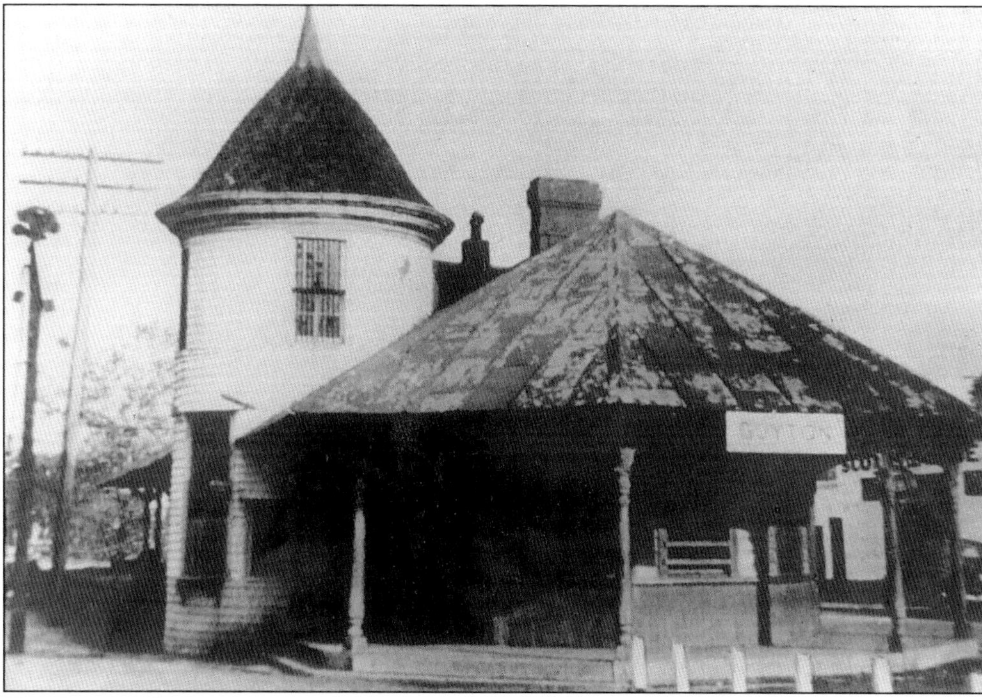

The Guyton Railroad Depot. Central of Georgia trains began operation in the fall of 1838. The City of Guyton was incorporated in 1888.

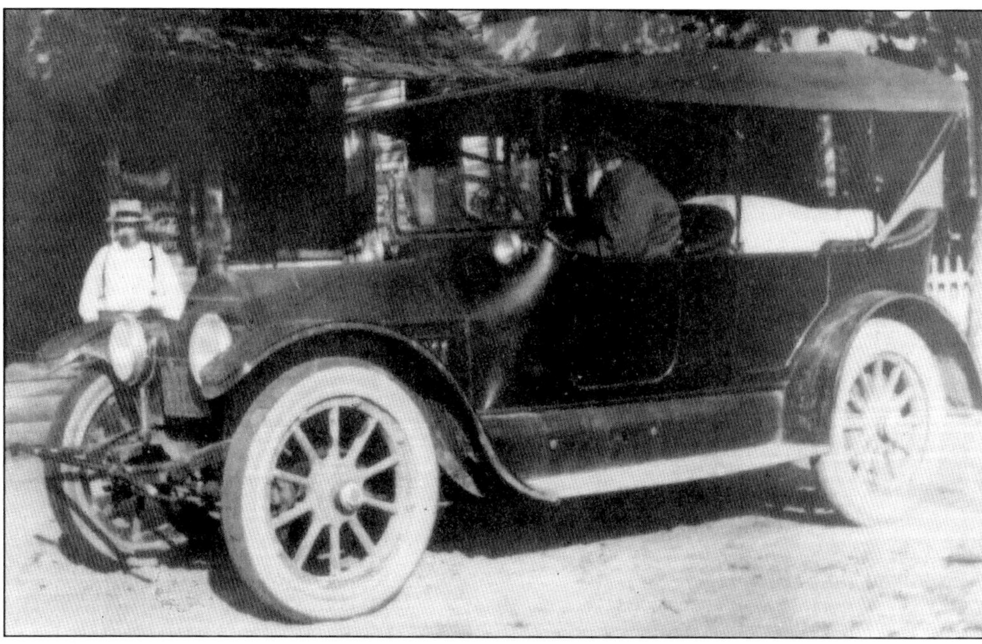

Mrs. Georgia Ewing, Mr. John Simmons, and a Model T.

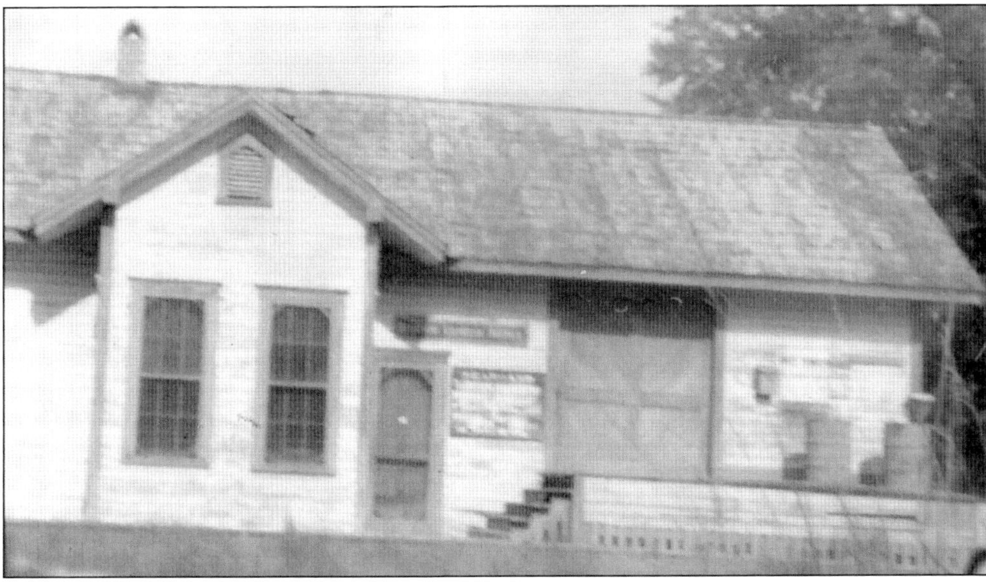

THE CLYO DEPOT.

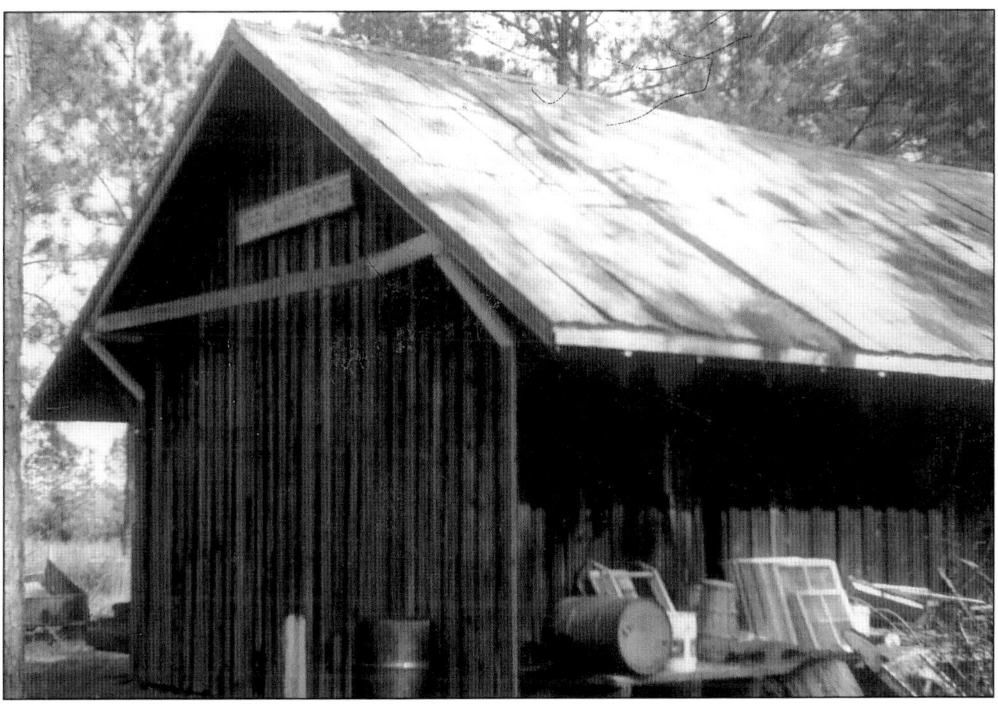

THE BLANDFORD DEPOT.

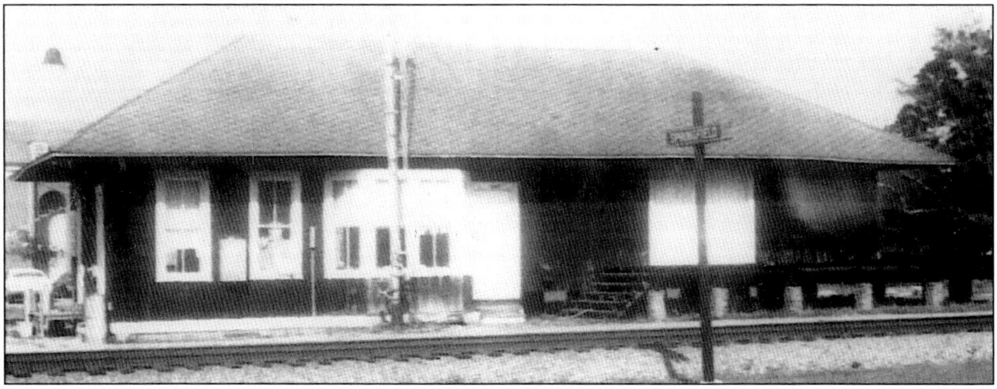

THE SPRINGFIELD DEPOT. In 1907 rail service came to Springfield with the building of the Brinson Railroad from Savannah, and this began the boom of growth in Springfield. Brinson Railroad shops were located in Springfield until they were moved to Savannah in 1916, when the Savannah and Atlanta (S&A) purchased the line.

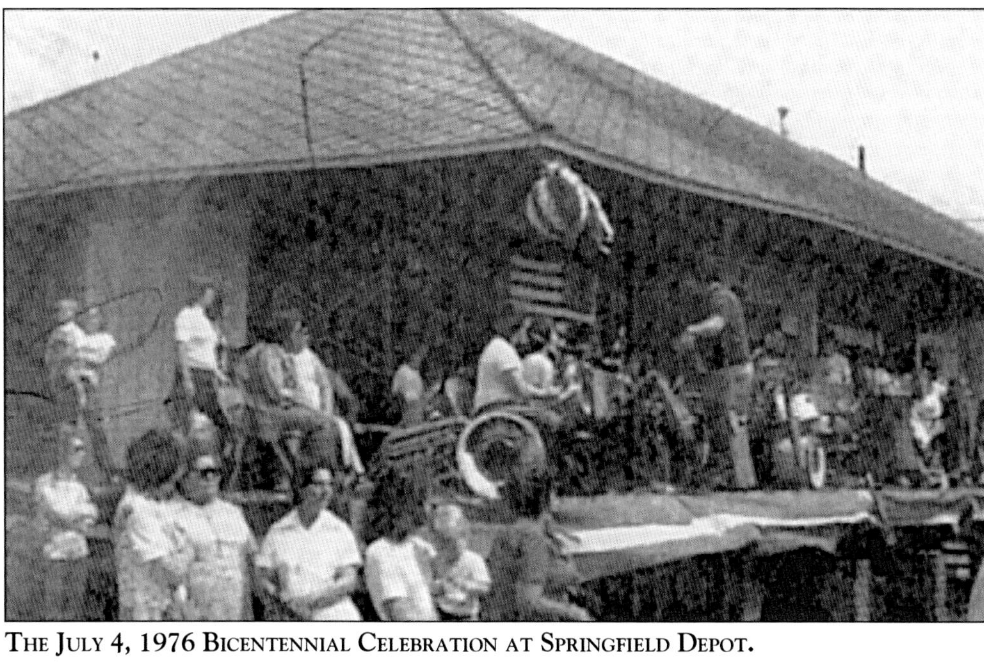

THE JULY 4, 1976 BICENTENNIAL CELEBRATION AT SPRINGFIELD DEPOT.

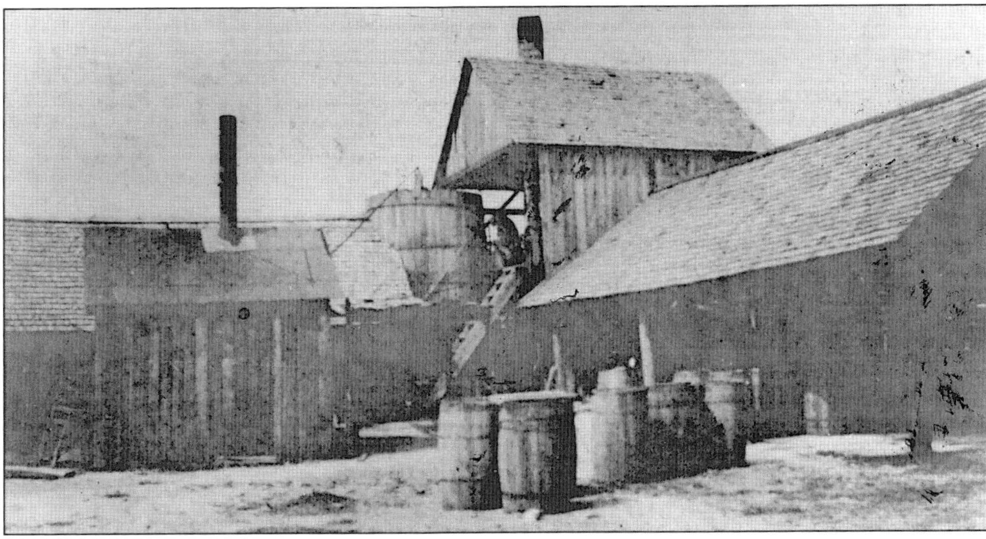

A TURPENTINE STILL. Timber products and farming were the main livelihoods of early Effingham residents.

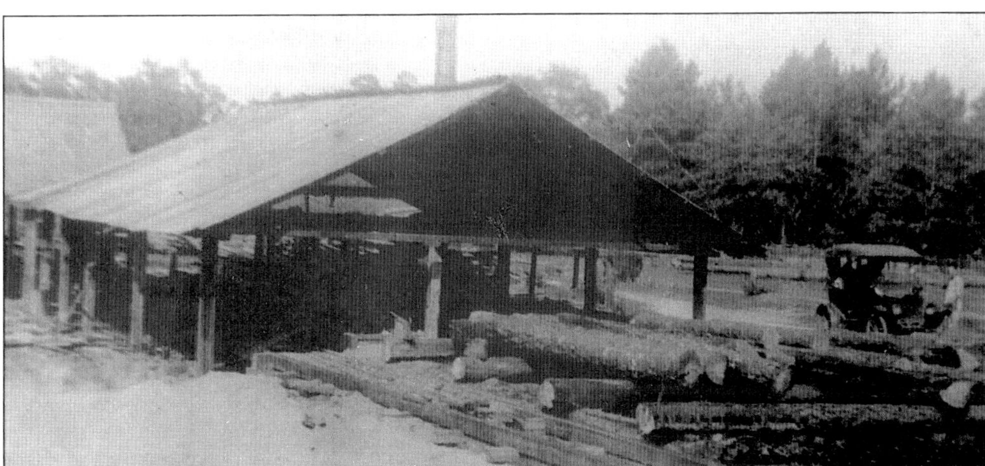

A SAWMILL. Sawmills were located throughout the county and offered jobs to many.

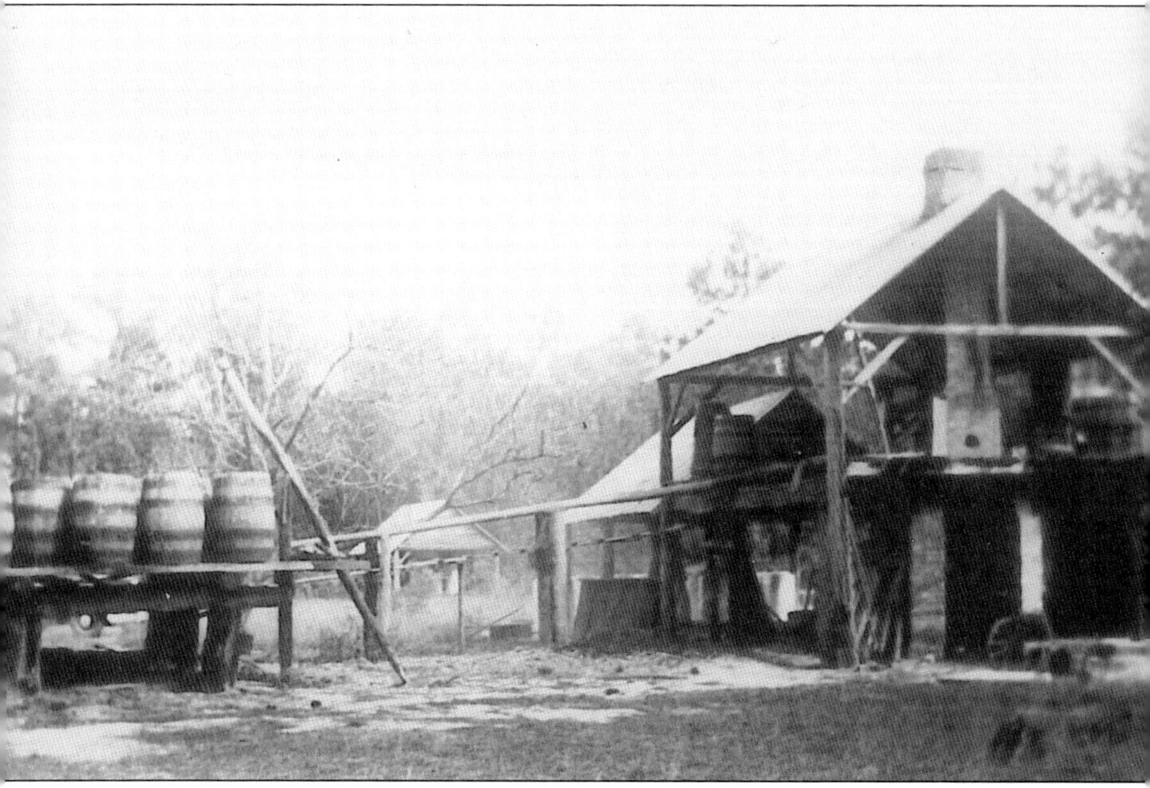

NAVAL STORES. Spirits of turpentine and rosin were shipped to Savannah during the years between 1910 and 1960. The raw gum, dipped from cups attached to faced pine trees, was gathered in barrels and hauled to a stilling plant. It was then cooked in a large furnace boiler with a copper condenser atop. The spirits of turpentine drained into wooden barrels, and the hot cooked gum "let out" into a trough strainer. The strained rosin was an amber, glass-like substance and was dipped out of the vat into barrels. The debris that remained after straining hardened when cooled, and this, known as "dross chips," was good for starting winter fires. The pineland was rented from landowners in agreements of leasing, the lease being 10,000 cups for a "crop." The trees were faced by laborers and the under brush was burned to clear workspace. When trees became inactive, they were milled for lumber. Many families of Effingham depended upon this for income.

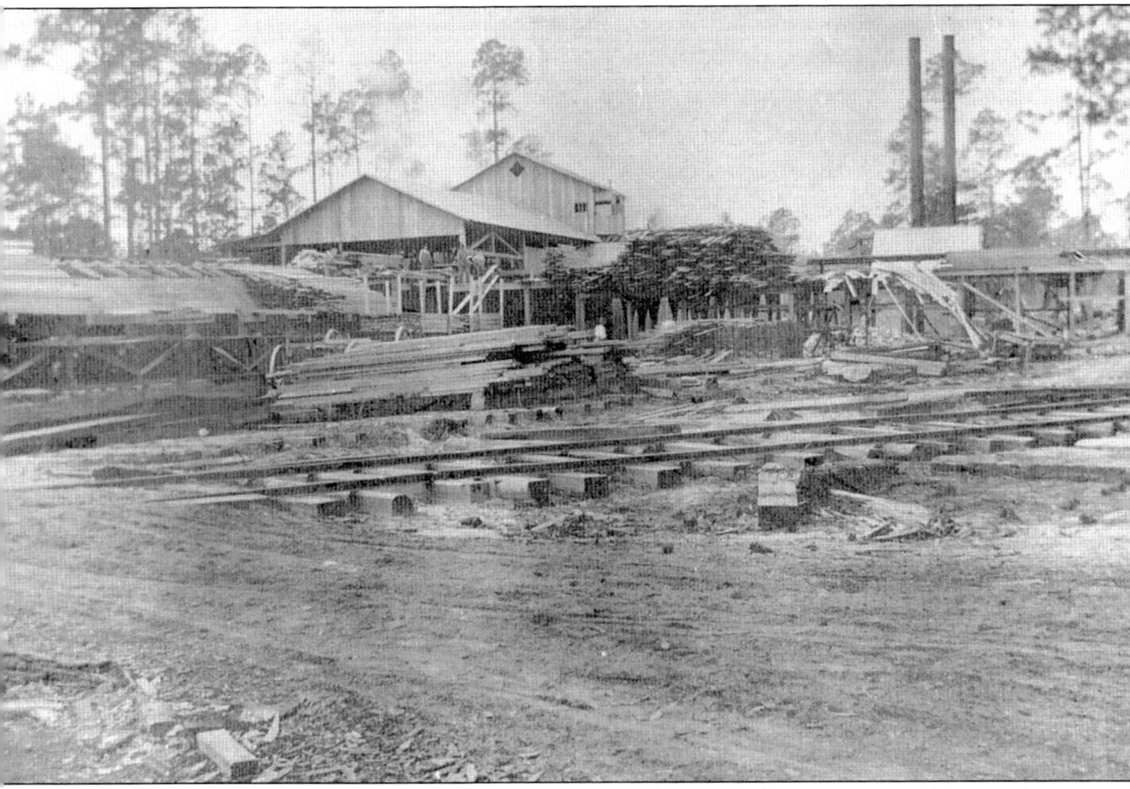

THE PINEORA MANUFACTURING CO. The Pineora Manufacturing Co. was a sawmill located on the Midland railroad tracks near Pineora in the early 1900s. It was owned and operated by Mallie Exley of Pineora and Thomas Hilton of Savannah. The flywheel, which was about 20 feet in diameter, provided the steam to pull the entire mill. Because of an abundance of prolific forests in Effingham County, saw mills made up a major part of the local economy and were located throughout the county. The first saw mill in the area may have been built by the Salzburgers near Ebenezer.

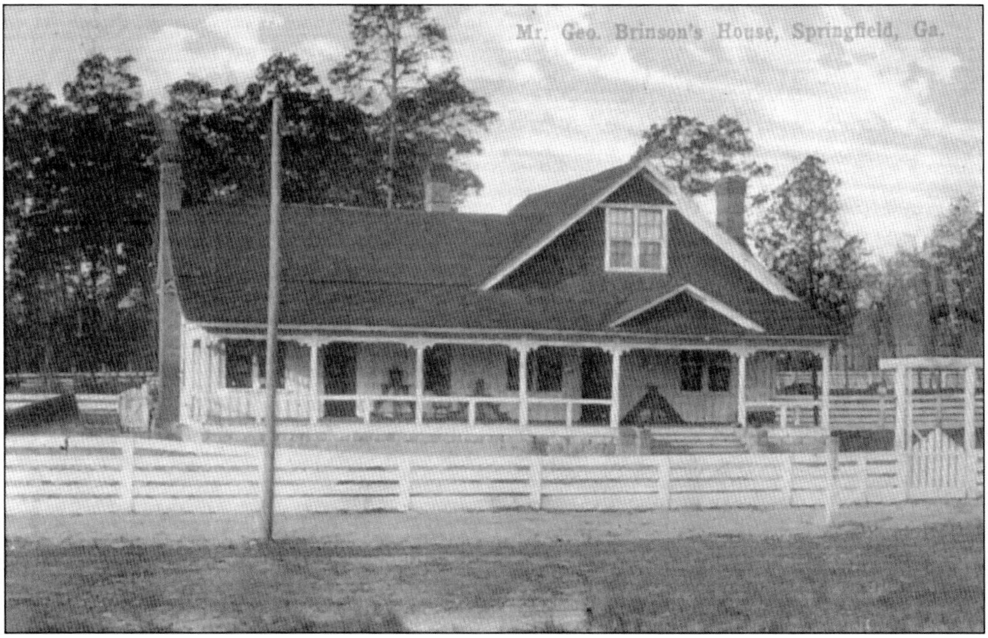

George Brinson's Home. The founder of the Brinson Railroad, George Brinson built his home in Springfield. Today, it is owned by Harold Rahn.

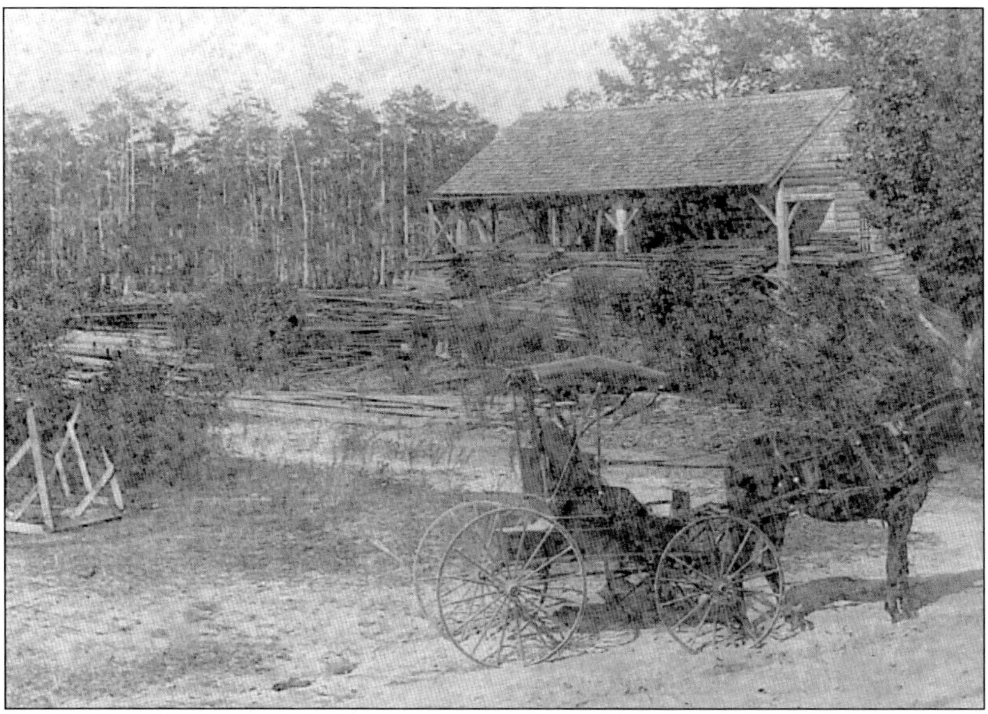

A Sawmill and Buggy. Owners of sawmills were greatly respected in the community.

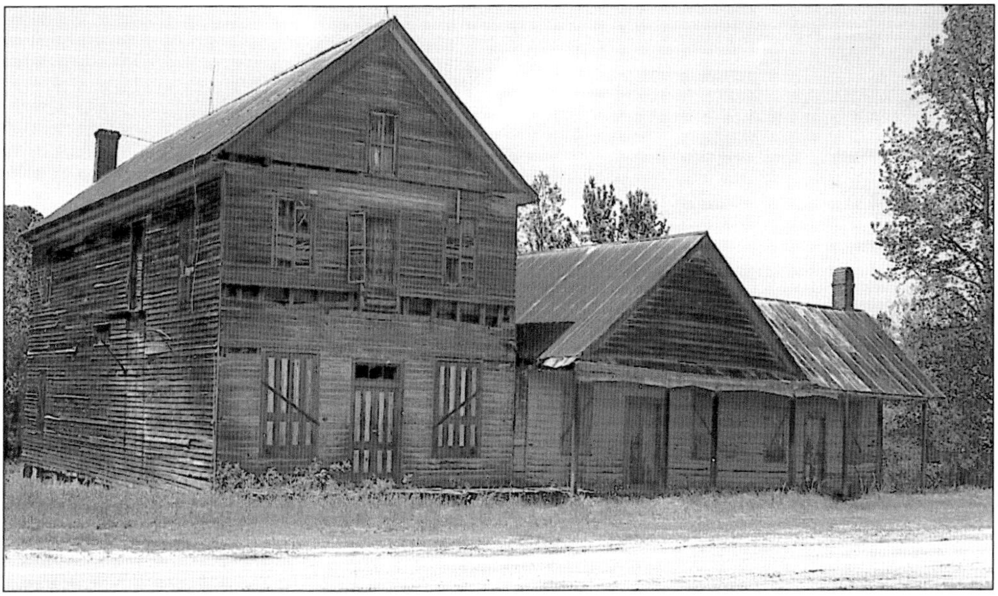

The Mallory Store. This picture doesn't do the Mallory Store justice because, in its heyday, the structure had a full porch and a shed roof across the front, in addition to another section of building on the right (or north) end, and a 40-by-80-foot buggy house. The store opened for business on July 19, 1893, and it finally closed in 1965. In the 72 years between those dates, Rance Mallory ran the store plus a gristmill, a sawmill, and a cotton gin. At the store he sold groceries, dry goods, hardware, buggies, wagons, plows, and fertilizer, but he didn't sell cards because that might encourage gambling in the community. He didn't sell firecrackers, either, as they might frighten the farmers' mules.

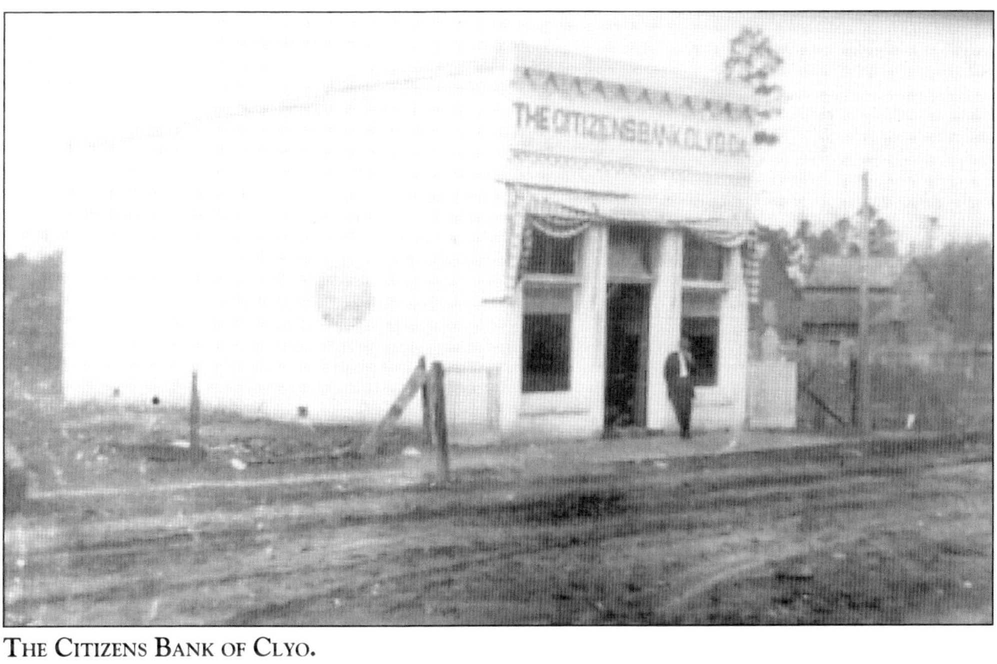

The Citizens Bank of Clyo.

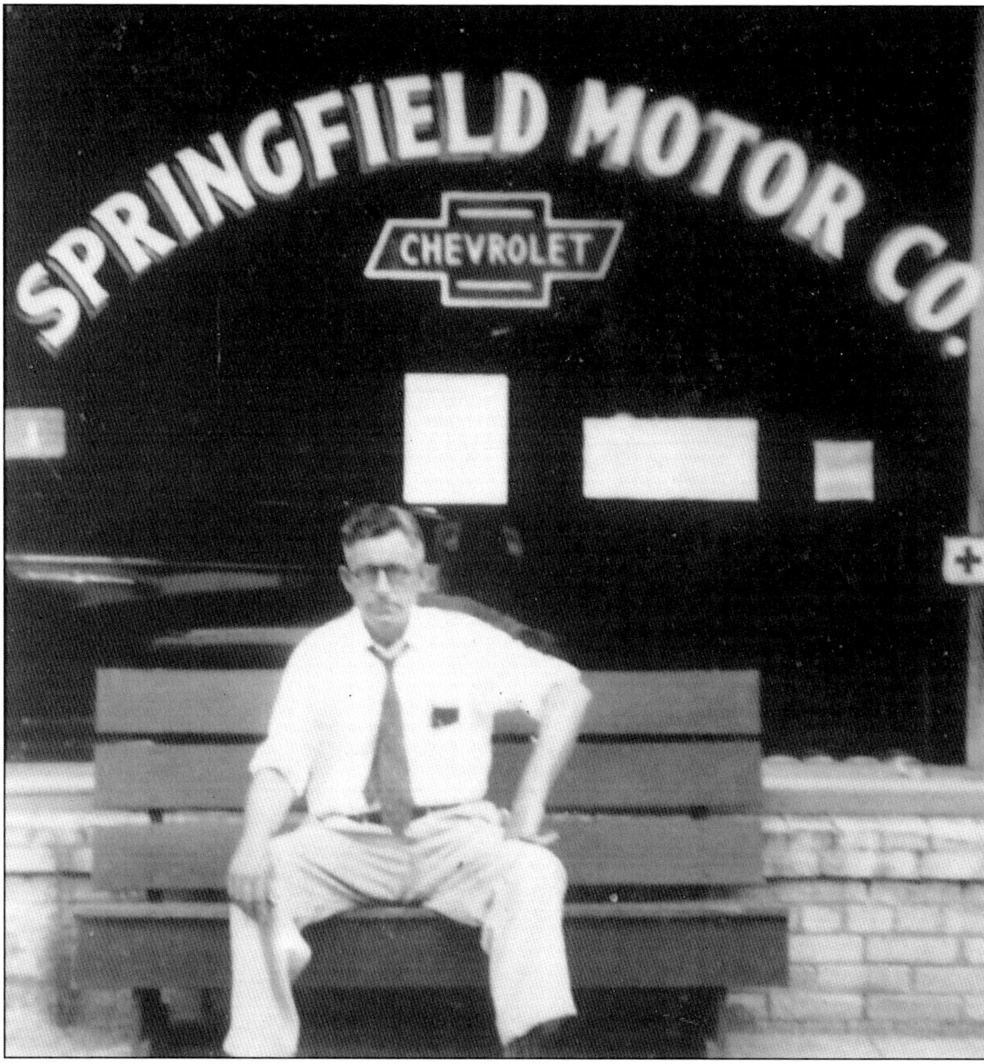

THE SPRINGFIELD MOTOR COMPANY. J.C. Varnell sits proudly in front of his Chevrolet dealership.

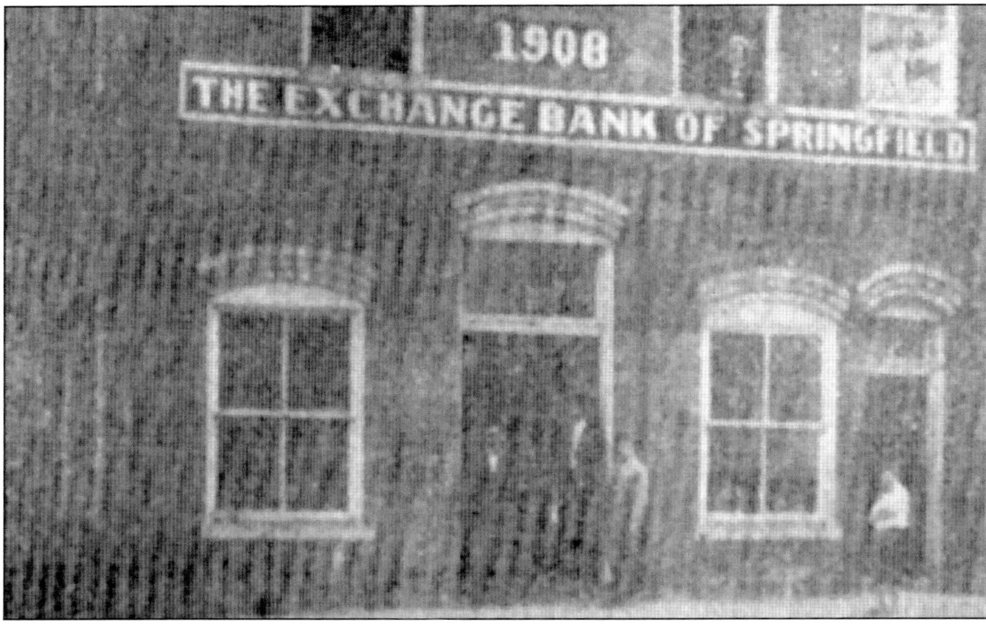

THE EXCHANGE BANK OF SPRINGFIELD. The Exchange Bank of Springfield was organized in 1908 by local stockholders, and J.W. McCareney of Virginia was its president and cashier. After several years, Chris Reiser and W.J. Hinely were hired. The bank eventually encountered hard times and was forced to close; however, Mac Marchman came to Springfield as a liquidating agent and issued certificates to stockholders, allowing the bank to reopen in 1921. The Exchange Bank of Springfield became part of the C&S National Bank in 1968 and was then known as the C&S Springfield Bank. The bank moved into a new structure in 1975 as the C&S of Effingham County with Charles E. Hartzog as president and Harry H. Shearouse as vice president. The building is now the home of Bank America.

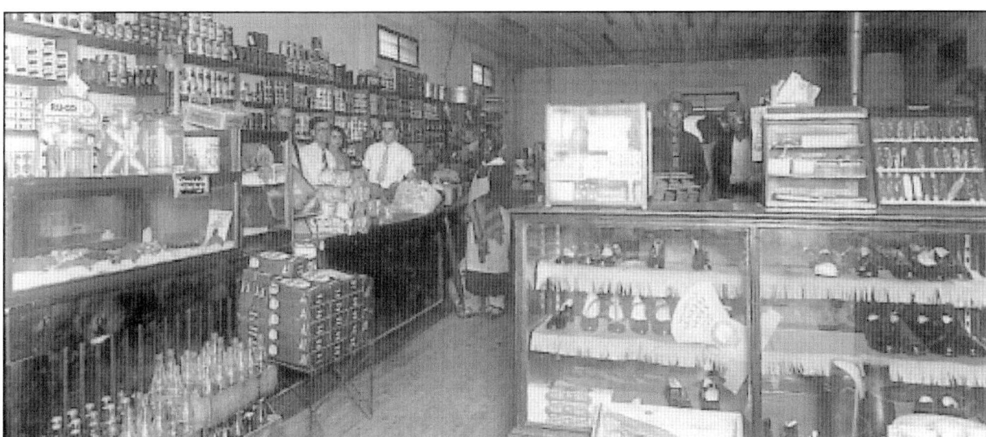

FARMERS UNION STORE. This store was begun in 1920 as a place where local farmers could purchase the supplies that they needed to get started, and Elmon C. Bragg was the first manager. During 1936, the shop was purchased as an independent store ownership of Bragg and Rahn (B&R). Standing behind the counter are Milton Bragg, Elmon C. Bragg, Mamie Hinely Morgan, and M.W. Bragg.

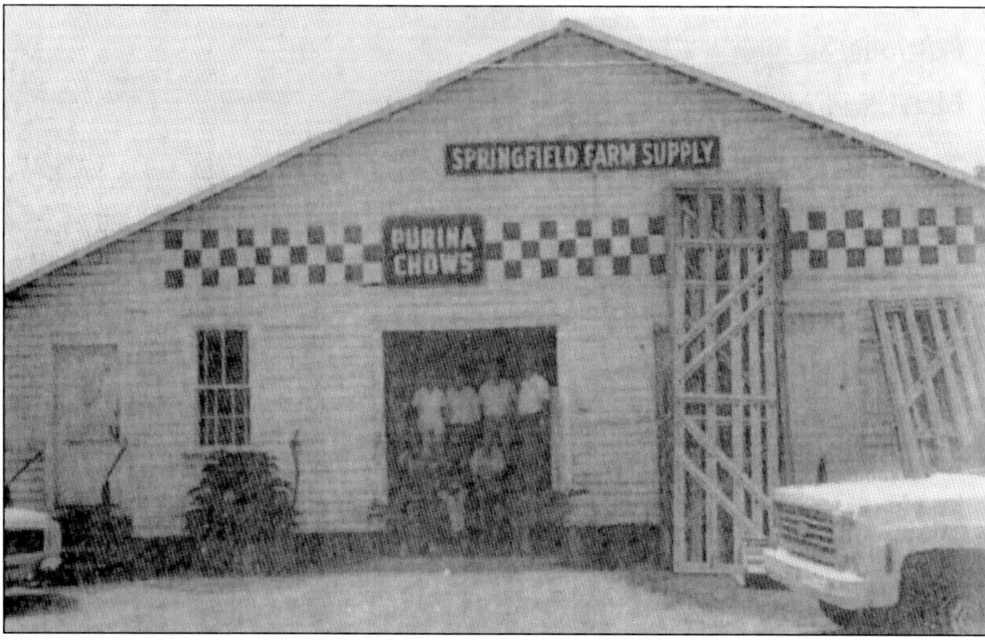

THE SPRINGFIELD FARM SUPPLY. The Springfield Farm Supply was originally established in 1935 by Ralph Rahn and W.R. Lee as an open potato shed where potatoes were graded and shipped. Mr. Rahn bought out Mr. Lee in a few years and he continued to ship potatoes, adding a farm supply business over the years. In 1962 George Chance and Durelle Hagin bought the business and ran it as partners until 1972, when Mr. Chance bought Mr. Hagin out. During 1975 Mr. Chance remodeled, displaying products in individual stalls. The business specialized in custom grinding and storing grains for livestock feed.

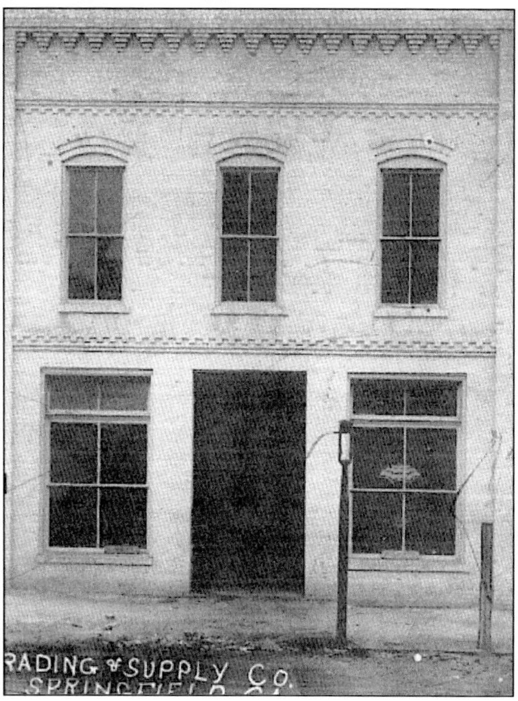

THE TRADING AND SUPPLY COMPANY. This store later became part of the Springfield Motor Co.

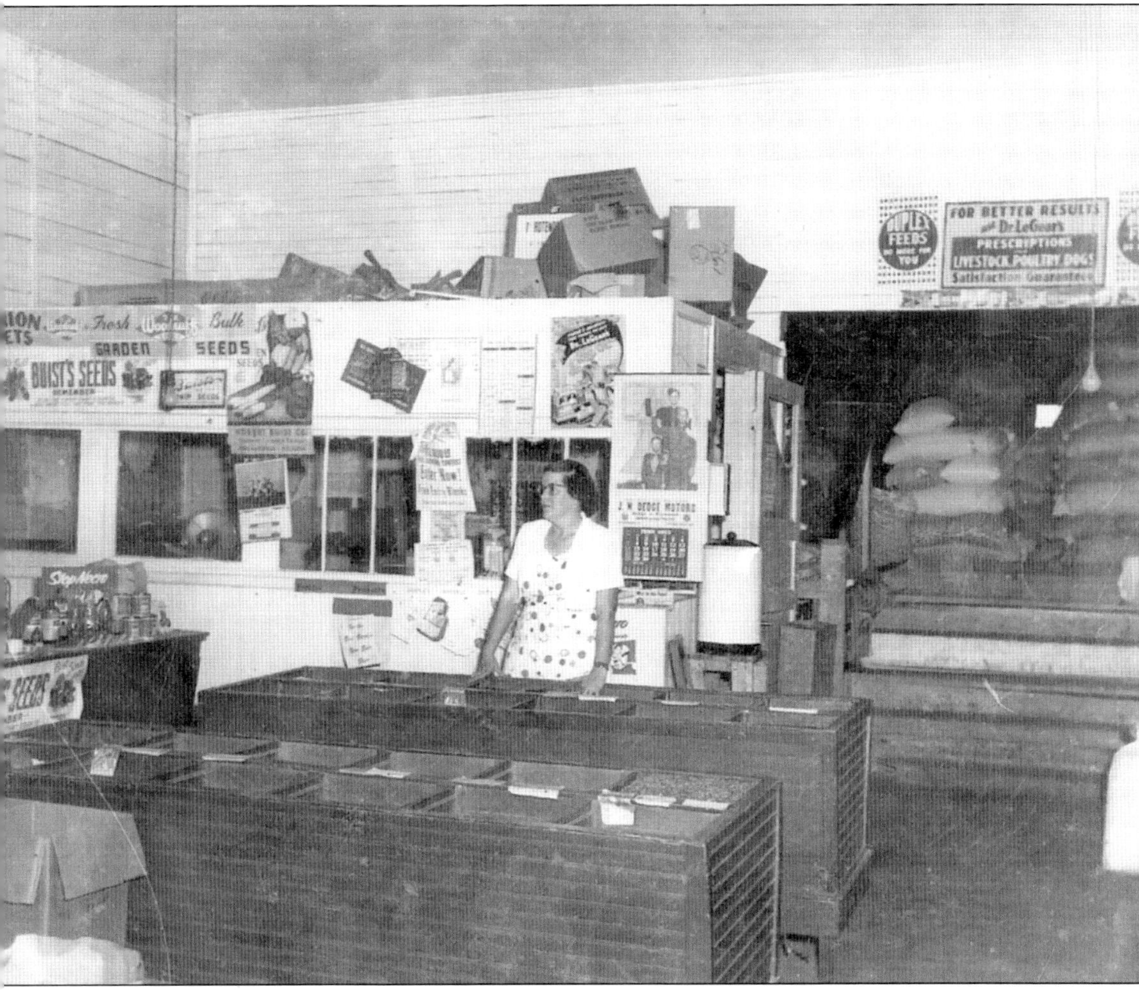

Rahn's Feed and Seed Store. Rebecca Exley Wilson is pictured here standing beside seed bins.

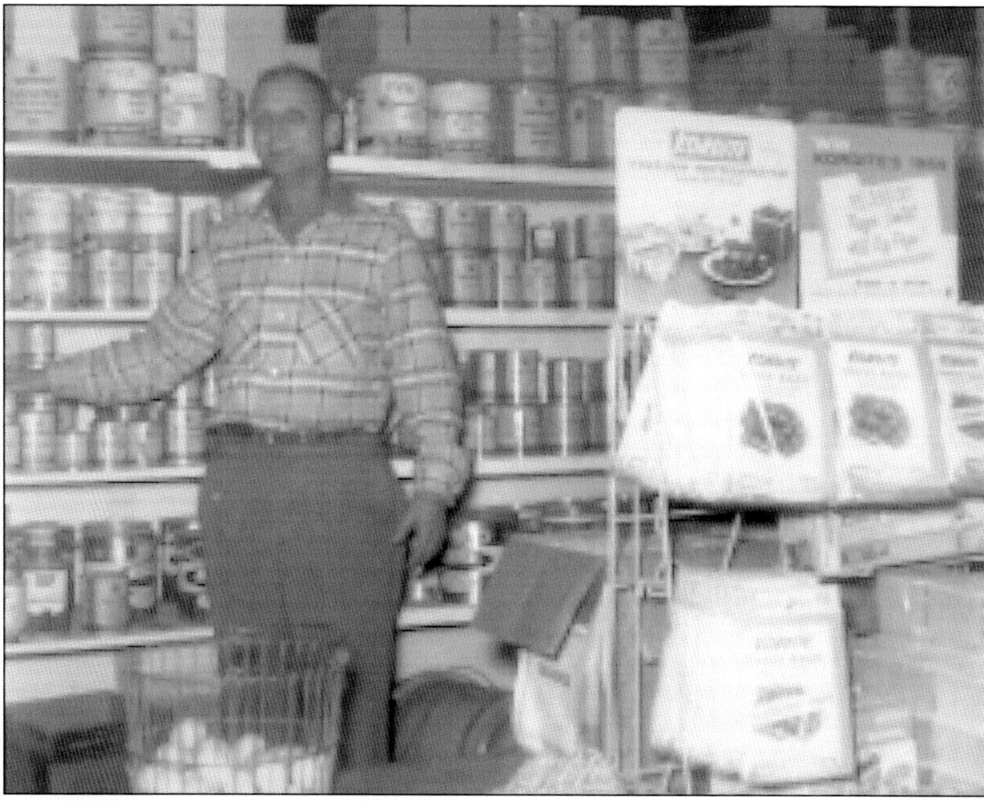

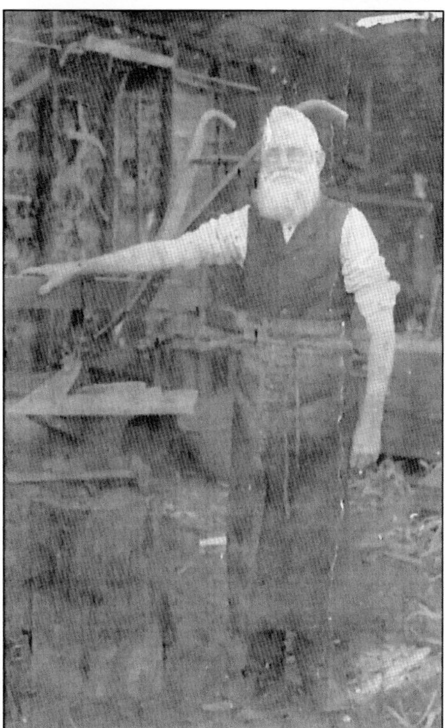

Rahn's Feed and Seed Store. Here, operator H.B. Rahn displays Southport Paint.

The Guyton Blacksmith. Micajah Futrelle, a blacksmith, worked near Pine Street in Guyton, close to the home of Doris Sweat Windsor.

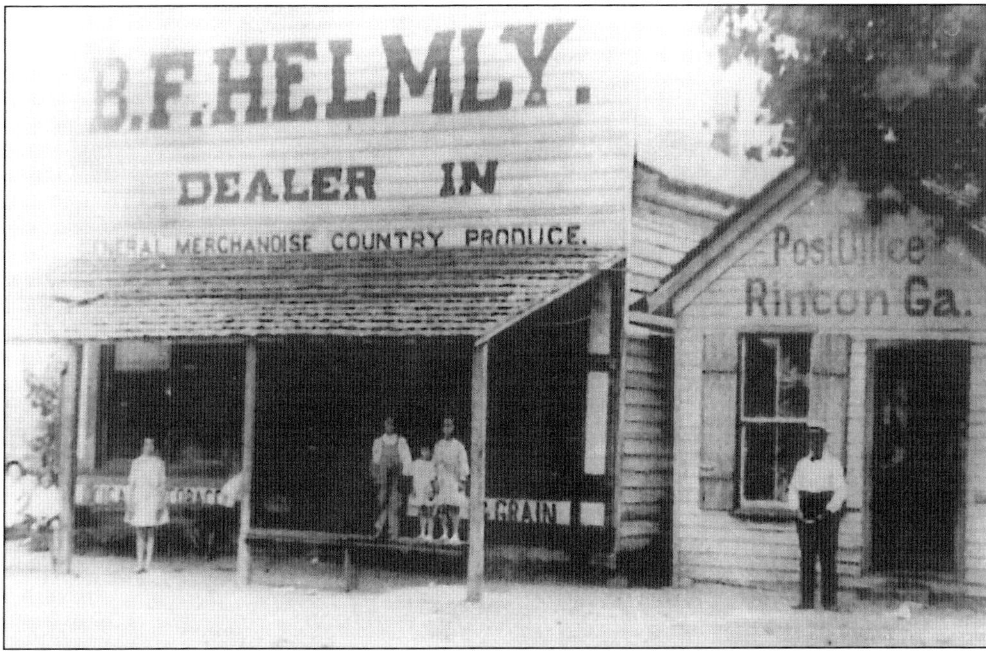

THE B.F. HELMLY STORE IN RINCON. In 1920 the post office and one of the leading retail stores in Rincon looked as they do in this picture. In front of the post office is the store owner and postmaster B.F. Helmly. To his immediate right are three of his children, C. Melanchthan Helmly, Louie Helmly, and Elizabeth Clyde Helmly. The others are unnamed. Can you identify them?

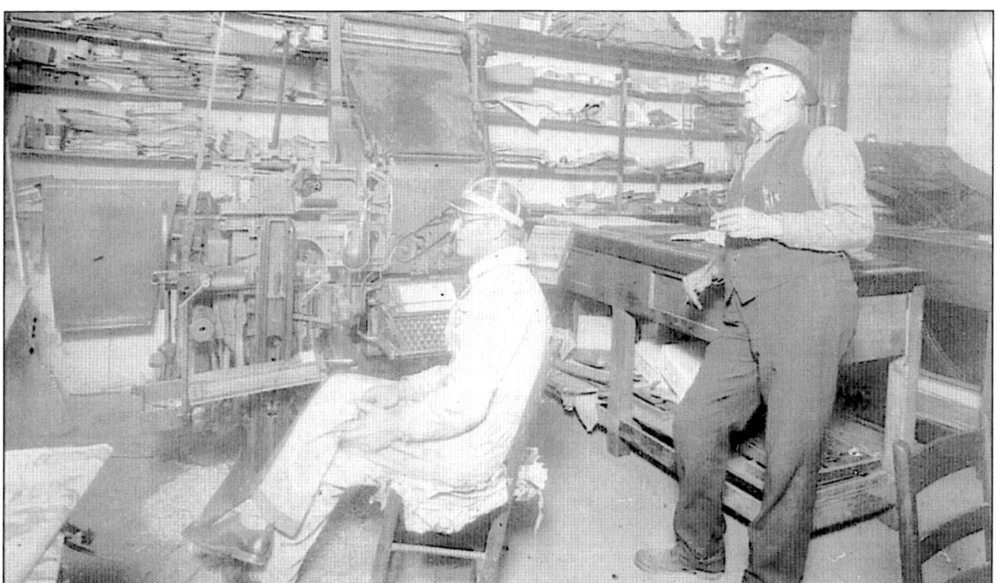

THE *SPRINGFIELD HERALD*. In 1925 Ted Dickey was the owner and Henry Morel was the printer of the local newspaper.

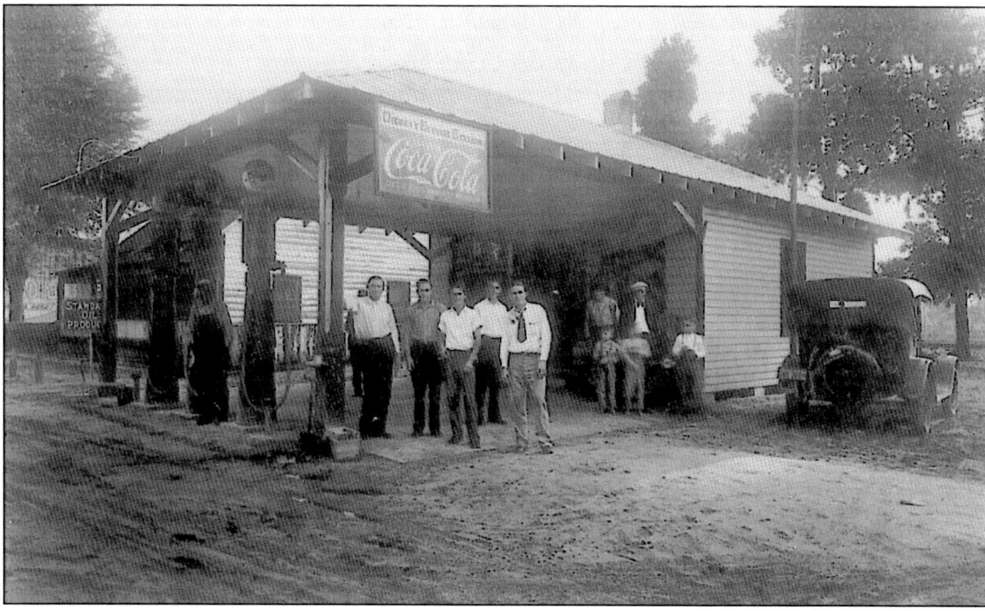

The Dickey Service Station. From left to right are owner Lawson Dickey, Leonard Dickey, Esten Barrs, Pat Ryan, George Dickey, L. Jefferson Dickey, and Green Dickey.

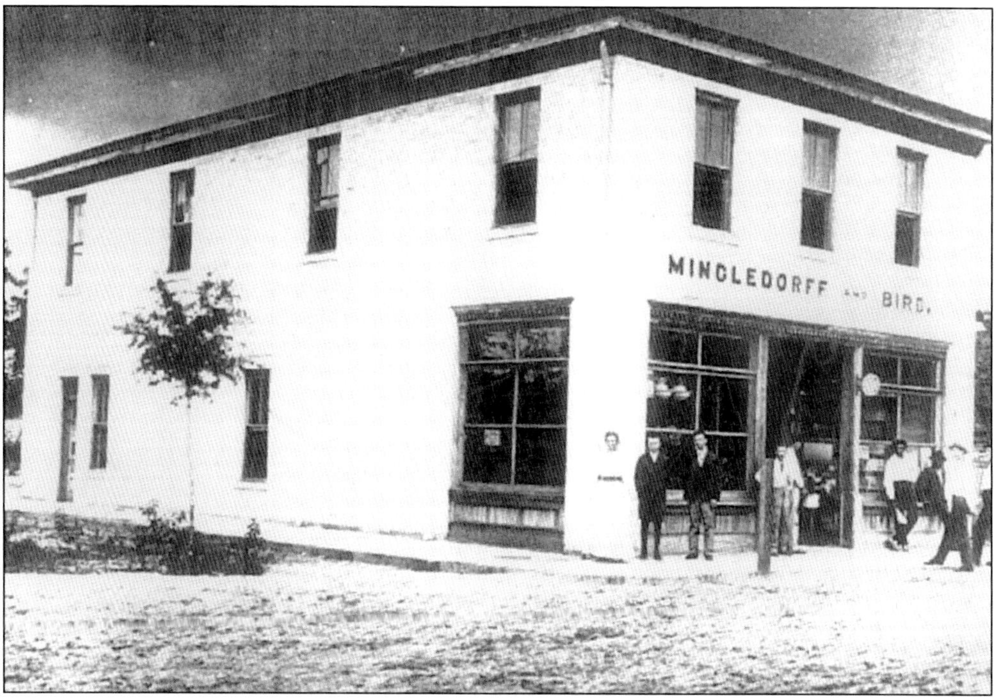

Mingledorff and Bird. There was only one retail store in Springfield in 1900 and it was operated by B.E. Mingledorff at Monroe (Oak) and Rabun Streets until 1907, when he and many others began the operation of stores on Washington (Laurel) Street in larger buildings and with more inventory. In 1908, there were three brick business buildings under construction at what is now the crossing of Laurel and First Streets. This location is still serving citizens today as Southern Frame and Art, owned and operated by the Lancasters.

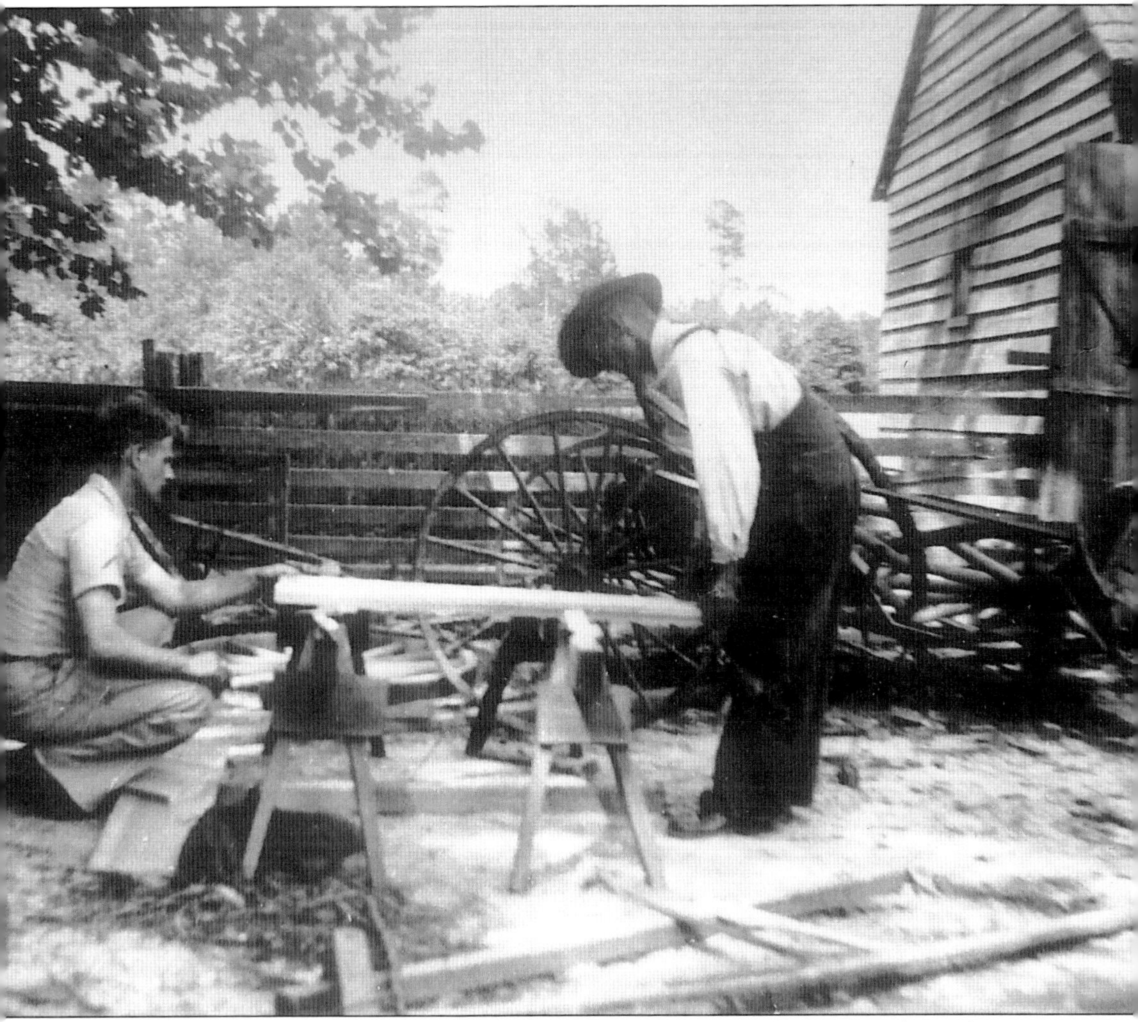

A JACK OF ALL TRADES. This timbercart was constructed *c.* 1927 for Diamond Match Co. by Abner Exley of Berryville Road. Abner was recognized as the best smitty in the county. He could shoe mules and horses, and repair or build wagons, carts, plows, hay rakes, etc. He made his own hubs from scratch and could cut, shape, weld, or thread metal or wood in his shop. Abner achieved his goals in life with a fifth-grade education, and he never served as an apprentice anywhere. His son Lawson was his regular helper.

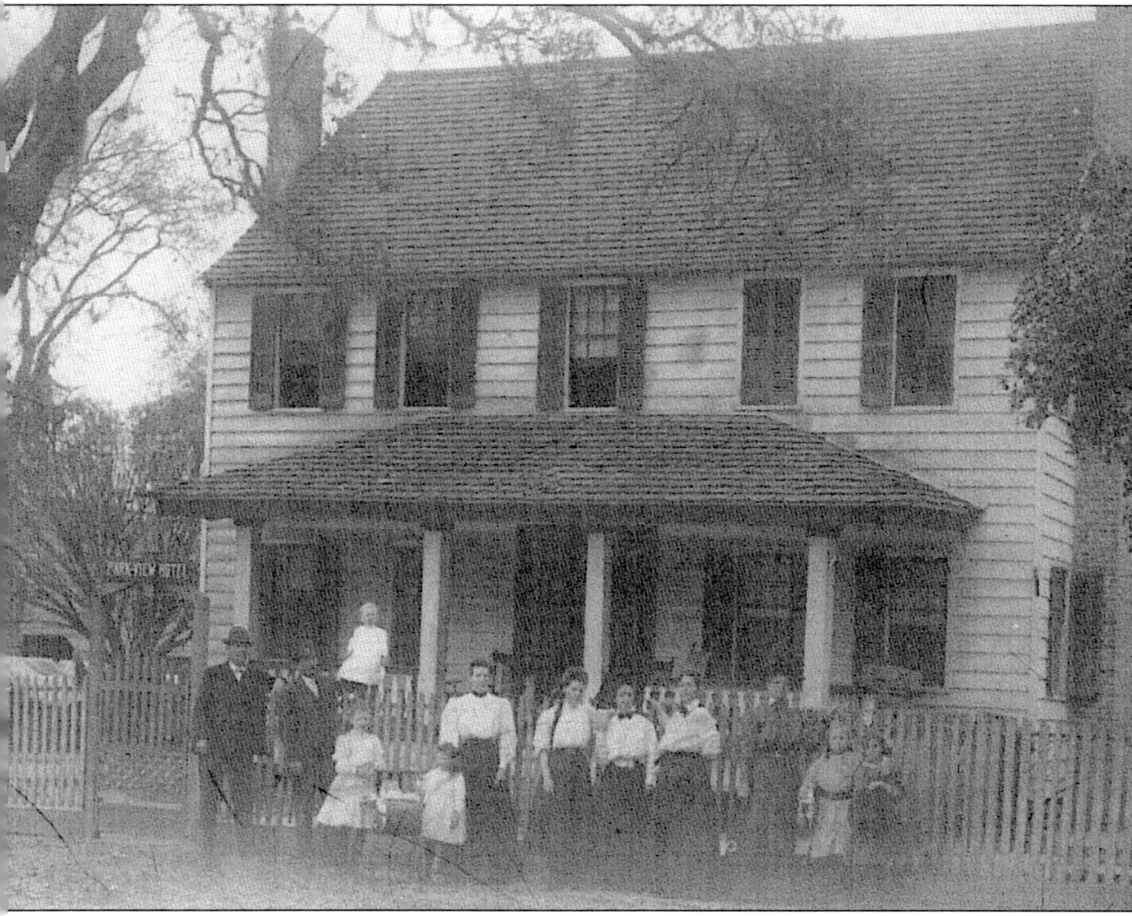

THE PARKVIEW HOTEL. The Parkview Hotel, which originally served as a bed and breakfast for out of town guests, was moved from Lot #4 in the town's early years. It was also the home of John Phillip Jones. In 1909 it became Parkview Hotel under the ownership and management of Mrs. Walton W. Seckinger. The hotel served many guests, including railroad officials and employees. It was later sold to the Mock family and served as their home for a number of years.

Four

Early Days of Education

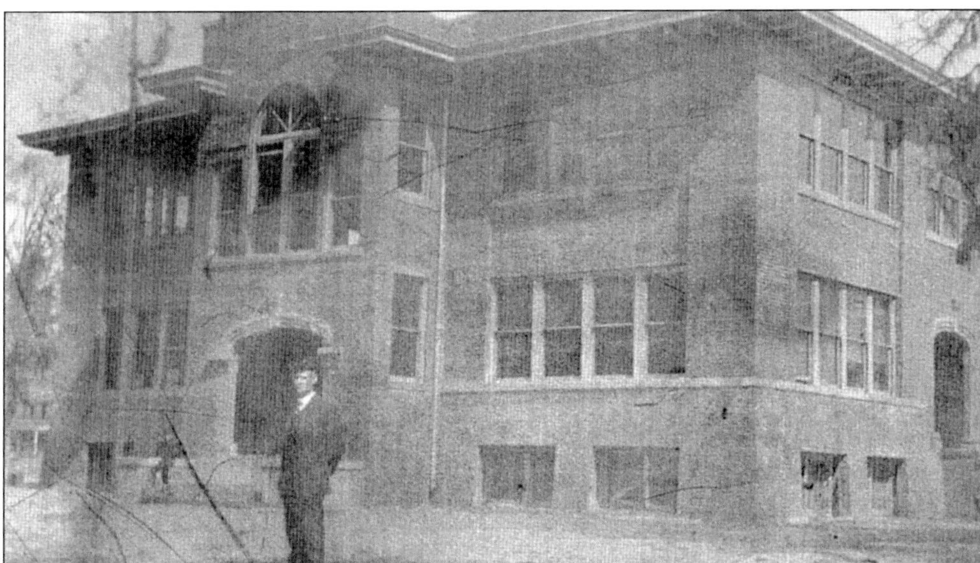

Effingham Academy. Money received from the sale of lots was to be used to build a courthouse and a jail on land reserved for county purposes. Any surplus money was to be used toward the building of an academy. During the 1840s, Effingham Academy was built using state and local funds in the block just west of where the present Treutlen Building is now located. The original building burned, and in 1911, the three-story brick structure shown above was completed. Standing beside the academy is Earnest Bascom Mingledorff, who began his teaching career in 1922. In 1938 he began his first term as superintendent of the county's schools. He served for 32 years.

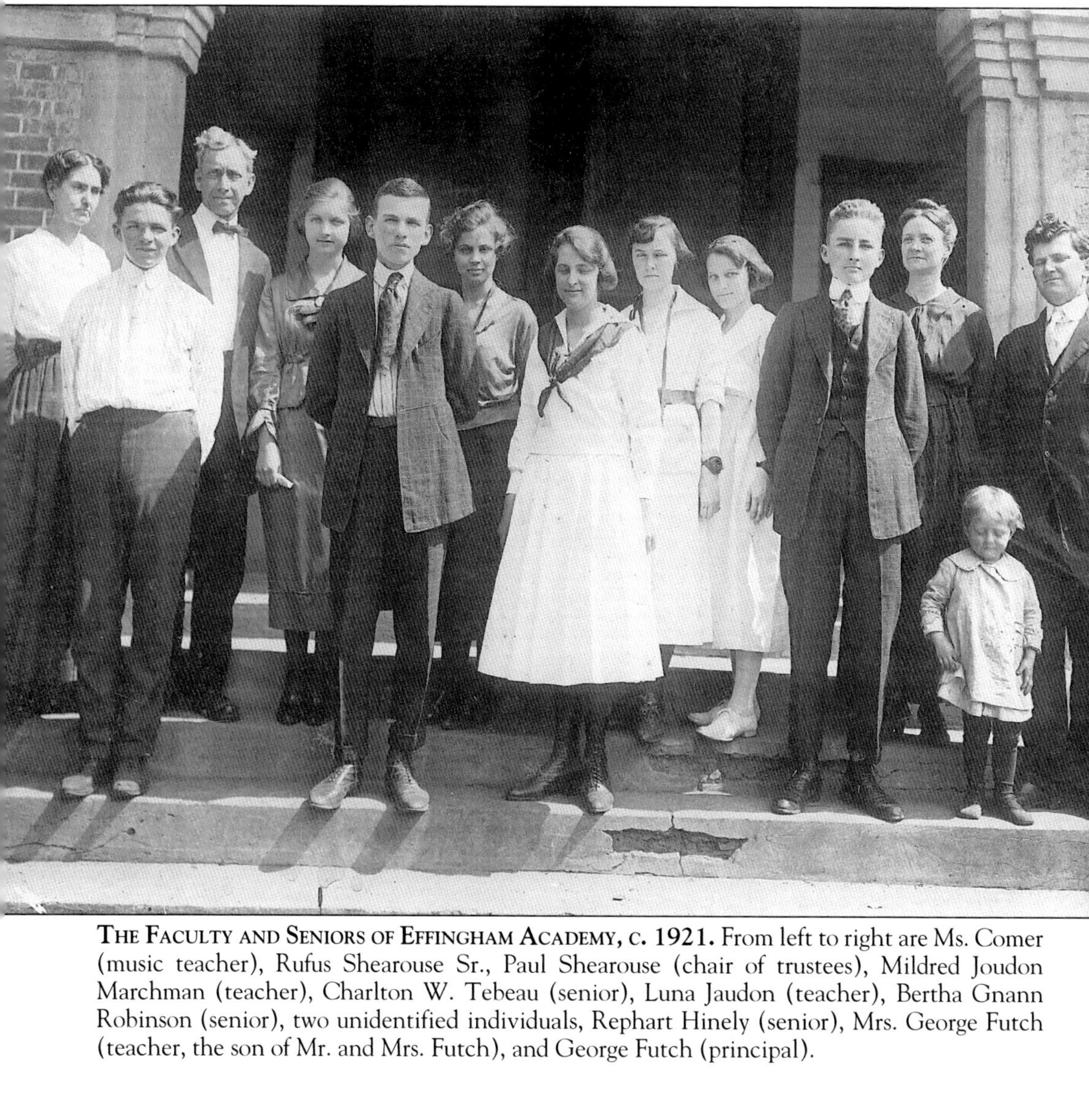

THE FACULTY AND SENIORS OF EFFINGHAM ACADEMY, C. 1921. From left to right are Ms. Comer (music teacher), Rufus Shearouse Sr., Paul Shearouse (chair of trustees), Mildred Joudon Marchman (teacher), Charlton W. Tebeau (senior), Luna Jaudon (teacher), Bertha Gnann Robinson (senior), two unidentified individuals, Rephart Hinely (senior), Mrs. George Futch (teacher, the son of Mr. and Mrs. Futch), and George Futch (principal).

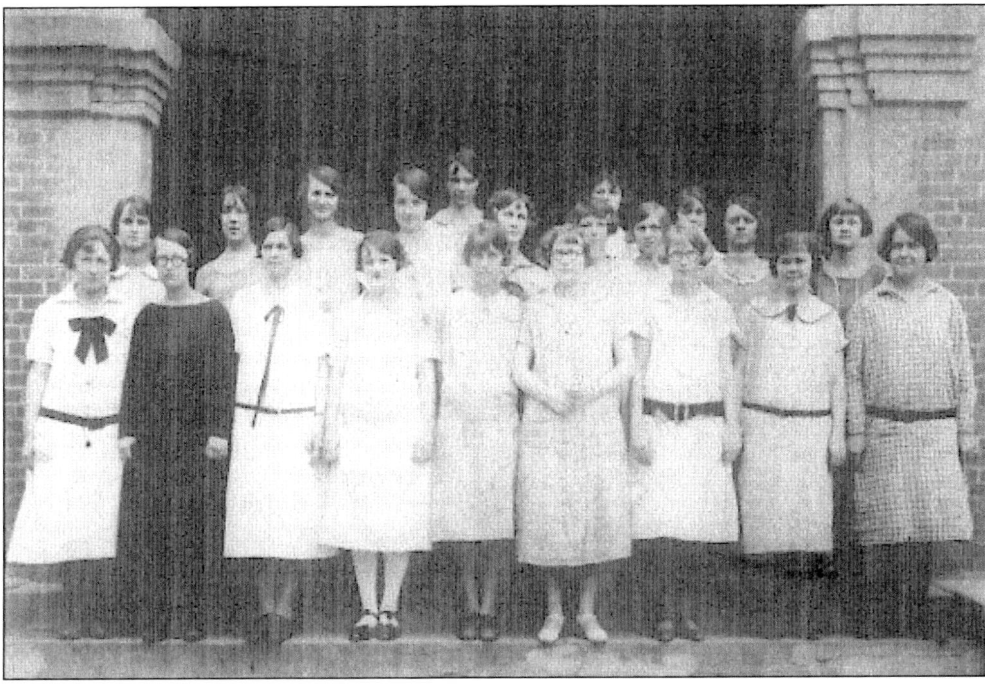

THE EFFINGHAM ACADEMY GLEE CLUB, 1925. Included in this group photograph are Jewel Helmly, Ruth Kieffer, Lina Usher, Helen Upchurch, Dorothy Neidlinger, Mrs. Cevie Robert (teacher), Lillian Neidlinger, Mary Dasher, Ethlyn Scott, Winnie ?, Sallie Low Atchison, Dorothy Arnsdorff, Nelwyn Scott, Lillian Seckinger, Mamie Lee Shipes, Jessie Mae Grovenstein, Gladys Jerald, Juctine Smith, and Nellie Mae Lee.

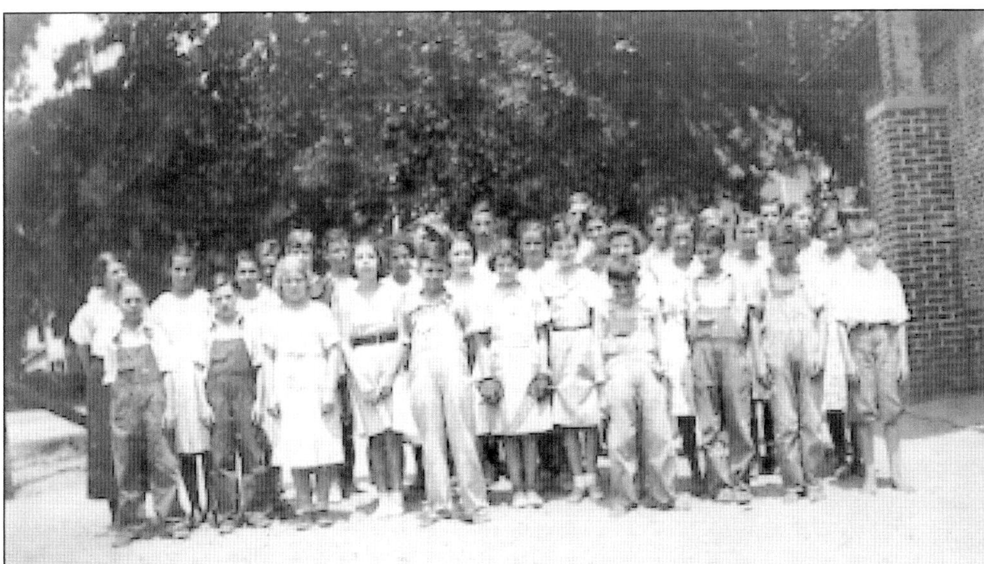

THE SEVENTH GRADE AT EFFINGHAM ACADEMY, 1933.

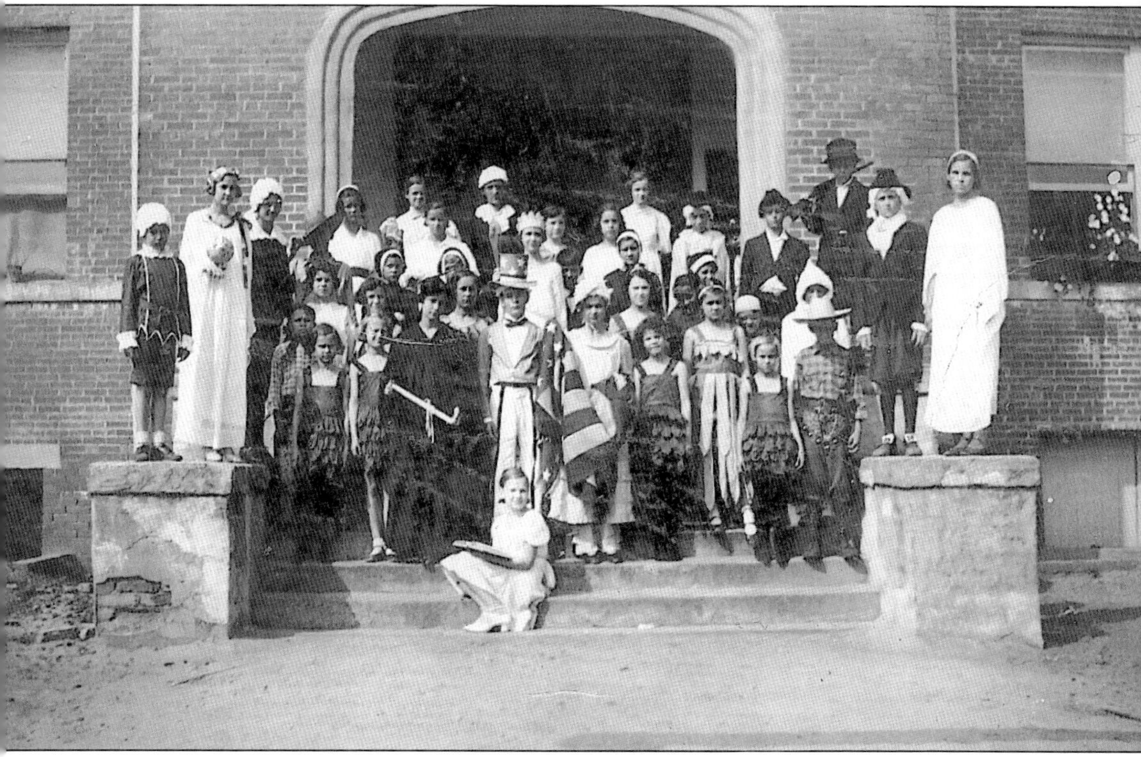

THE HISTORICAL PAGEANT AT EFFINGHAM ACADEMY ELEMENTARY, 1933.

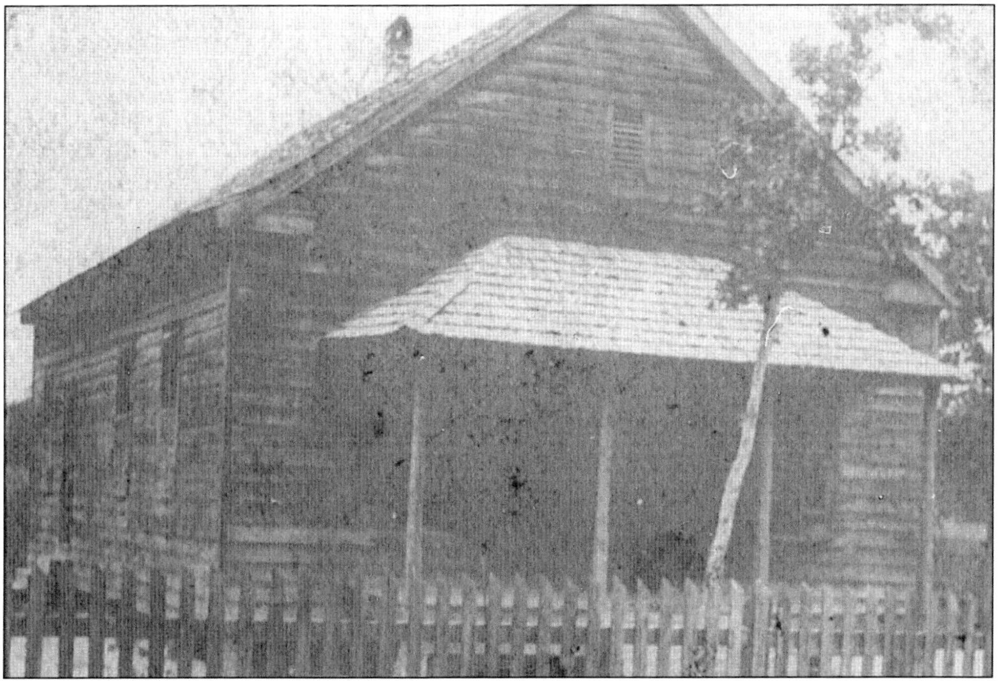

THE EBENEZER SCHOOL. Wesley Exley donated land for a schoolhouse on Rincon-Stillwell Road. The trustees were M.C. Exley, G.W. Seckinger, B.C. Zeigler, and J.A. Helmly.

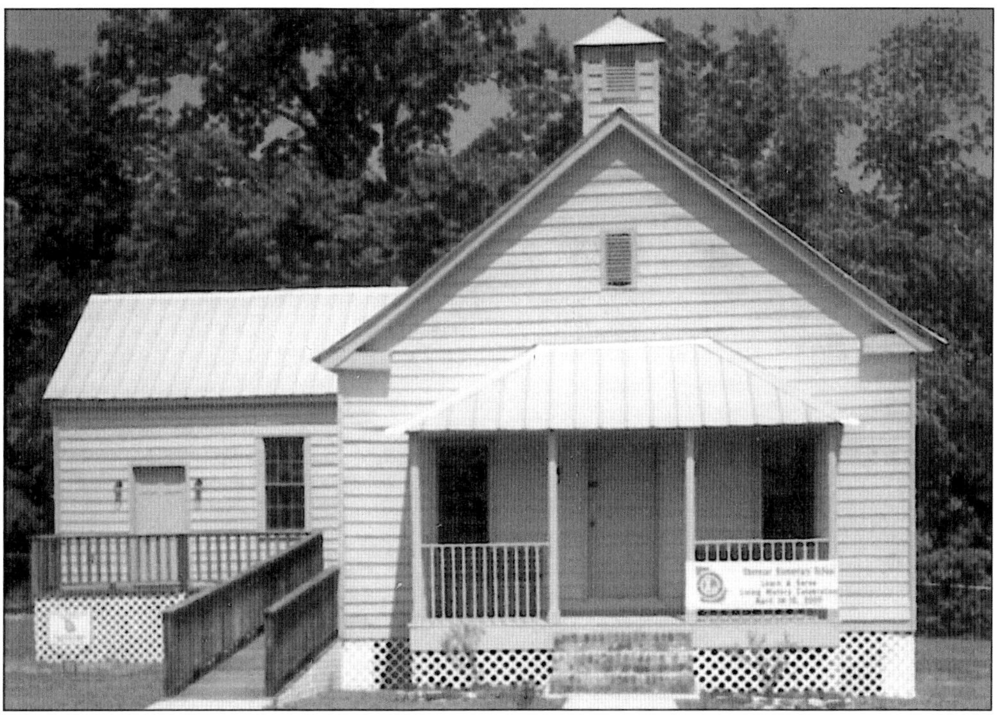

THE OLD EBENEZER SCHOOL. The old Ebenezer School has been restored as a living history museum on the campus of the modern Ebenezer Elementary School. Mrs. Angie Wendelken was principal when the restoration was completed.

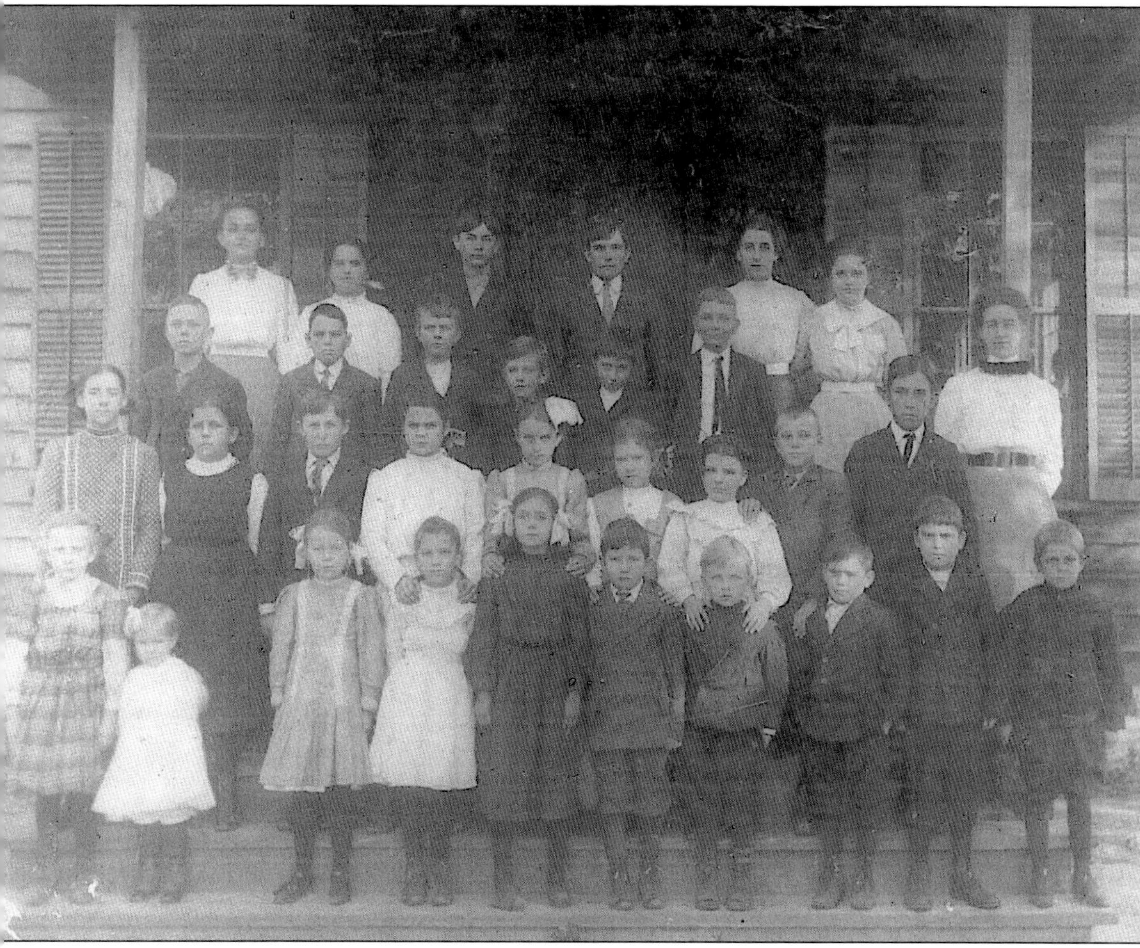

THE LEBANNON SCHOOL, 1928.

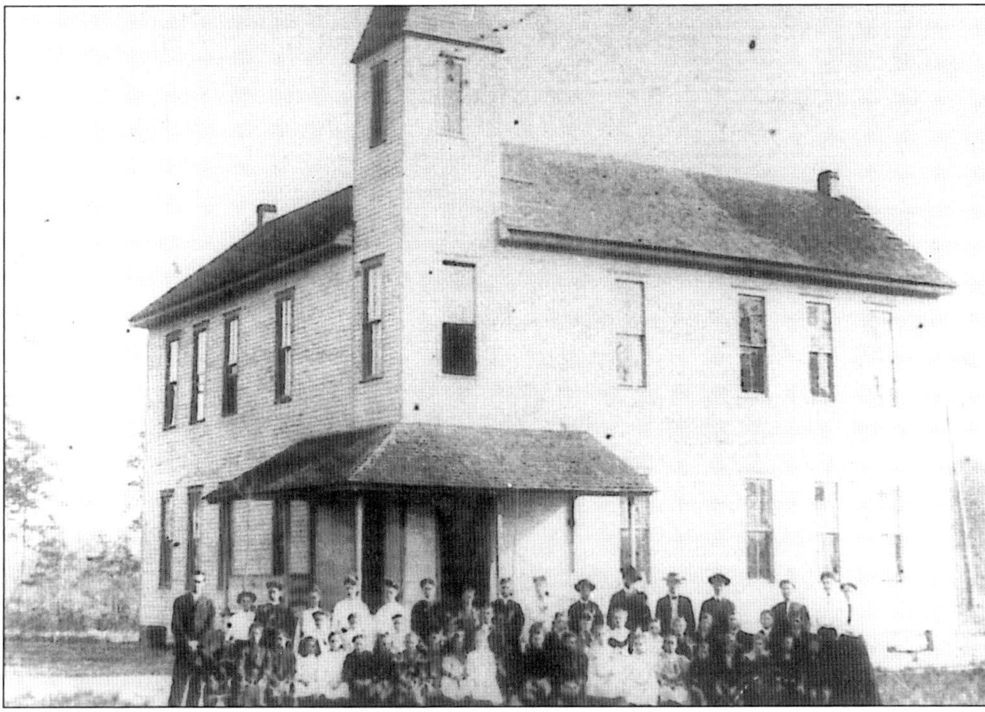

THE RINCON SCHOOL.

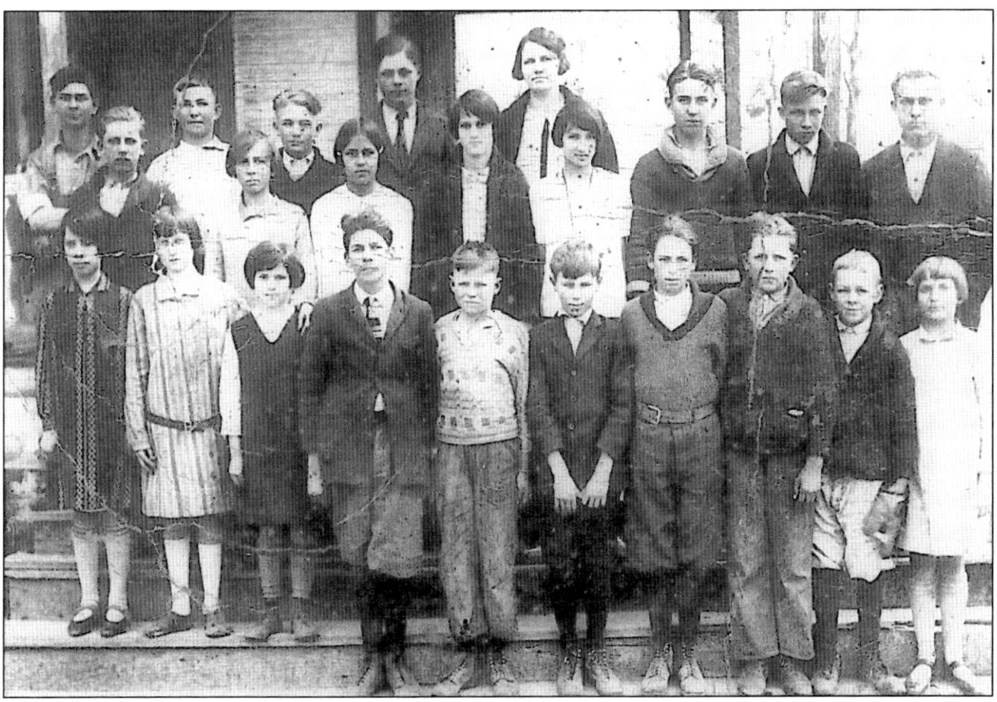

PUPILS OF THE RINCON SCHOOL.

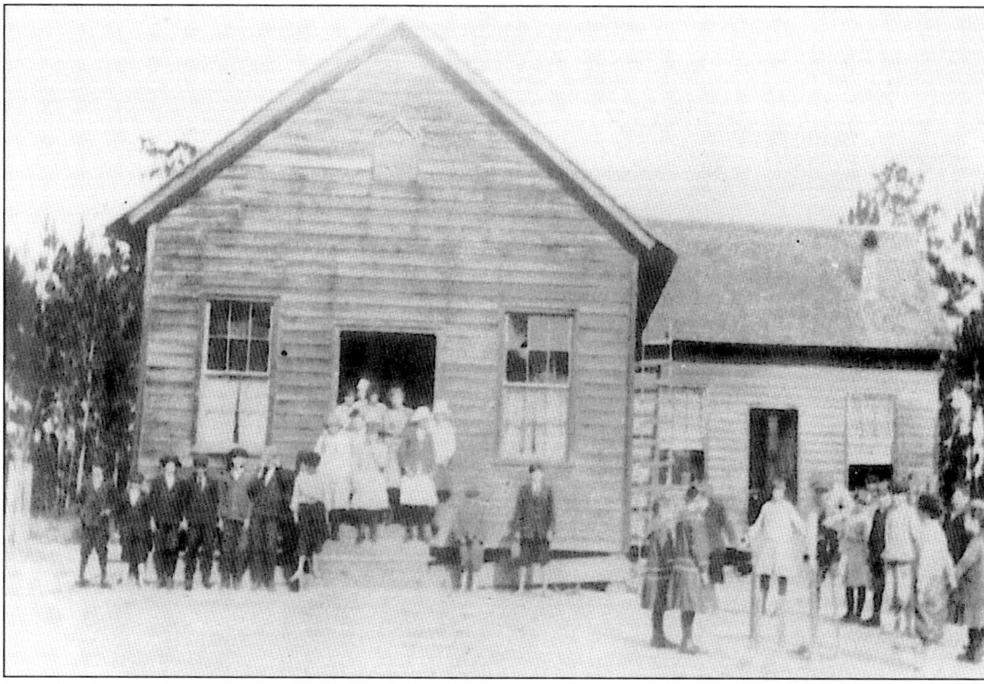

THE STILLWELL SCHOOL.

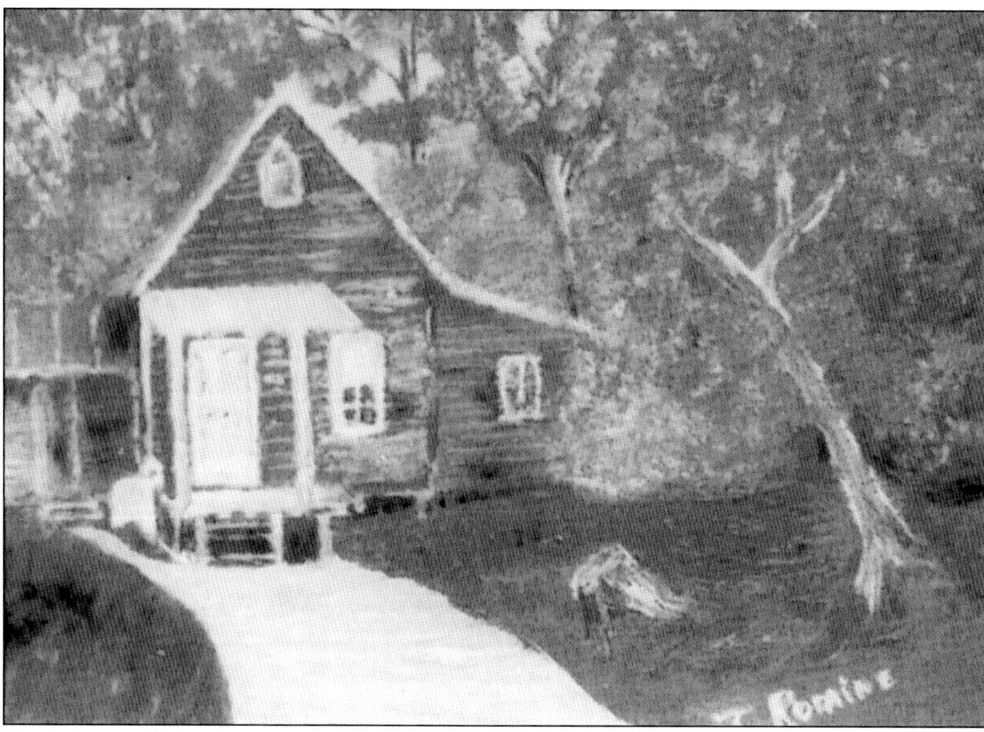

THE MIDWAY SCHOOL.

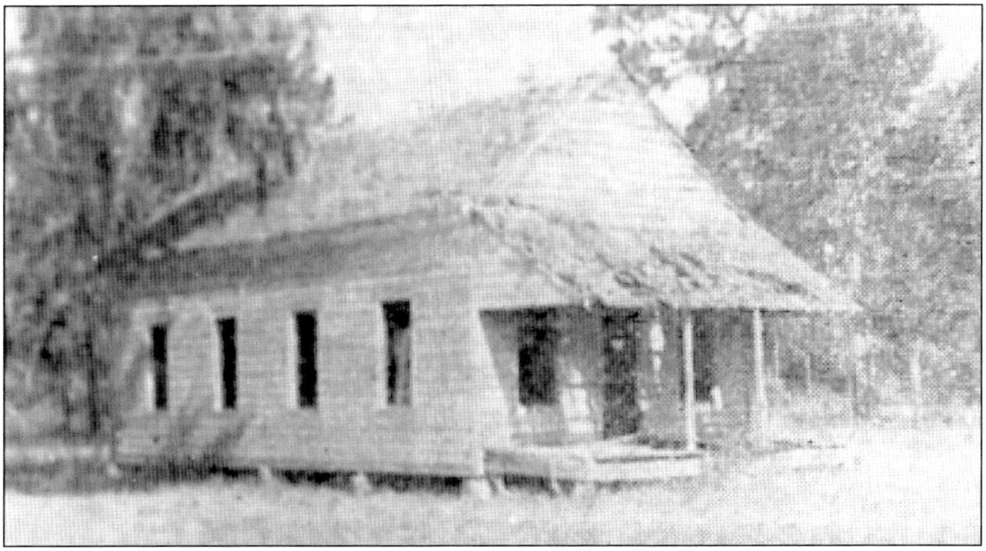

THE MARLOW ZION SCHOOL.

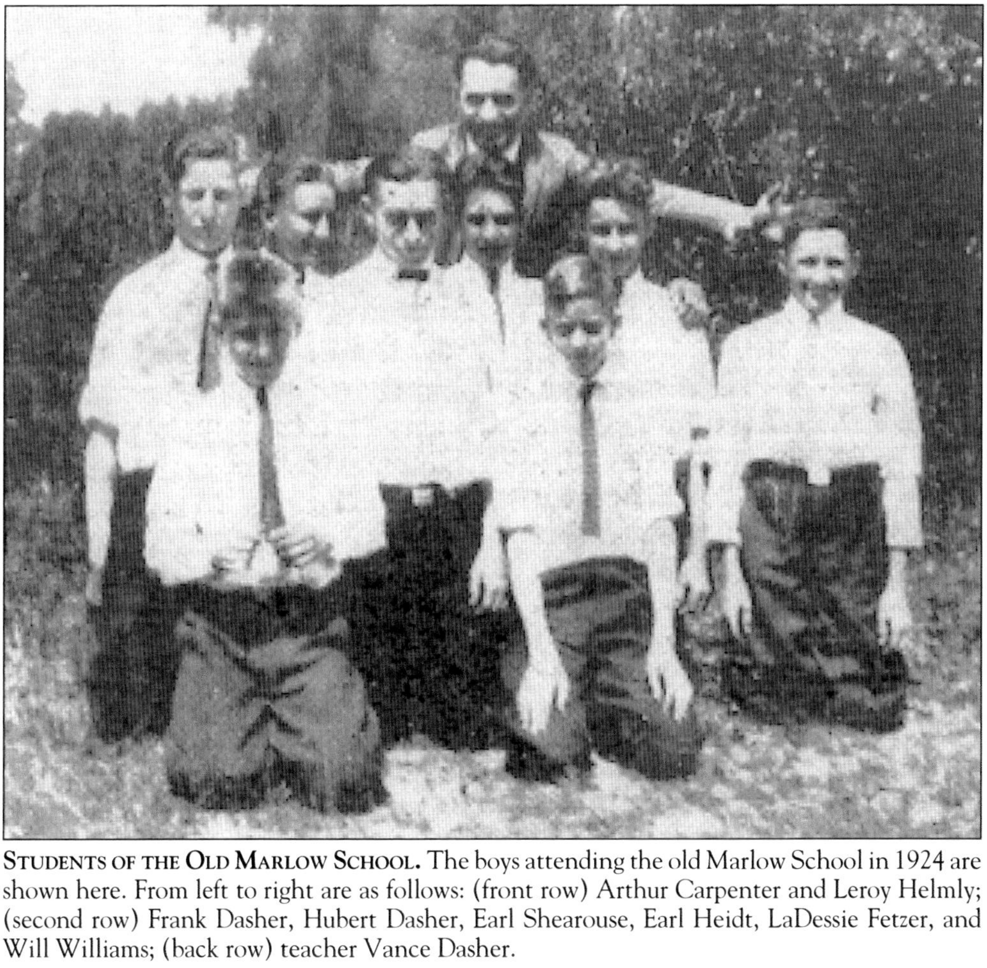

STUDENTS OF THE OLD MARLOW SCHOOL. The boys attending the old Marlow School in 1924 are shown here. From left to right are as follows: (front row) Arthur Carpenter and Leroy Helmly; (second row) Frank Dasher, Hubert Dasher, Earl Shearouse, Earl Heidt, LaDessie Fetzer, and Will Williams; (back row) teacher Vance Dasher.

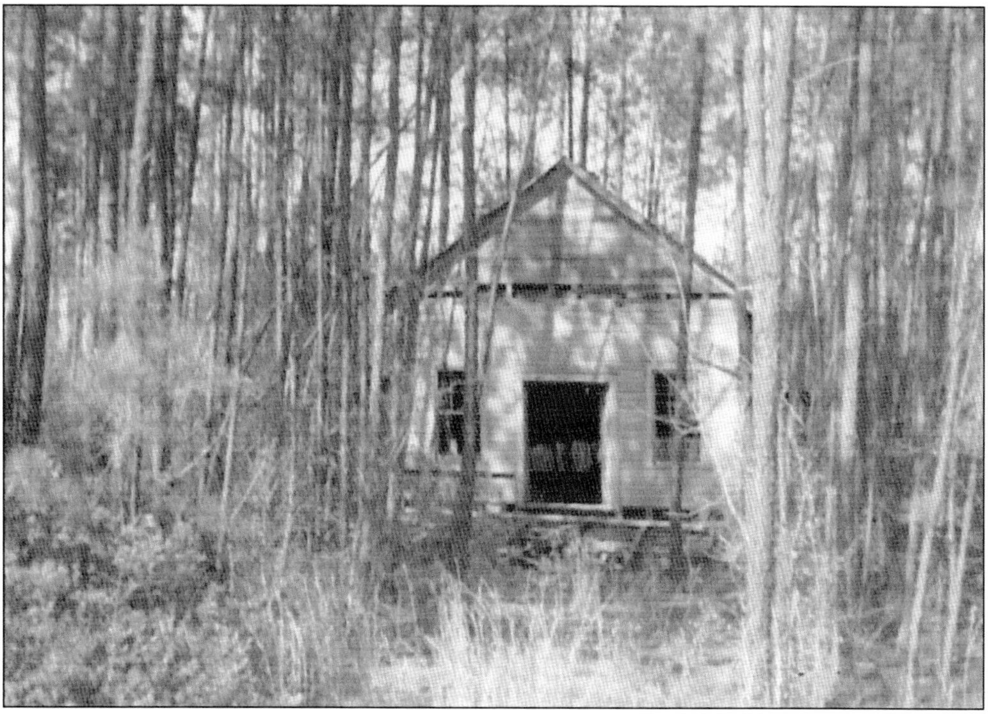

THE RACE PATH SCHOOL.

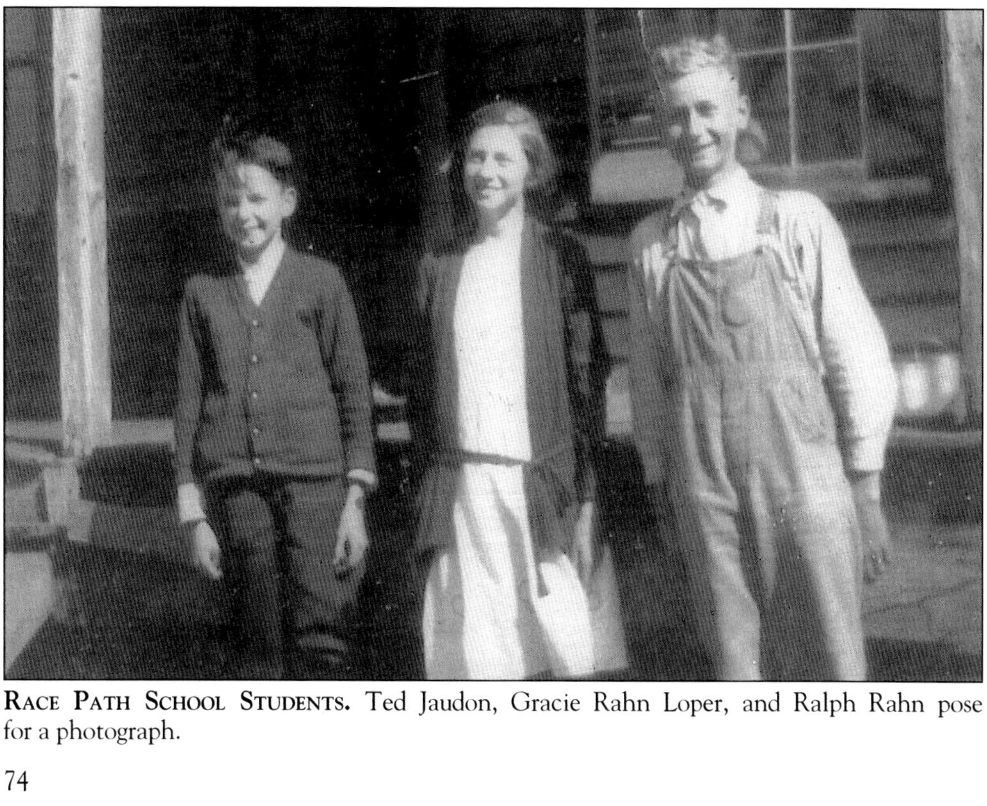

RACE PATH SCHOOL STUDENTS. Ted Jaudon, Gracie Rahn Loper, and Ralph Rahn pose for a photograph.

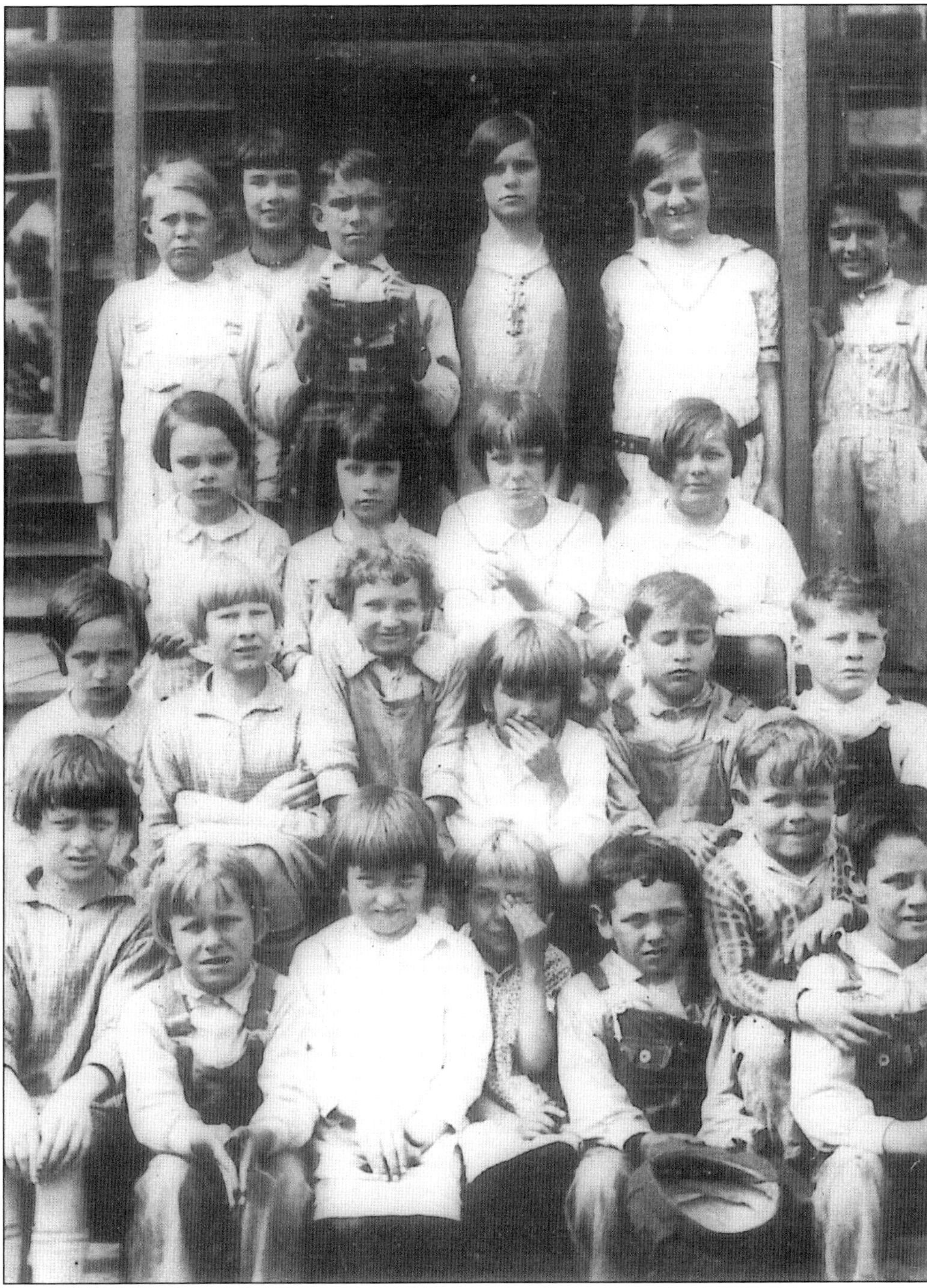

The Green Morgan School. This one-room school was located on Green Morgan Road, about one-and-one-half miles east of the old Dixie Highway and about four-and-one-half miles west of Clyo. One teacher taught the primer through the seventh grade. The Green Morgan School was built about 1900 and served families in that community until the late 1930s. Clara Freyermuth inherited the land on which the school was located. George, her husband, had been a student there and decided to save the building by moving it to their backyard near Guyton.

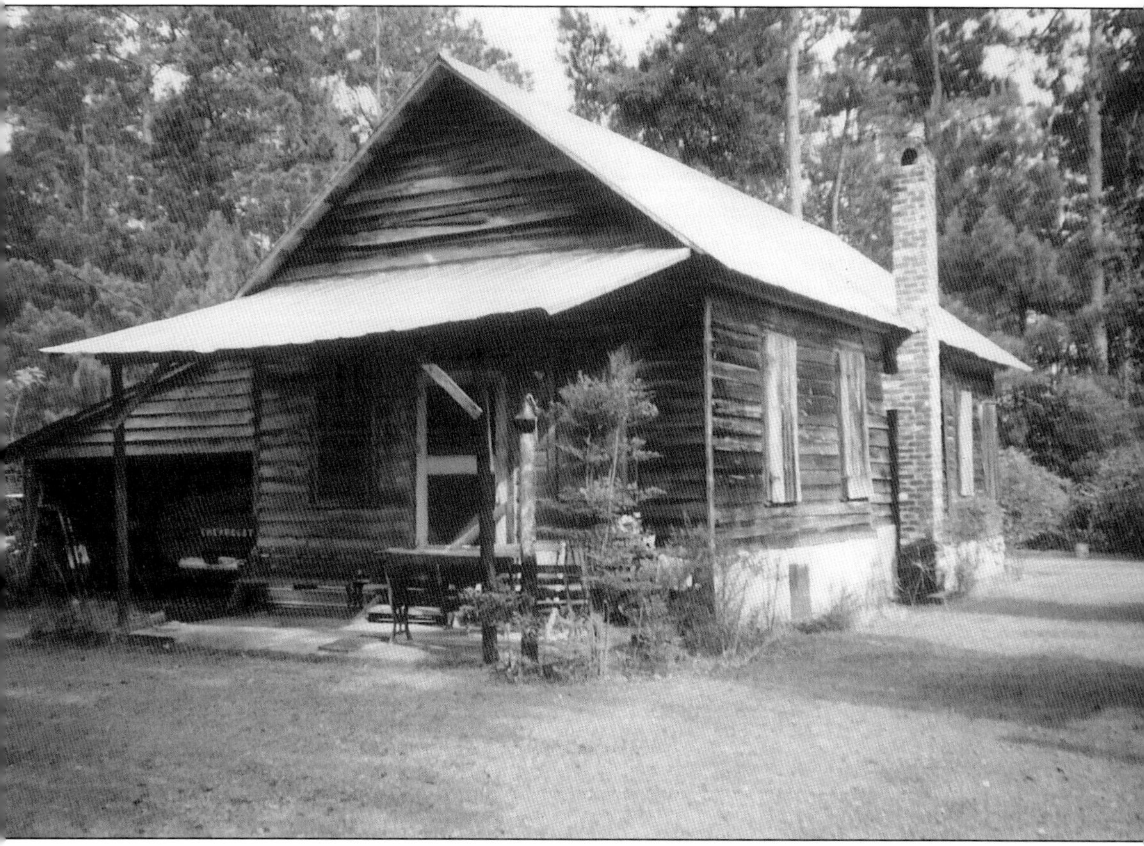

THE GREEN MORGAN SCHOOL.

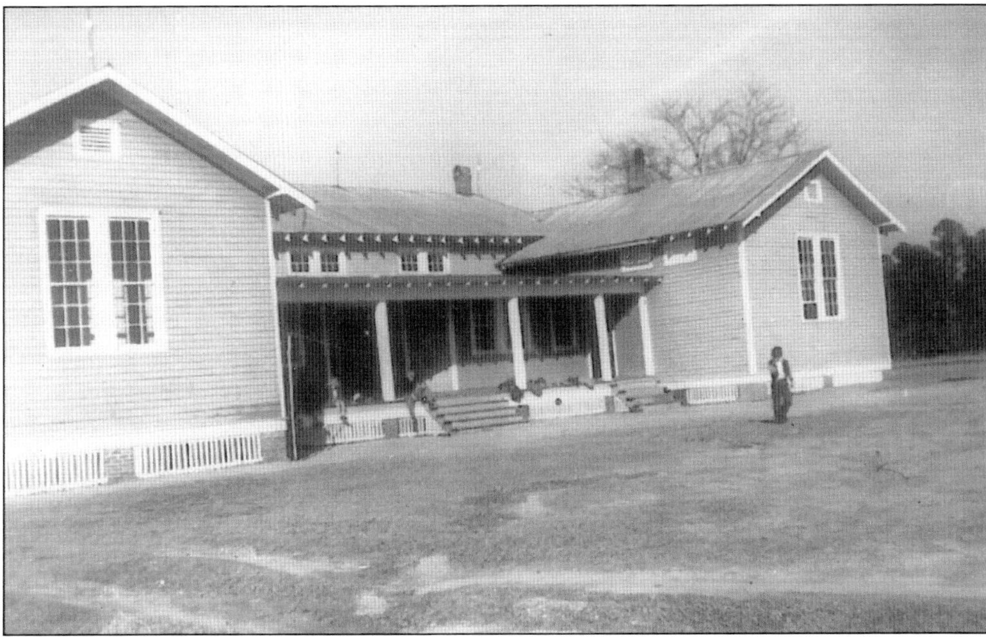

The Clyo Consolidated High School. Graduating seniors of this high school in 1926 included Madison Morgan, Valda Compton, J. Edmund Exley, Marion N. Exley, Myrtie Johnson, and Sadie Wheeler. Hollis Morgan graduated in 1927.

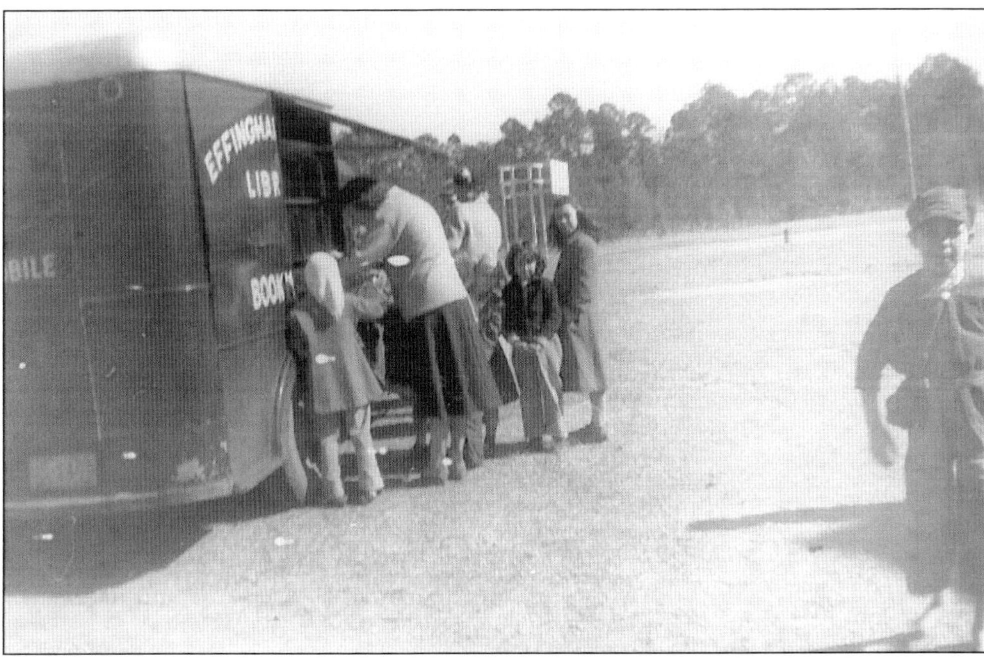

The Effingham County Bookmobile. Edna Morgan and students at the Clyo School are shown getting books from the bookmobile.

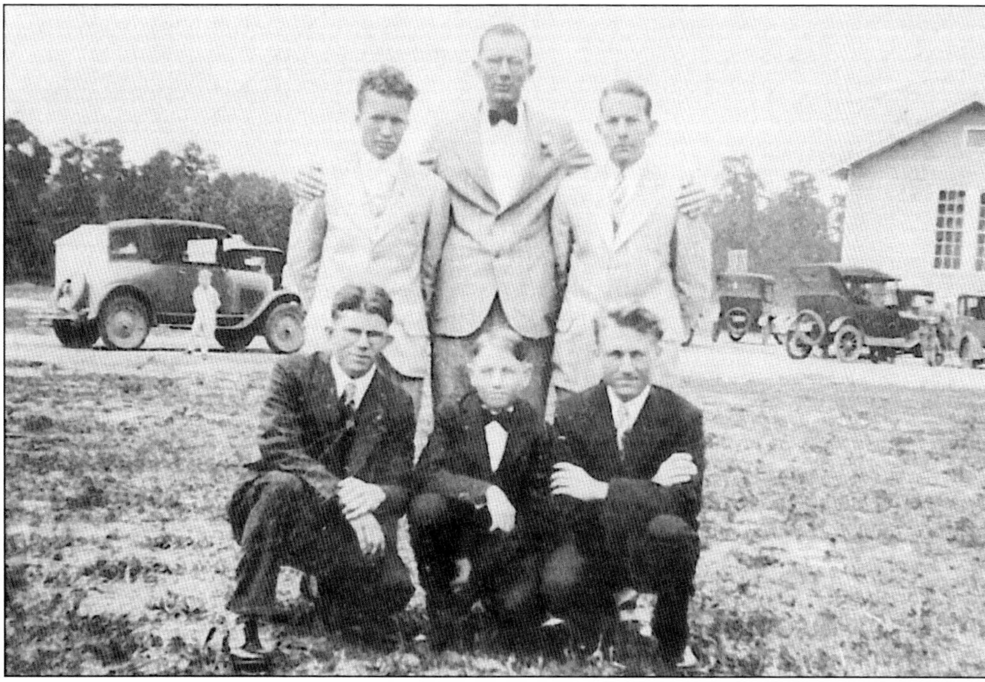

CLYO STUDENTS. From left to right are (front row) Claude Seckinger, unidentified, and Buck Morgan; (back row) Rudolph DeLoach, Bill Mingledorff, and Wyberg Hanberry.

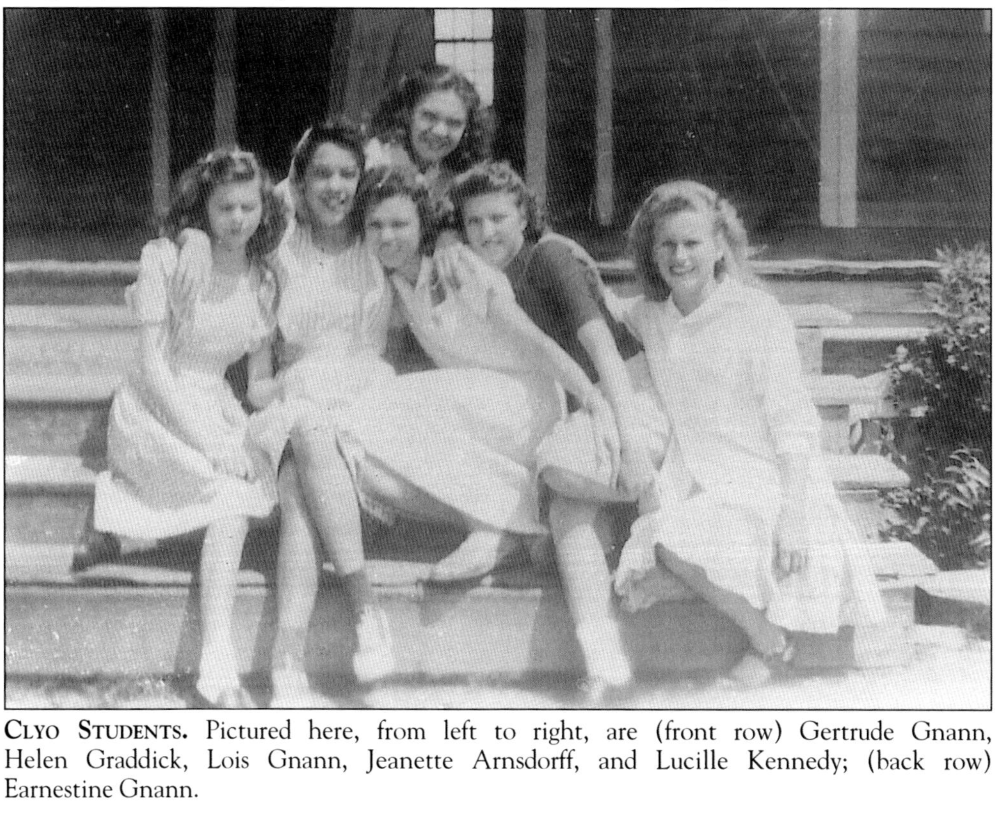

CLYO STUDENTS. Pictured here, from left to right, are (front row) Gertrude Gnann, Helen Graddick, Lois Gnann, Jeanette Arnsdorff, and Lucille Kennedy; (back row) Earnestine Gnann.

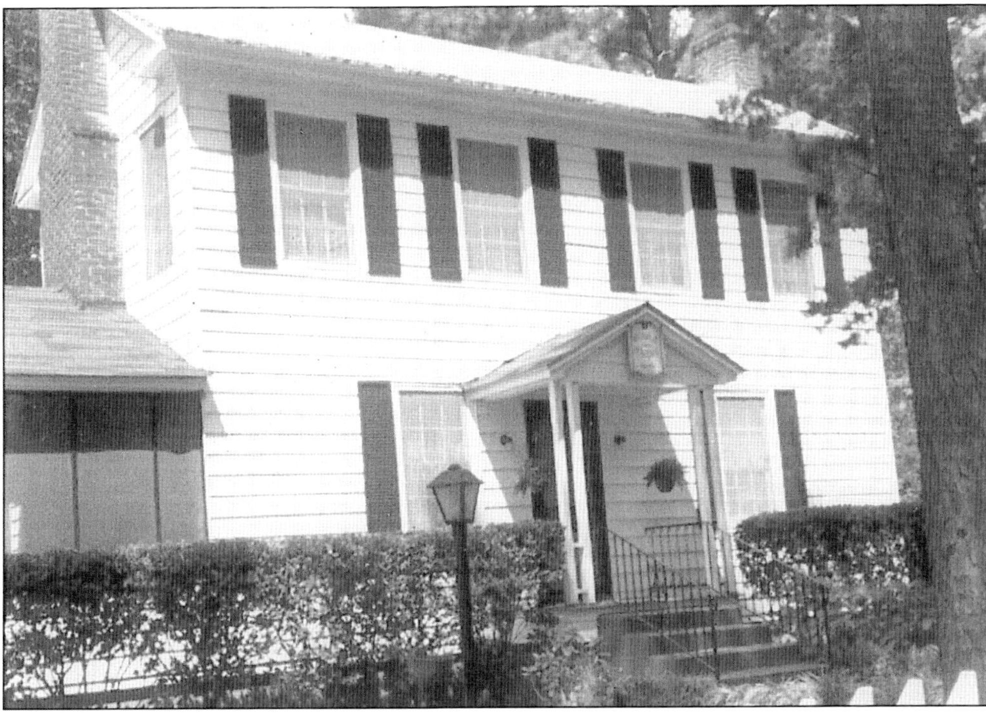

WHITESVILLE ACADEMY IN GUYTON.

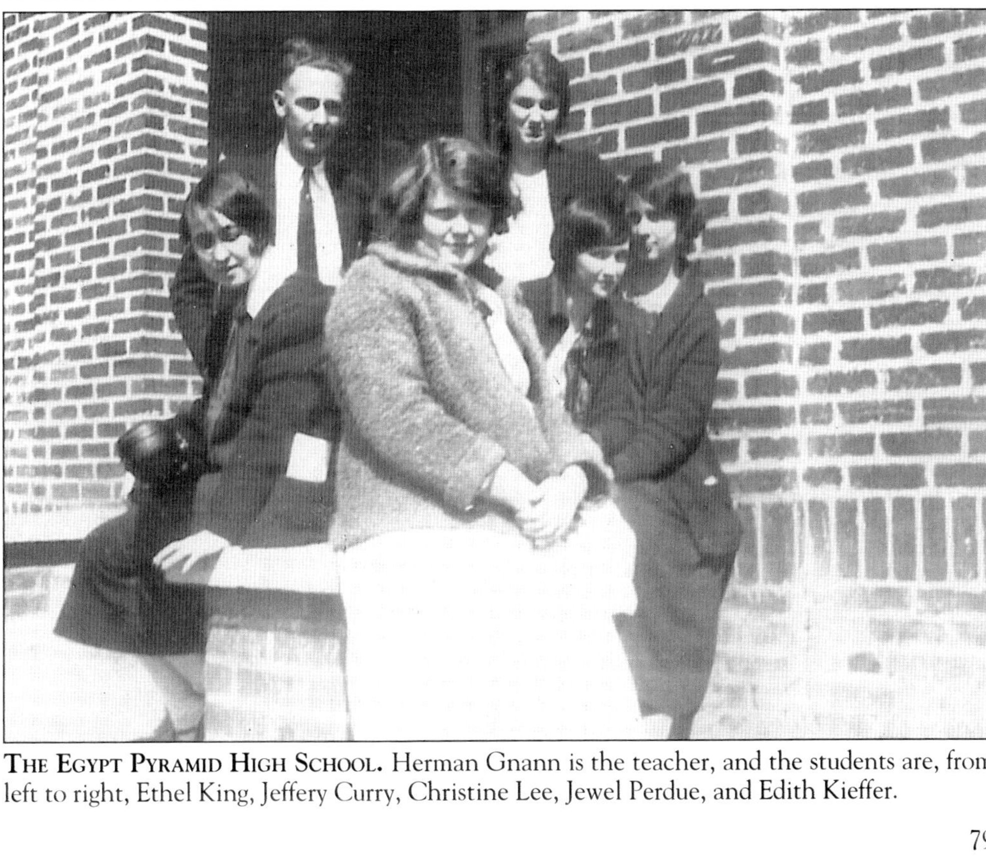

THE EGYPT PYRAMID HIGH SCHOOL. Herman Gnann is the teacher, and the students are, from left to right, Ethel King, Jeffery Curry, Christine Lee, Jewel Perdue, and Edith Kieffer.

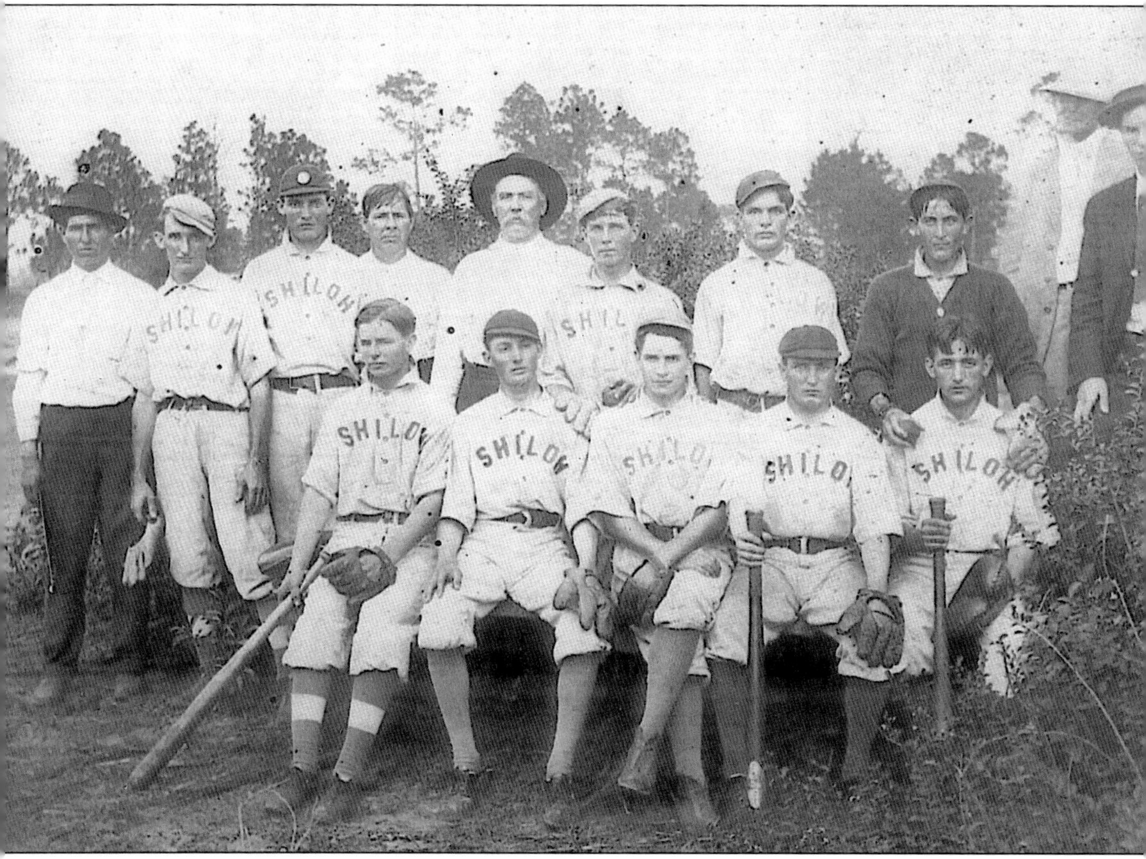

The Shiloh Baseball Team. Included in this team picture are Burgsteiner, Hinely, Carr, Rahn, Neidlinger, and Ford.

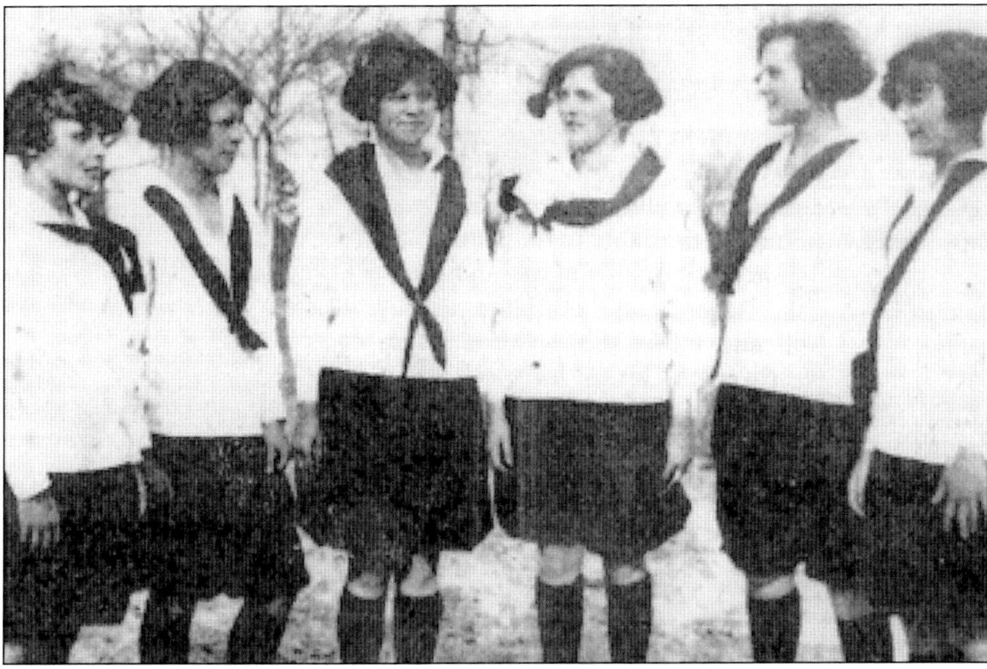

The Rincon High Basketball Team in the Late 1920s. From left to right are Georgia Helmly Wessinger, Grace Waldhour Arnsdorff, Daisy Kessler Rahn, Gladys Lynch Helmly, Rita Hinely Davis, and Clyde Helmly Walcher.

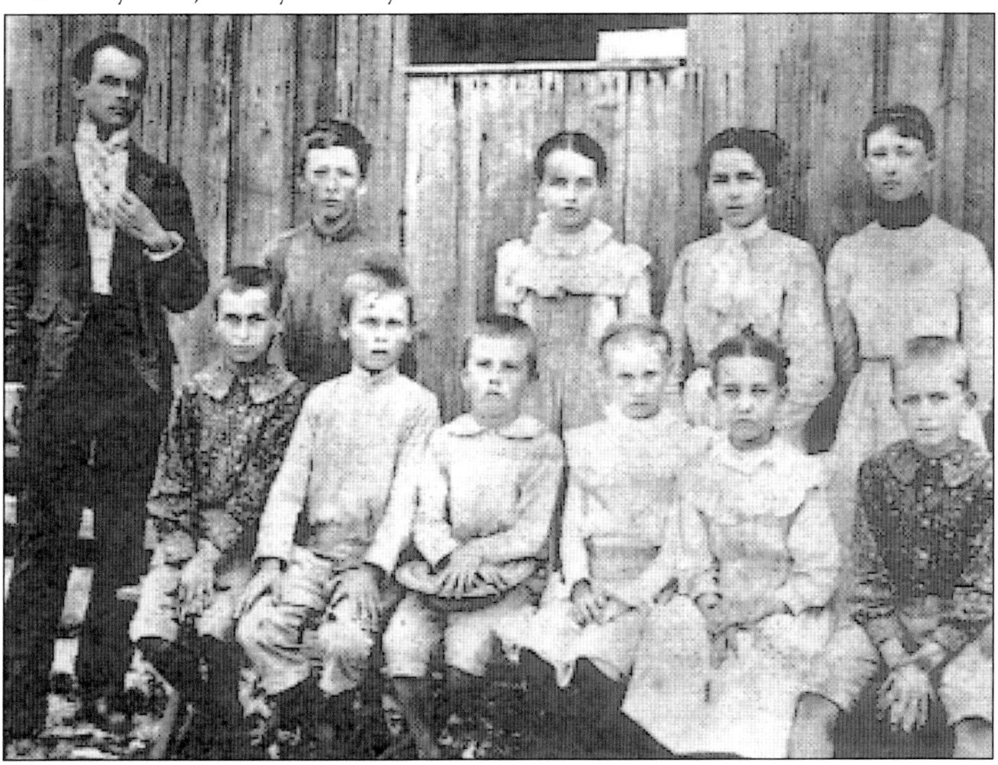

The Indigo School and Students.

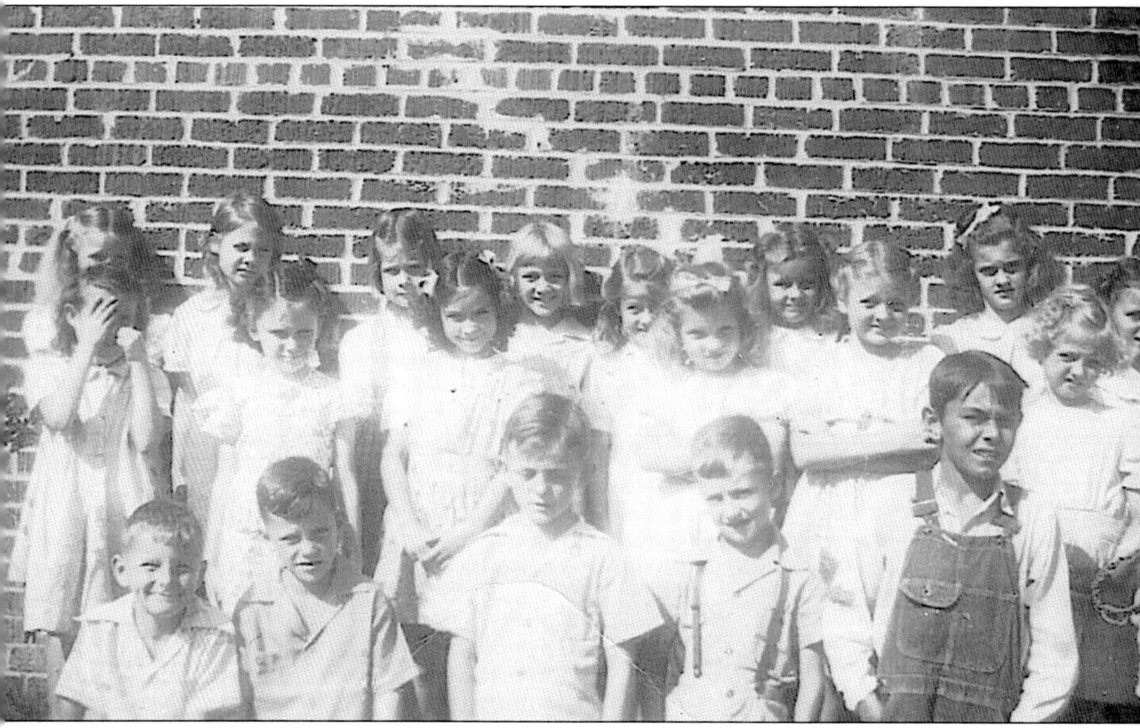

The First Grade at Effingham Academy. These students graduated as the last seniors from Effingham Academy (Springfield High School). From left to right they are as follows: (front row) Orville Beckwith, Donald Hodges, Wiley Thomas, Charles Hinely, and Roger Williams; (middle row) Margie Mae Boyles, Catherine Morgan, Rachel Wilson, Betty Lee Rahn, Mary Will Marchman, and Mary Jane Rahn; (back row) Barbara Boyles, Jewel Boyles, Margie Anderson, Ava Gnann, Carol Morgan, Paula Zittrouer, Norma Jean Hodges, and Joyce Rahn.

Five

Churches

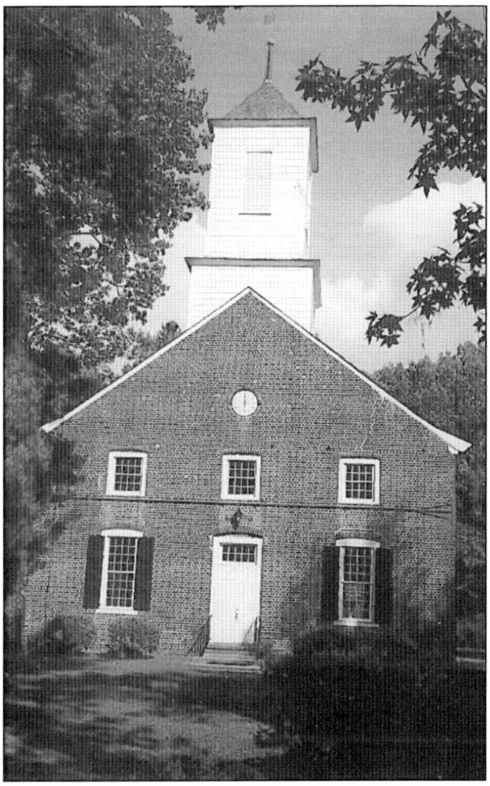

The Jerusalem Lutheran Church. This church was organized in 1733 in Augsburg, Germany by Protestant exiles from Salzburg, Austria. The building shown here was built in 1769 and was the focal point of the thriving village of Austrian colonists who sought religious freedom. In 1779 the town of Ebenezer was captured by the British under Col. Archibald Campbell. During the town's occupancy by the British, the church was used first as a hospital and later as a stable for calvary horses. In 1782, Continentals under Gen. Anthony Wayne drove the British out of Ebenezer, and in July 1782, the Georgia Legislature met in the church. John Adam Treutlen, Georgia's first elected governor, was raised in the orphanage here, taught school here, and was an active member of the church. The walls are 21 inches thick and are constructed of handmade brick fashioned from local clay deposits. The church members remain an active congregation of the Southeastern Synod of the Lutheran Church in America.

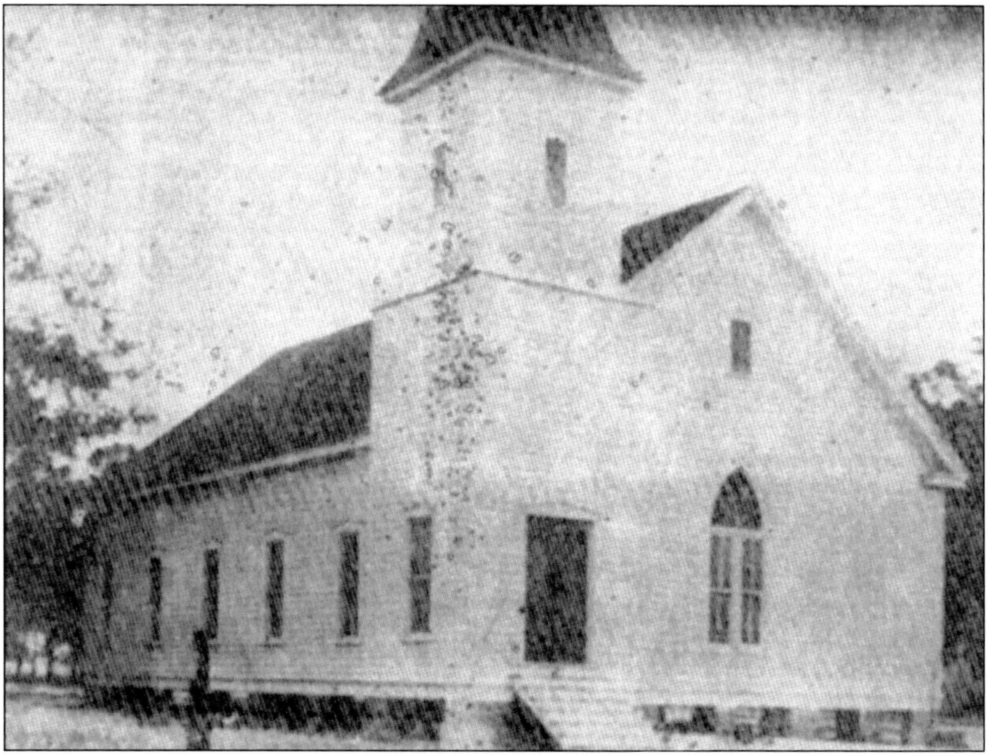

The Springfield Baptist Church. The Springfield Baptist Church began in 1848 with a membership of five people: W.W. Wilson, C. Bevill, J.T. Wilson, Henrietta Strobhor, and F.C. Solomon. The church was constituted on January 16, 1848, and G.S. Jackson was elected as the first pastor. The site of Springfield First Baptist, Lot #60, is reported to be on Jack's Branch, near Springfield's present water. The new church site and building were dedicated in 1995.

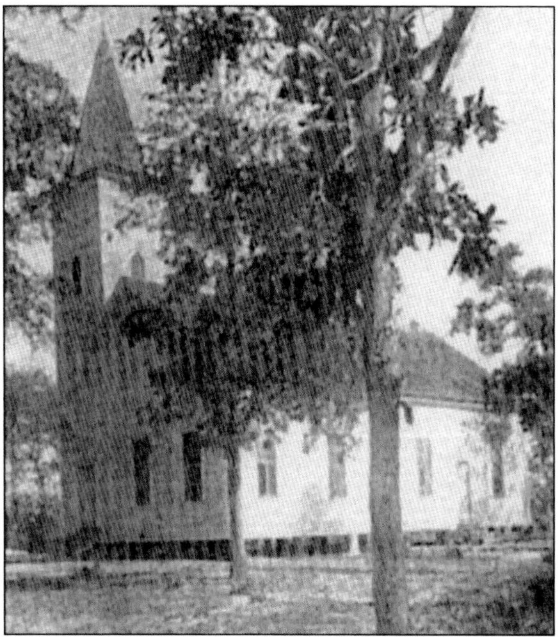

The Springfield Methodist Church. The Georgia Conference of 1835 appointed T.C. Benning to the Springfield Circuit. The General Assembly of Georgia passed an act in 1838 to incorporate the Wesleyan Methodist Episcopal Church in the town of Springfield, to be known by the name of Springfield Church. This church building burned in 1902, was replaced by another wooden structure, and then in 1949 the present Springfield United Methodist Church was dedicated debt free. The church faces Cleveland Street.

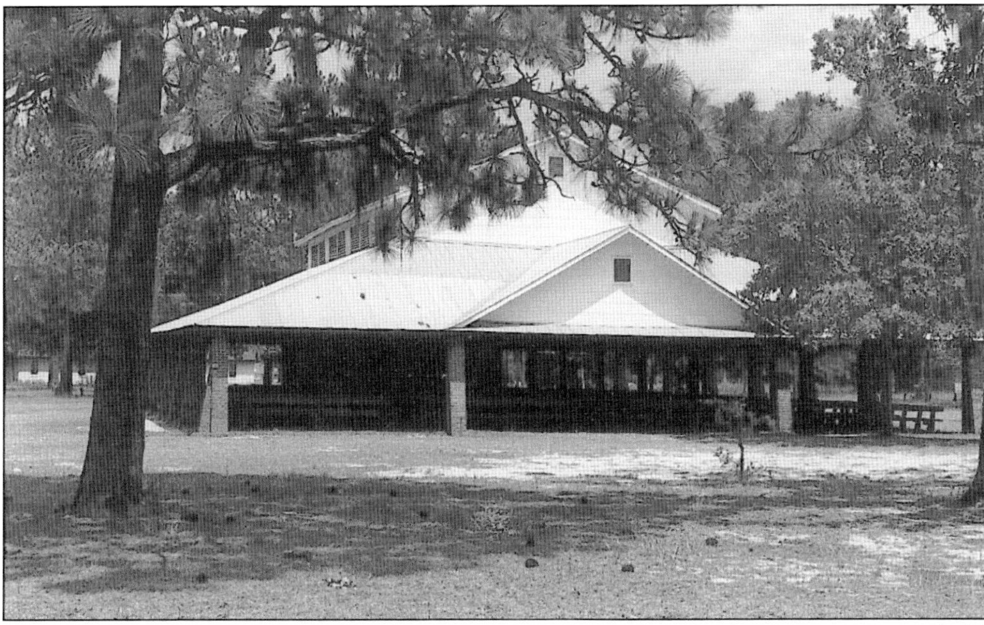

The Effingham Methodist Campground. The Effingham Methodist Camp Meeting holds the record for continuous campmeeting services in South Georgia. The campground has operated from 1790 to the present, and encampment includes the third week in July. The first campground was located off Sisters Ferry Road on land belonging to George Powledge and later sold to Gideon Mallette. In 1864, this site was burned during Sherman's March to the Sea. In 1864 and 1866, encampment was held at Turkey Branch Methodist Church. In 1867, the campground was rebuilt on the Edward Bird tract at Springfield. The present site was occupied after an exchange with G.M. Brinson in 1907.

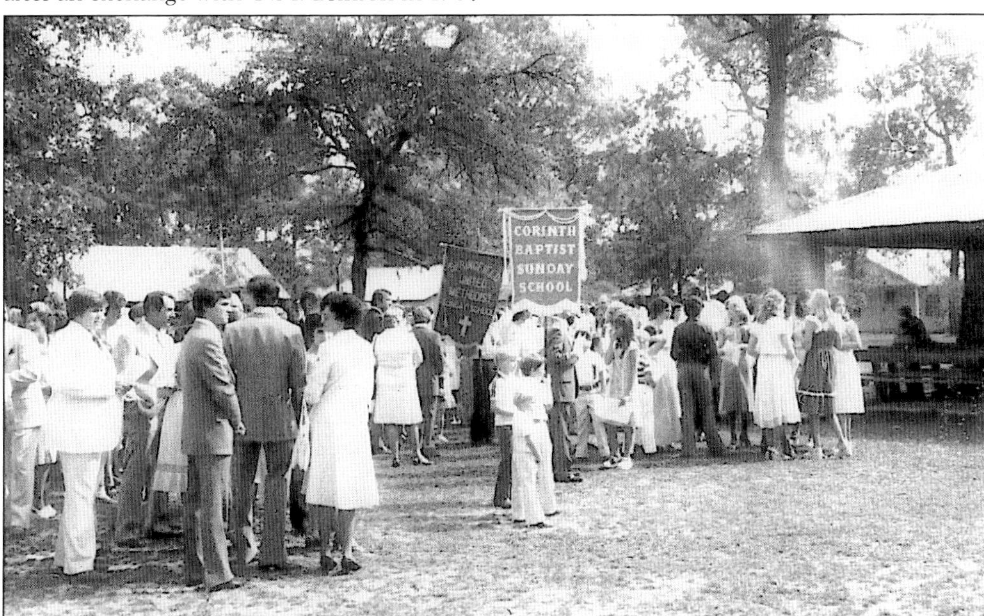

A Sunday School Convention. Each year on the first Sunday in May all churches in the county are invited to the campground for a day of singing, preaching, and basket lunches.

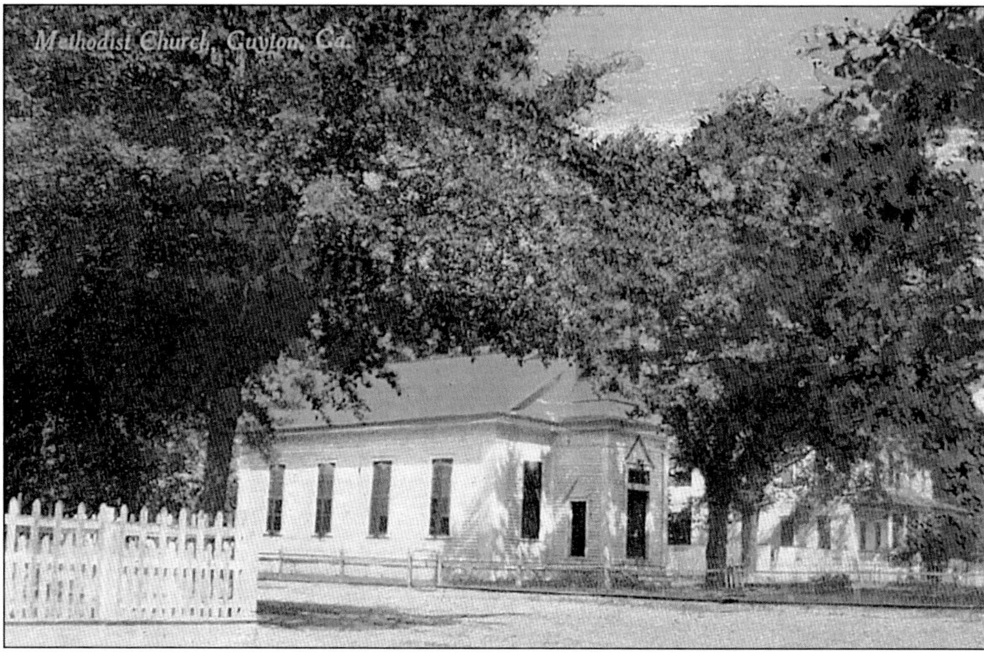

THE GUYTON UNITED METHODIST CHURCH.

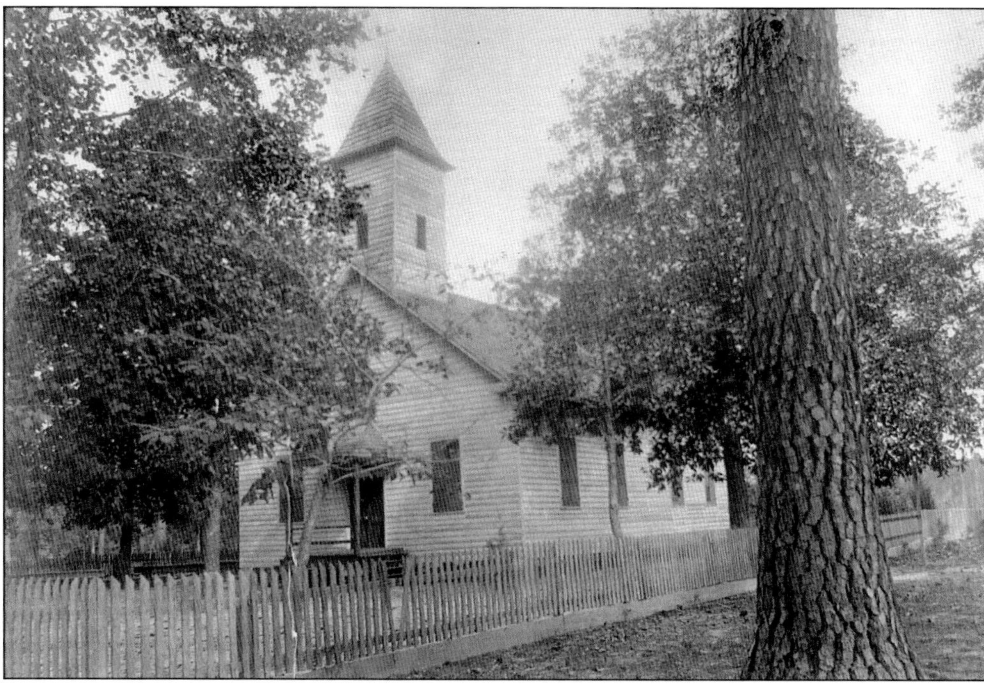

THE LAUREL HILL LUTHERAN CHURCH, 1862. The property for this church was given by Will Washington Metzger as a Christmas gift to the community. Other founders of this church include Christopher Louis Gnann, John Israel Reiser, and James Jonathan Exley. Mr. Exley was a member of the Old Antioch Methodist Church near Berrysville and moved to Laurel to be within walking distance of his place of worship. The church pews were homemade and there were wooden shutters at the windows.

THE ZION LUTHERAN CHURCH, 1845. The Reverend P.D. Strobel became pastor of Ebenezer in the summer of 1844. On page 269 of *The Salzburgers and Their Descendants* by Strobel is written "During Mr. Strobel's stay at Ebenezer, a new church was built near the Ogeechee River. This church was designed for the accommodation of those members who moved so far from Ebenezer that it was impracticable for them to attend preaching at the parent church." The people called their church "Zion" no doubt in memory of the church dedicated on March 7, 1743, and located four miles south of Ebenezer. Soon after the first church building was completed, a one-room schoolhouse appeared by its side. This school continued to operate, changing with the times. When tax money was used for schools, it became a public school. Consolidation closed the school about 1925.

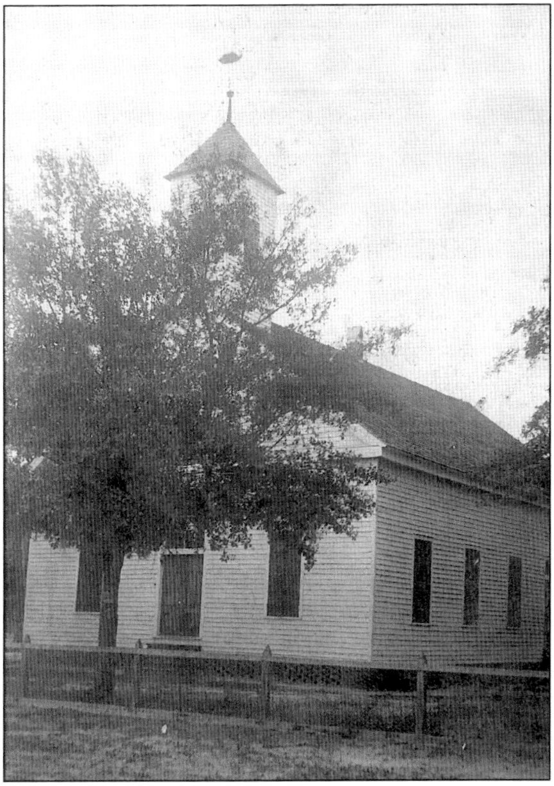

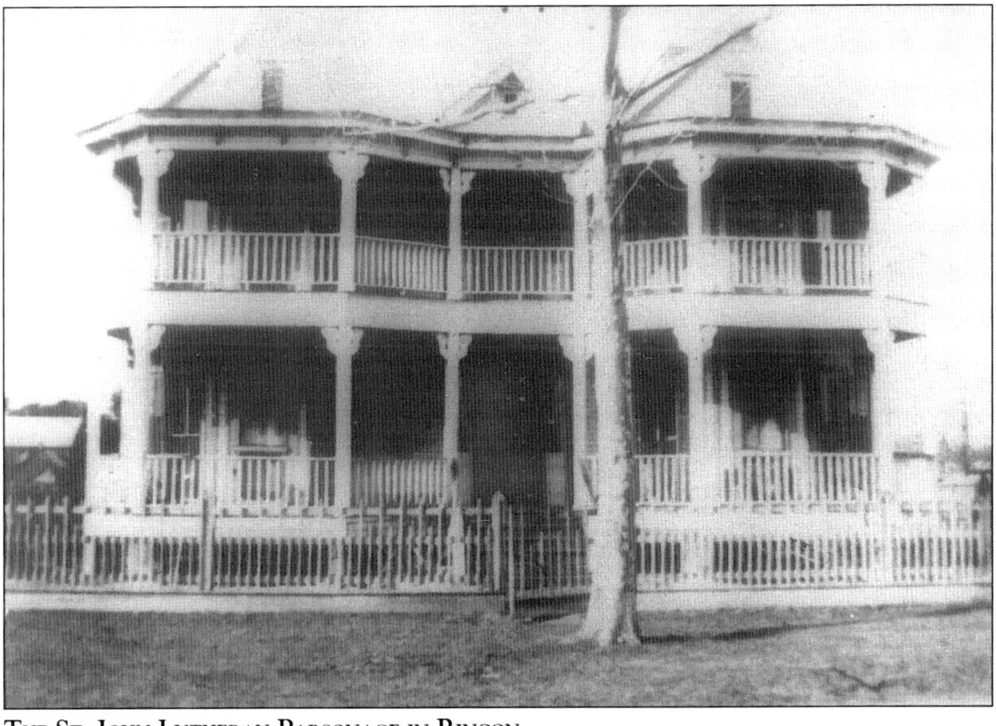

THE ST. JOHN LUTHERAN PARSONAGE IN RINCON.

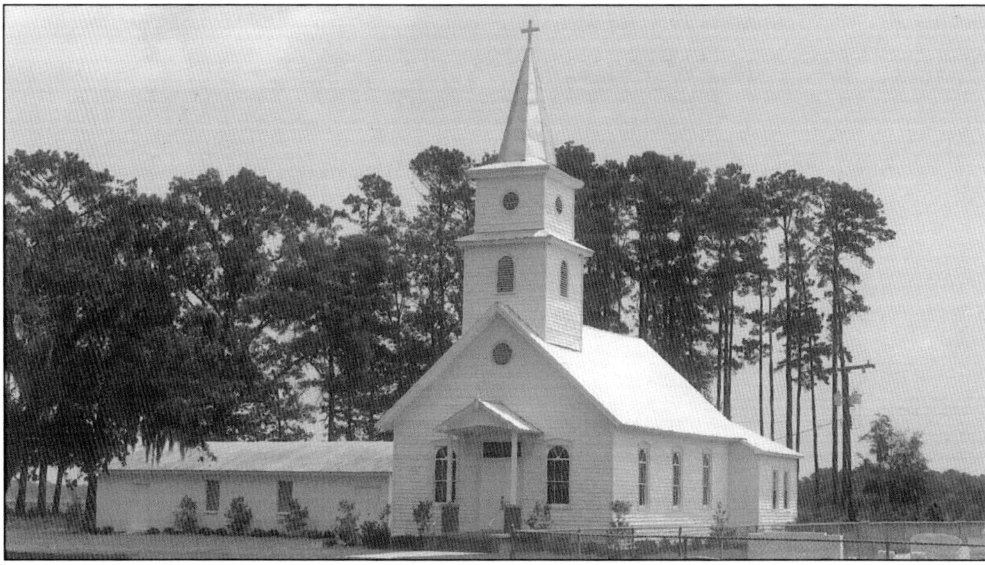

The Goshen Church. The Goshen Church was built about 1751 and was served by the early pastors of the Salzburgers and, later, for a short time by the Moravian missionaries. The church remained a part of the Ebenezer Charge until after the Revolutionary War. In 1820, the Methodist church was organized at Goshen under the direction of Rev. James O. Andrew and was allowed to use the Goshen church building. The actual deed to the property was transferred to the Methodist Conference several years later. Rev. Lewis Myers moved to Goshen about 1823 and served the Methodist Church here for many years.

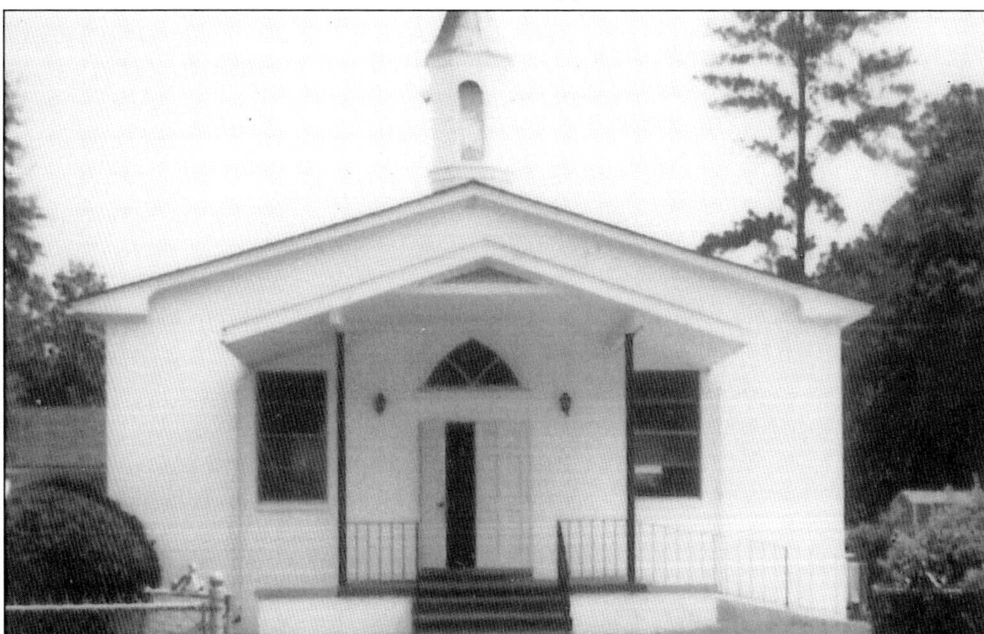

The Macedonia Baptist Church. This congregation was founded in 1870 by a group of descendants of the New Providence Baptist Church of Guyton. The Reverend Inman Bryant served as the first pastor of Macedonia, and the Reverend Samuel Hutchinson III is the present pastor. The church is located near Highway 17 in Guyton.

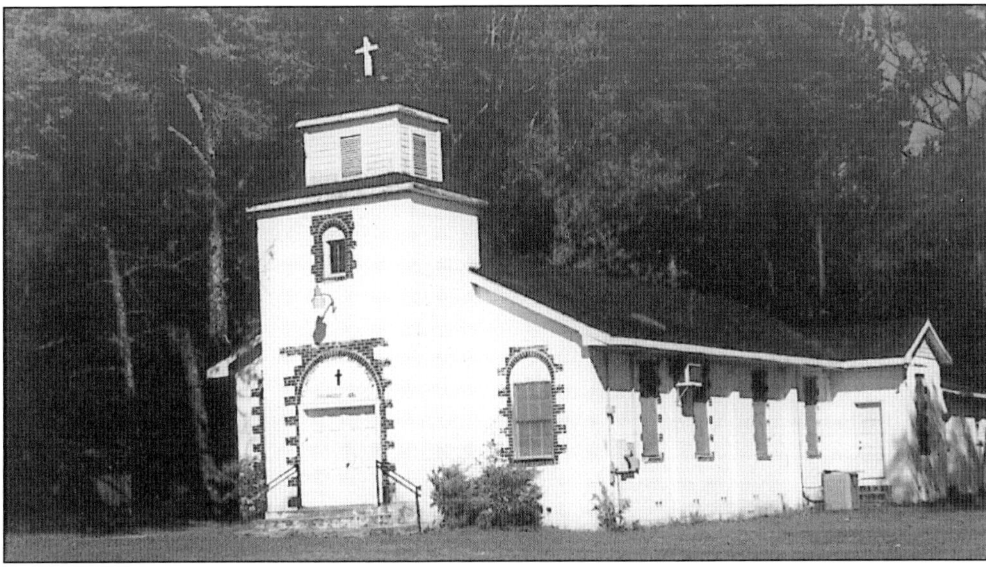

THE ST. MATTHEW MISSIONARY BAPTIST CHURCH. This church was first organized in 1886 in Springfield.

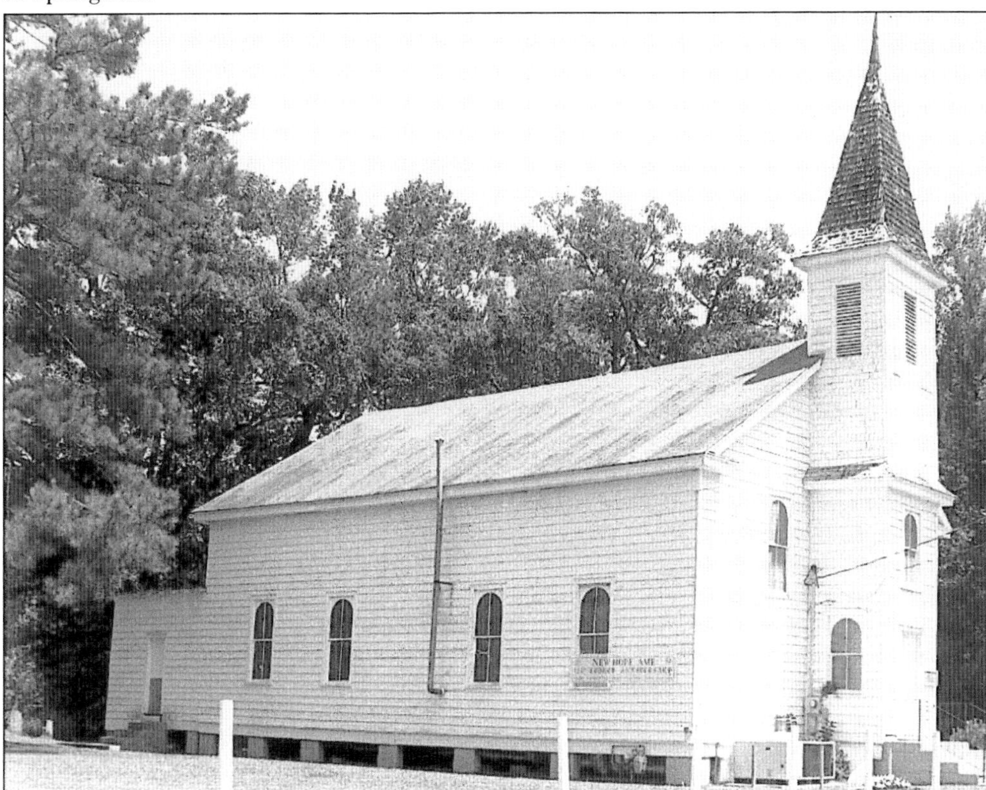

THE NEW HOPE AME CHURCH. The New Hope African Methodist Episcopal Church was organized on August 4, 1869, under the leadership of Rev. W.H. Wells. The church joined the Georgia Conference in November of that same year, and the presiding bishop was Alexander Washington Wayman. The conference was held in Macon, Georgia on November 12, 1869.

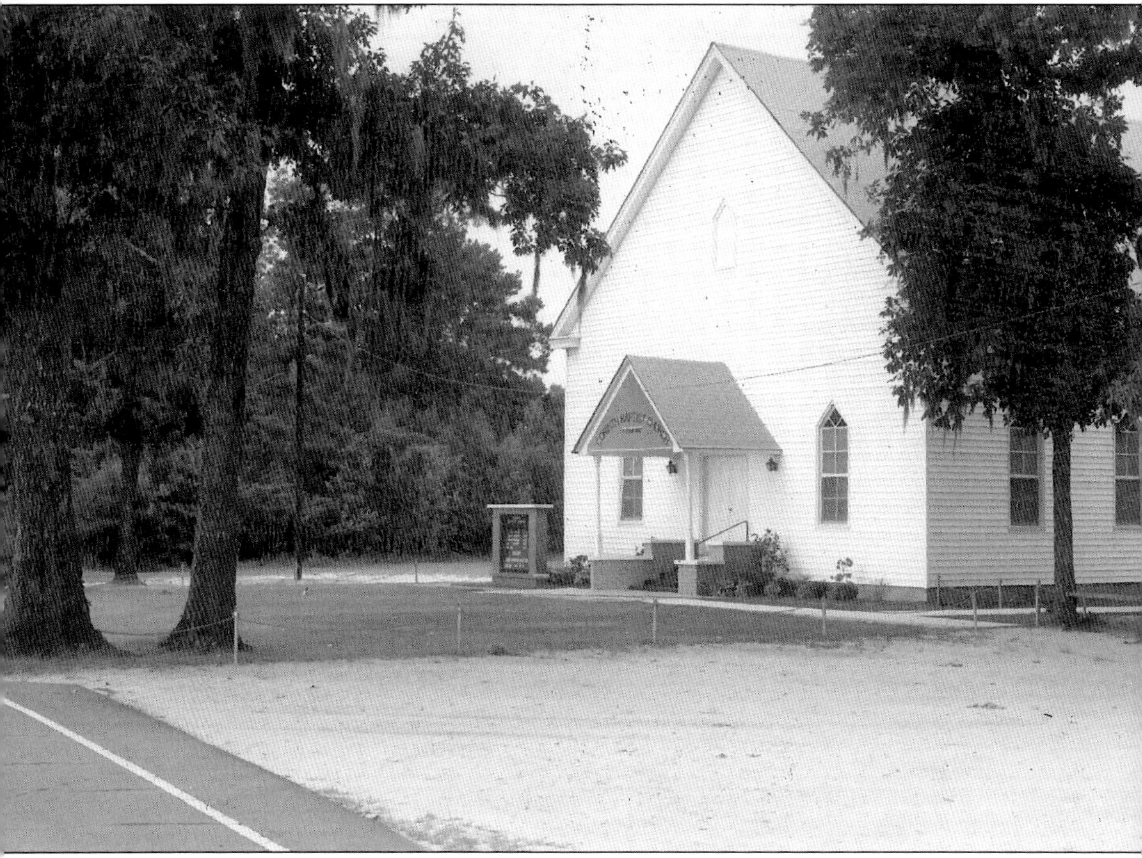

THE CORINTH BAPTIST CHURCH.

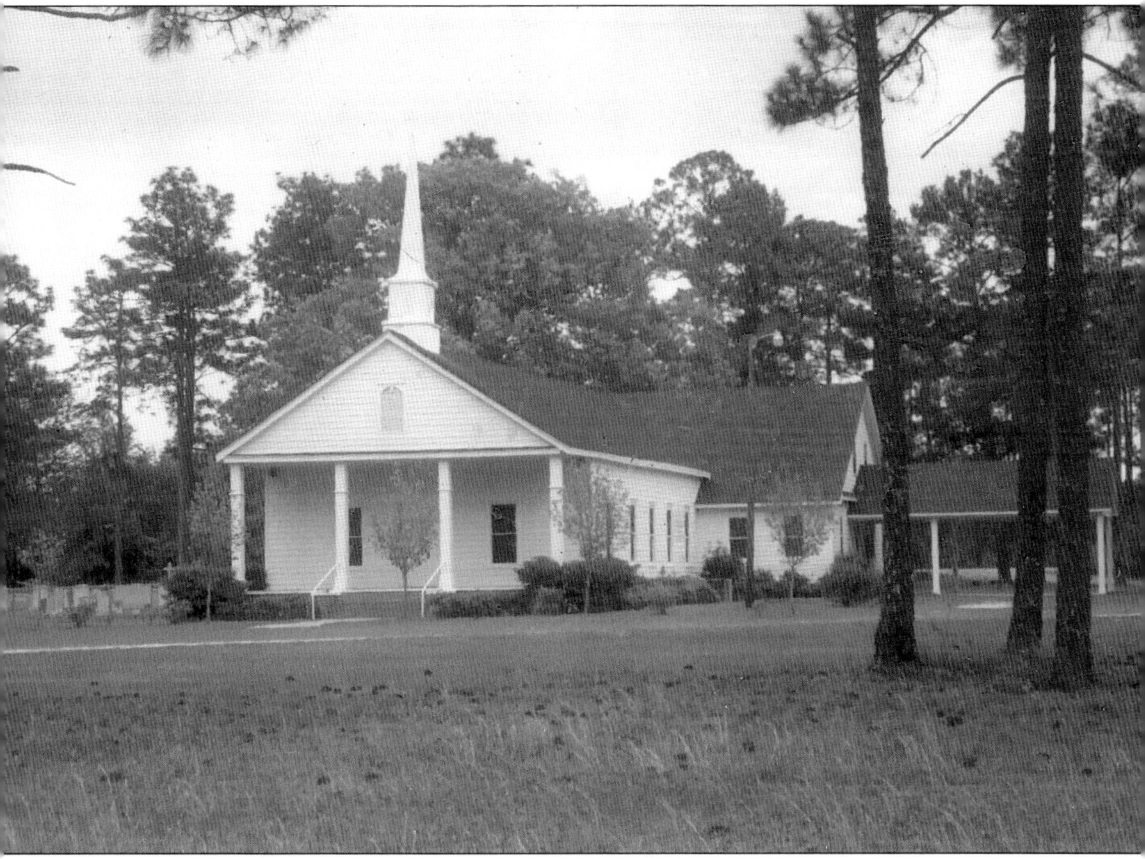

THE MIZPAH METHODIST CHURCH, 1859. L.A. Malone was hired to build the church from materials that were donated by the members. The church was completed December 20, 1859, but Sunday school rooms and a social hall were added later. Some of the family names listed among the charter members of the church are Porter, Pitts, Morel, Enecks, Burns, Brauder, Coursey, Mallard, Longstreet, and Smith.

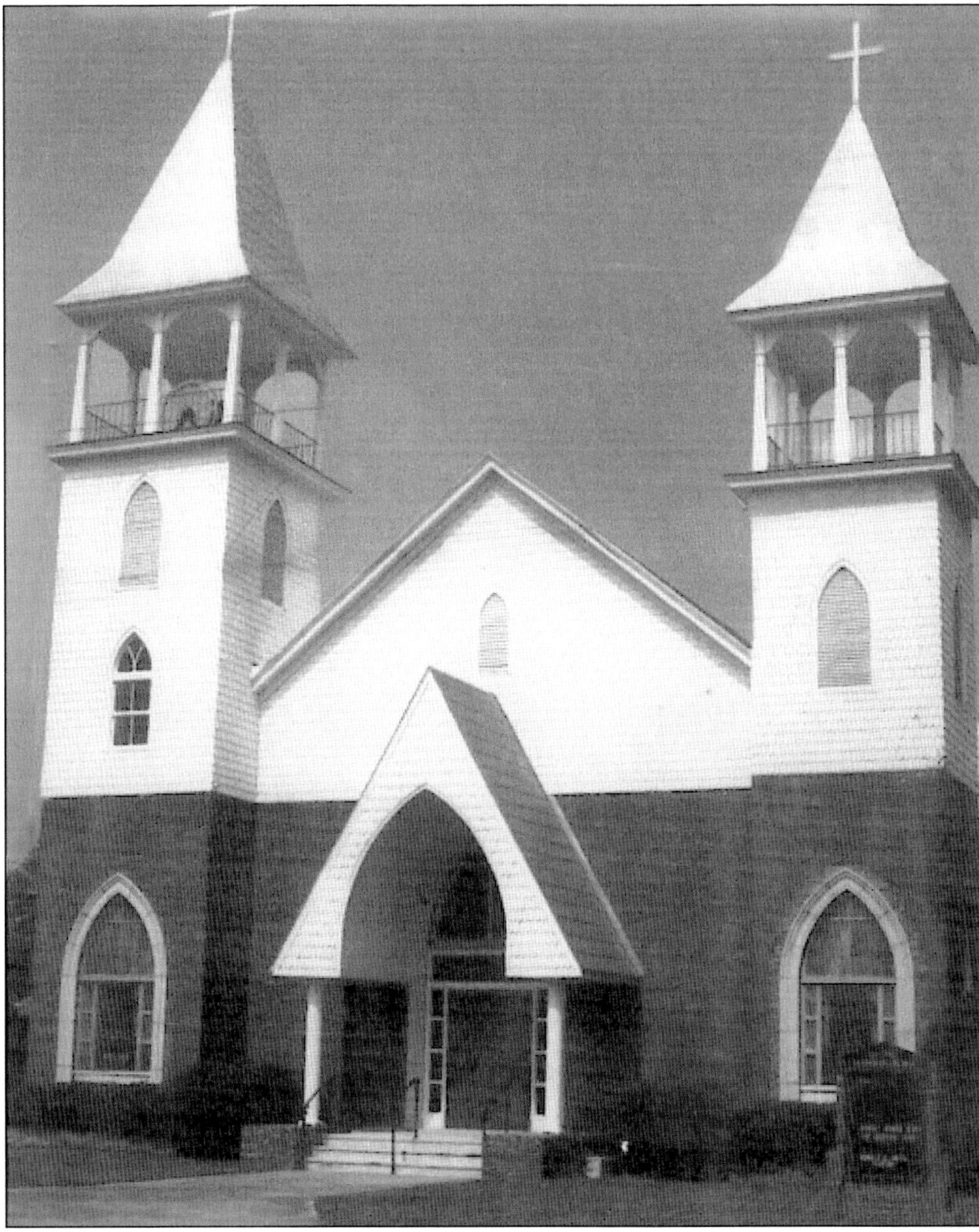

THE HOLY TRINITY LUTHERAN CHURCH. This congregation was formally organized on June 9, 1912 with 51 charter members. The beautiful church was built through volunteer work and gifts, and the building was dedicated on November 9, 1912. The Reverend Dr. T.W. Shealy served as pastor from the time the church was organized until his death on July 10, 1936.

Six

KINFOLKS

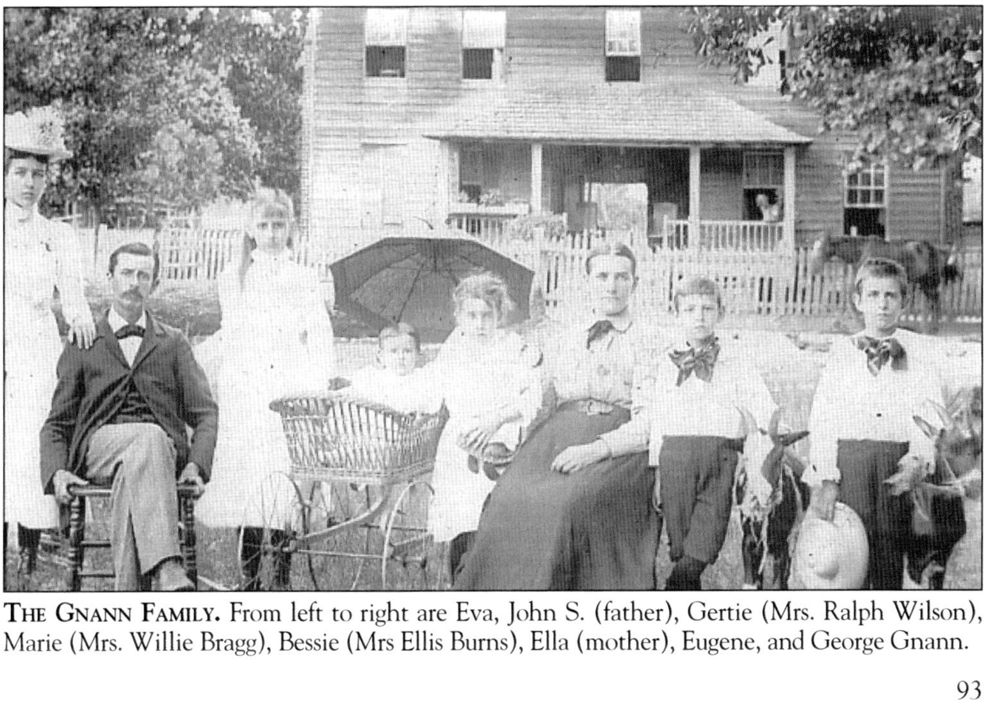

THE GNANN FAMILY. From left to right are Eva, John S. (father), Gertie (Mrs. Ralph Wilson), Marie (Mrs. Willie Bragg), Bessie (Mrs Ellis Burns), Ella (mother), Eugene, and George Gnann.

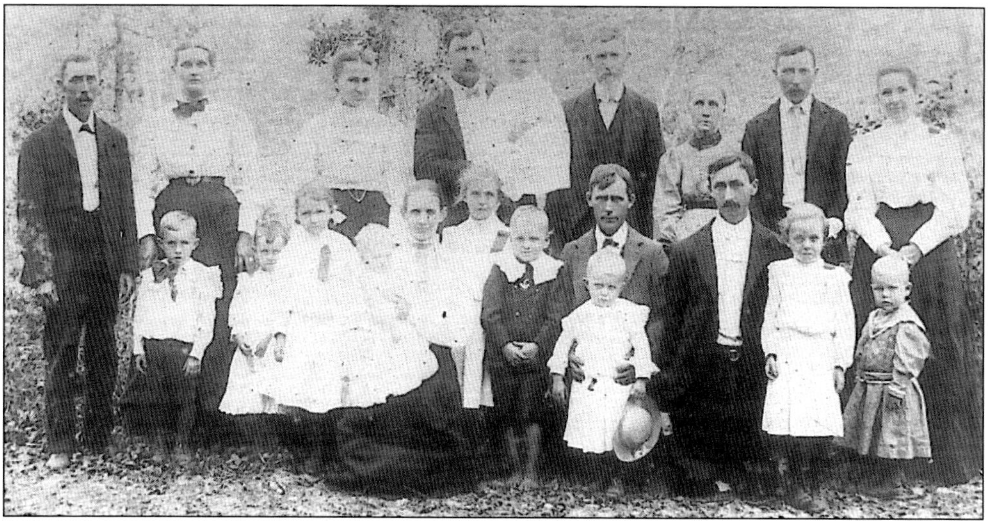

MEMBERS OF THE ARNSDORFF FAMILY. From left to right are as follows: (front row) Tillman Arnsdorff, Mattie A. (Thomas) Arnsdorff, Marie A. (Hinely) Arnsdorff, Hattie Gnann Arnsdorff (holding Cecil), Gertrude A. Arnsdorff, unidentified, J. Claude Arnsdorff (holding James A.), Ollie Arnsdorff, Anna Julia A. (Bragg) Arnsdorff, and Bertie Arnsdorff; (back row) George Arnsdorff, Ella W. Arnsdorff, Albert Arnsdorff (holding Grace A.), David B. Arnsdorff (father), Julia Mallette Arnsdorff (mother), Johnnie Arnsdorff, and Lilly (Edwards) Arnsdorff.

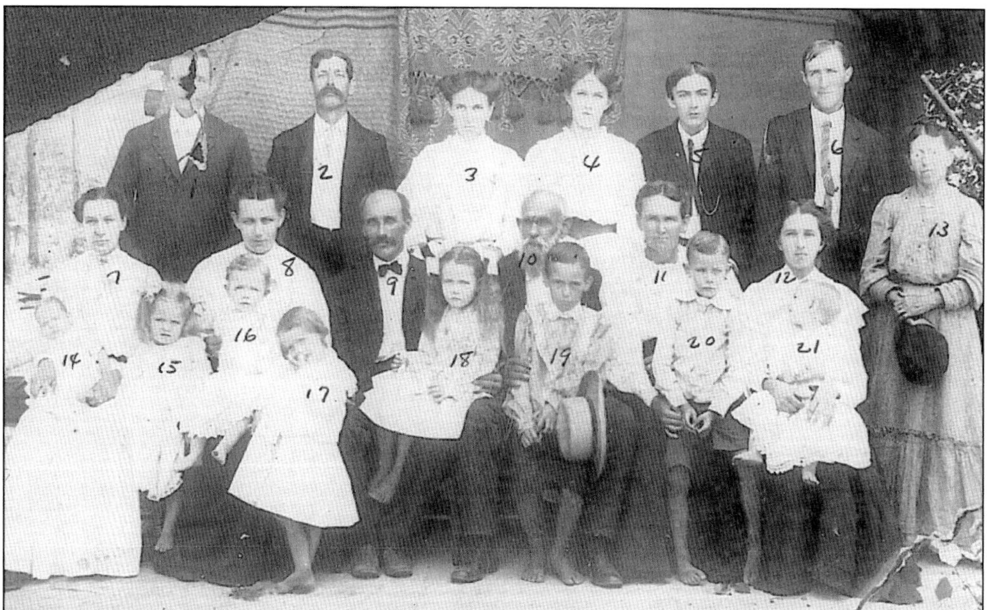

THE FREYERMUTH FAMILY, C. 1907. Pictured, from left to right, are the following: (front row) 14] Rose (Arlene's child), 15] Lucile (Arlene's child), 16] Spy Morgan, 17] Sam Morgan, 18] Lillian Ashmore, 19] Harold Freyermuth, 20] Louis Morgan, and 21] Olivia ?; (middle row) 7] Arlene Hinely, 8] Hattie Morgan, 9] Marion Freyermuth, 10] Grandpa Hodges, 11] Annie Hodges Freyermuth, 12] Mattie Morgan, and 13] Aunt Jane Reiser (second wife of Lewis Morgan); (back row) 1] Gazzie Hinely, 2] Thomas H. Morgan, 3] Mell Morgan, 4] Maybelle Crapps, 5] Leo Freyermuth, and 6] Hugh Morgan.

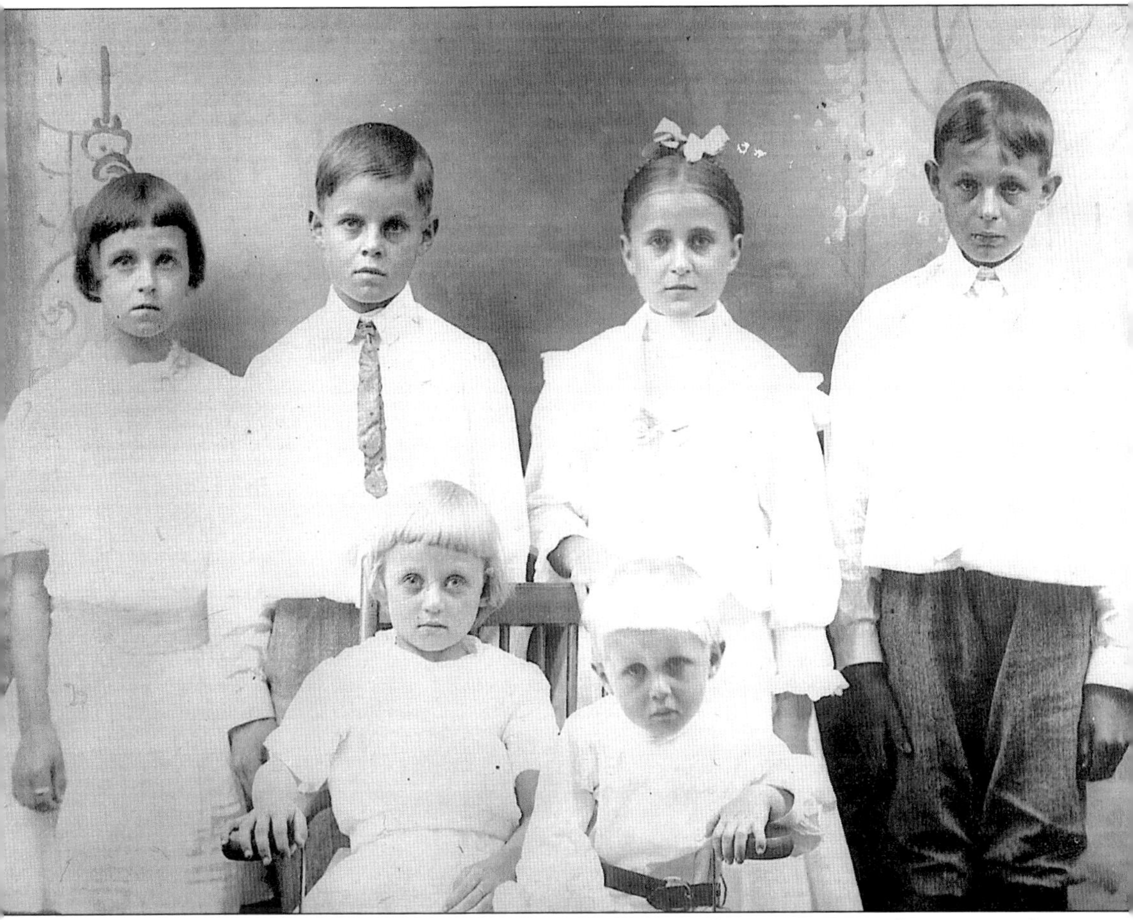

THE ZITTROUER FAMILY. John Robert Zittrouer and Carrie Smith Zittrouer were the parents of the children pictured above. From left to right, they are (front row) Freeda Z. Rahn and John Robert Zittrouer Jr.; (back row) Carrie Mae Z. Reiser, Henry Lovick Zittrouer, Louise Z. Hinely, and George Franklin Zittrouer.

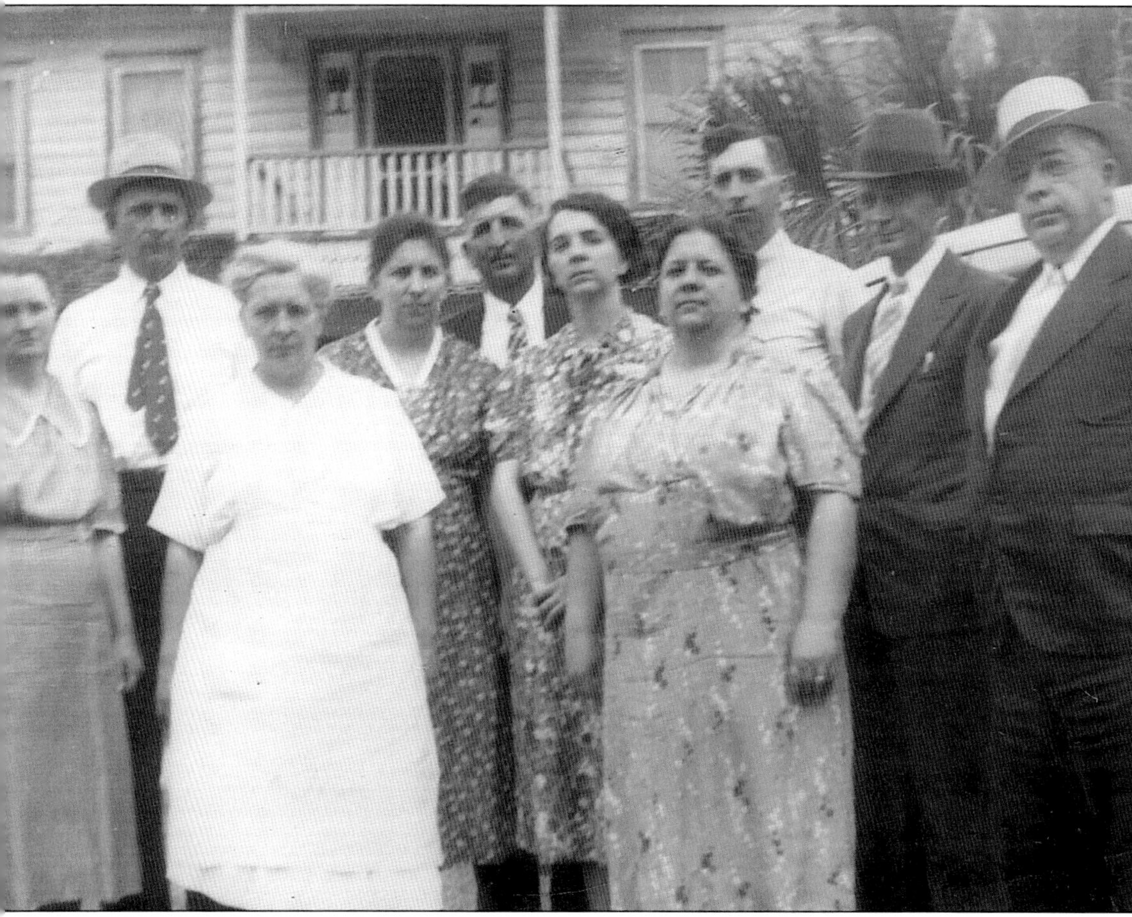

Hinely Brothers and Sisters. Shown here are, from left to right, Lulie, Frank, Annie, Alice, Judd, Mimmie, Amy, Bruce, Hugh, and Emmitt.

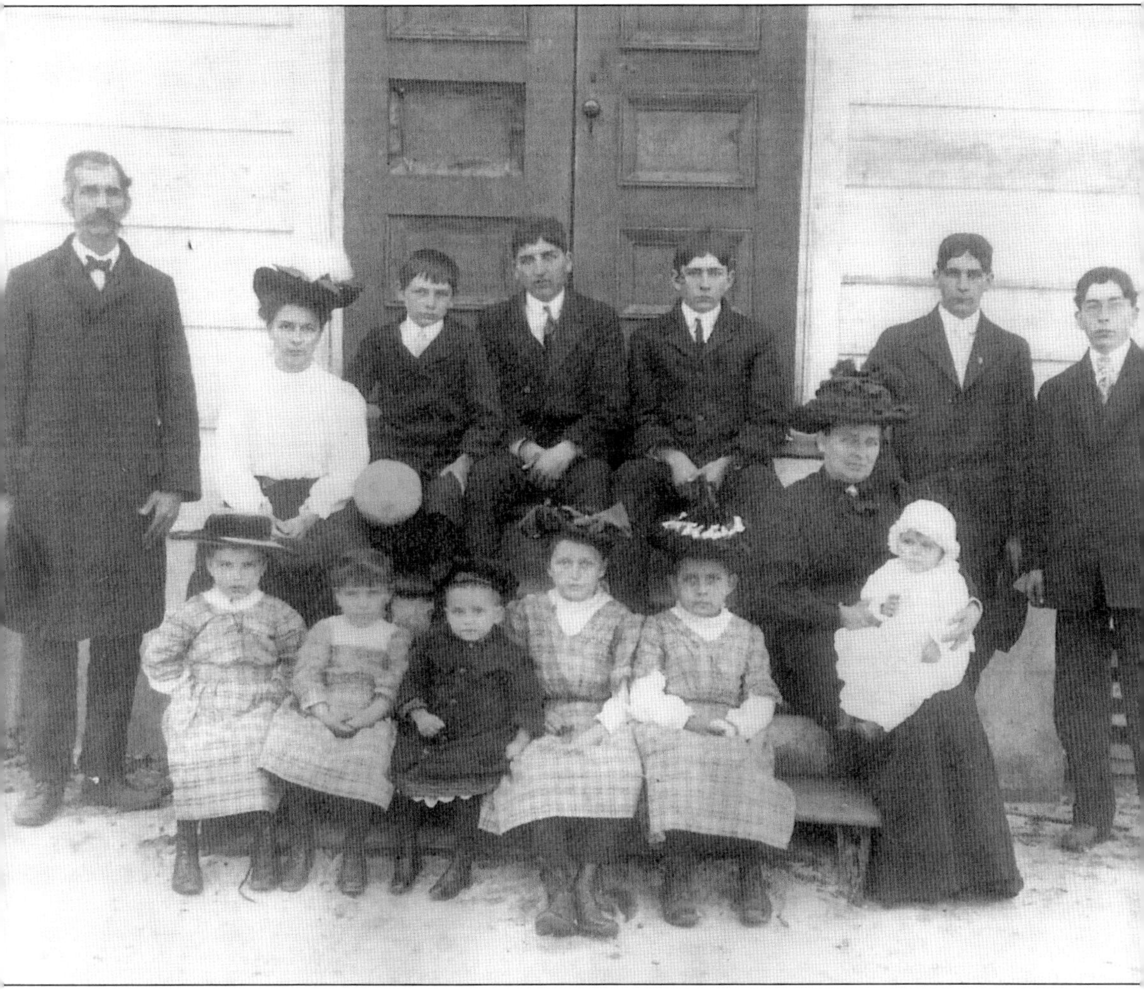

The Hinely Family. From left to right are as follows: (front row) Addie, Alice, Bruce, Lulie, Amy, Julia Ellen, and Mamie (baby); (back row) Horace, Annie, Hugh, Judd, Frank, Harry, and Emmitt.

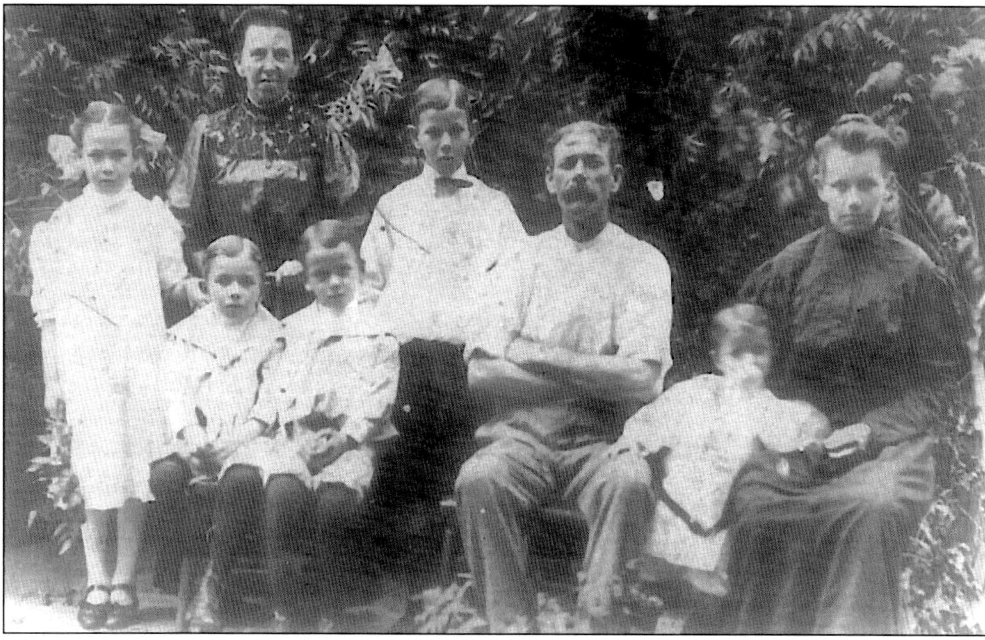

The Morgan Family. Shown here are, from left to right, (seated) Spy, Millon, Tom, Elton, and Hattie (Freyermuth) Morgan; (standing) Lillian, Jane (Reiser), and Lervia Morgan. The old house in the background behind the wisteria burned in 1928.

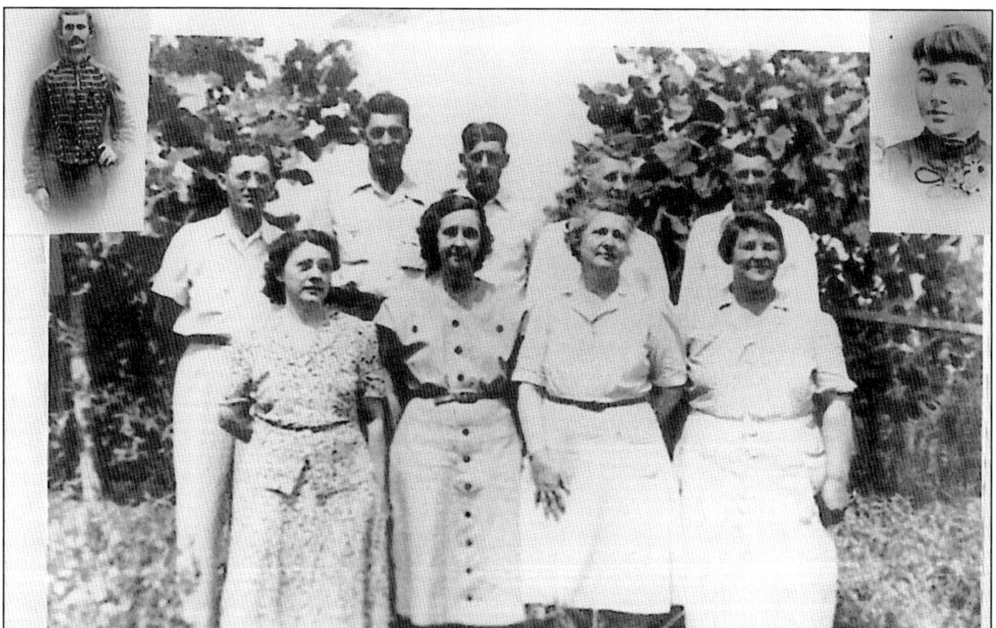

The Exley Family. From left to right are (front row) Hazel Blanche Exley Groover, Mamie, Clarie Exley Dasher, Helen Victoria Exley, and Hattie Fay Exley Joyner; (back row) Eldred (Chub) Walton Exley, Barnard Exley, Chancy Exley, Slade Heyward Exley, and Leon Grady Exley. The parents are James Alfred Augustus Exley (inset left) and Ora Walton Rahn Exley (inset right).

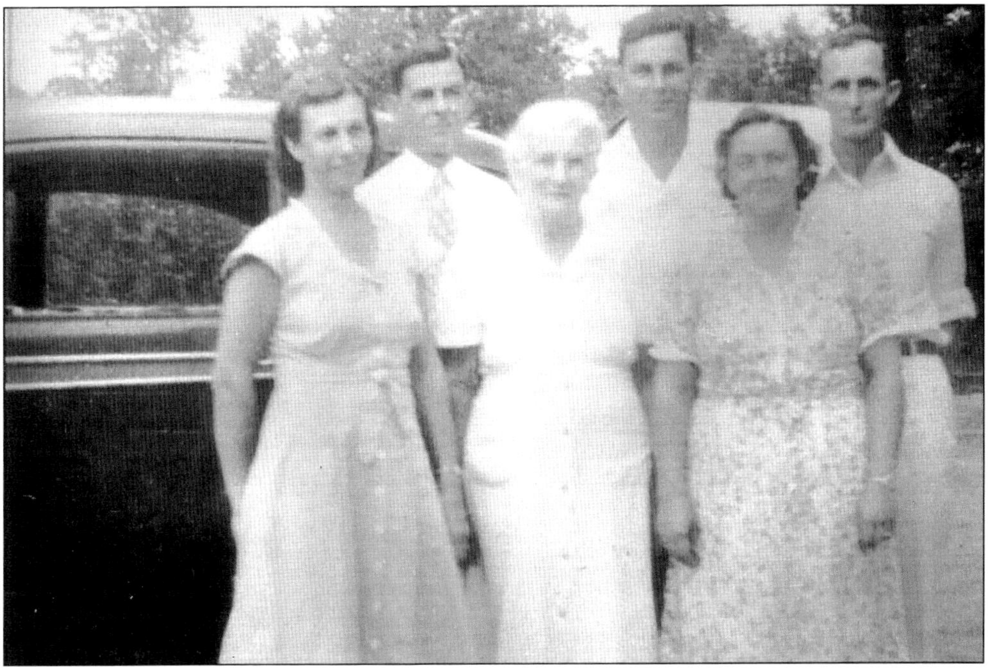

Morgan Brothers and Sisters. From left to right are as follows: (front row) Zona Morgan Combs, Susan Gugie Morgan, and Melba Morgan Weitman; (back row) Nesbit Morgan, Raby Morgan, and Hollis Morgan.

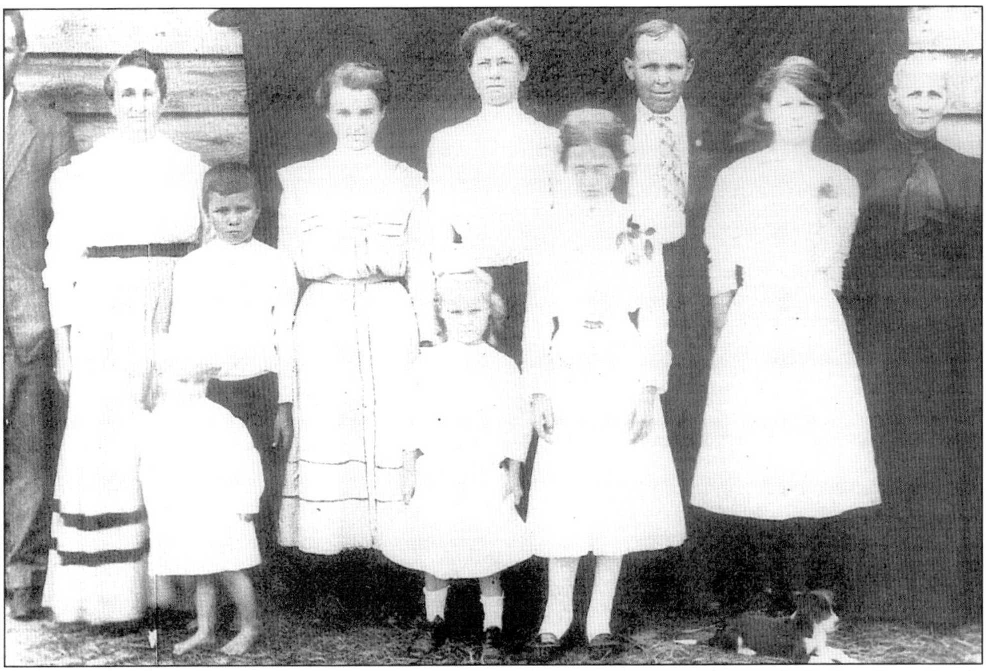

The Rahn Family. Shown here, from left to right, are (front row) Ralph Rahn (barefoot), Mae Rahn Seckinger, Ethel Rahn Brinson, and Ruby Rahn Beckwith; (back row) Orville Rahn (partially visible), Katie (Kieffer) Rahn, Frank Rahn, Maud (Rahn) Grovenstein, Anna Rahn, Shelton Rahn, Lula Freyermuth Rahn, and Thadeus Madison Rahn (not visible).

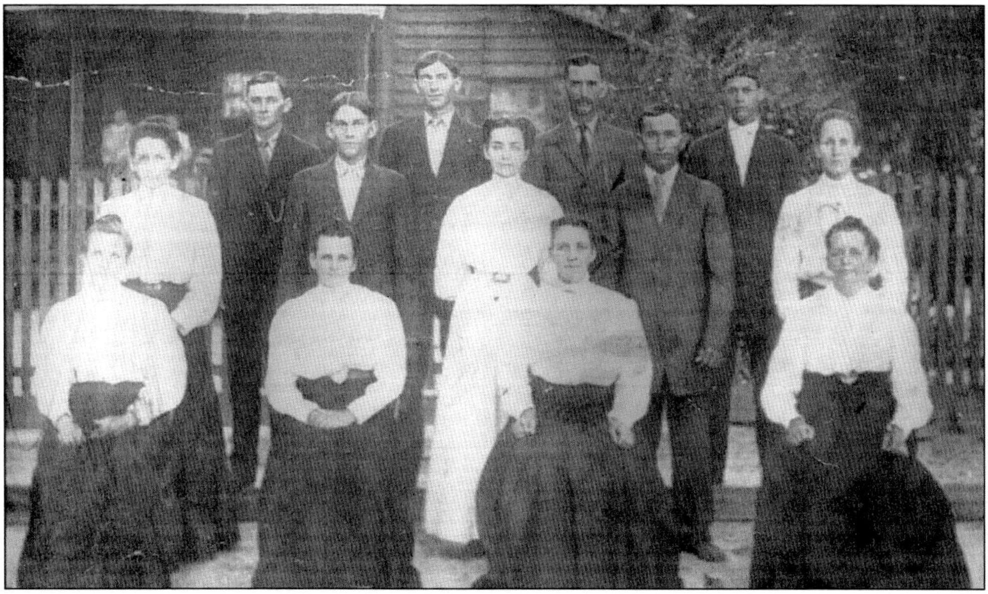

The Rahn Family. From left to right are as follows: (seated) Sophie (Rahn) Grovenstein, Addie (Rahn) Helmly, Emma (Rahn) Helmly, and Irene (Rahn) Kessler; (standing) Lydia (Rahn) Futrelle, Victor Rahn, Stacy Rahn, Claudie Rahn, Lavinia (Rahn) McLeod, Israel Rahn, Furman Putman Rahn, Angus Backman Kessler, and Ada Rahn.

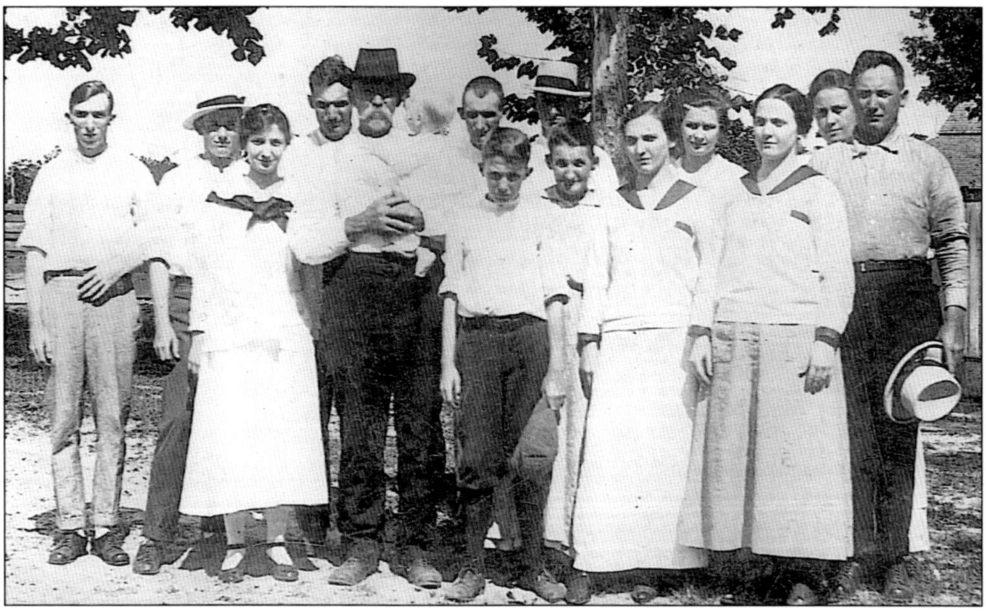

The Ford Family Reunion, 1917. Shown here are the following, from left to right: (front row) Corrie Ford, James William Ford (1858–1922), baby Earl Patrick Ford Jr. (born 1916), Parker Ford, Ella (Arnsdorff) Ford, Lula Ford, and Hattie Ford; (back row) William T. Ford, Hardy Ford, Hugh Ford, Edward Palmer Ford, Earl P. Ford, Cassie Elkins Ford, Ruth (Baily) Ford, and James Porcher Ford.

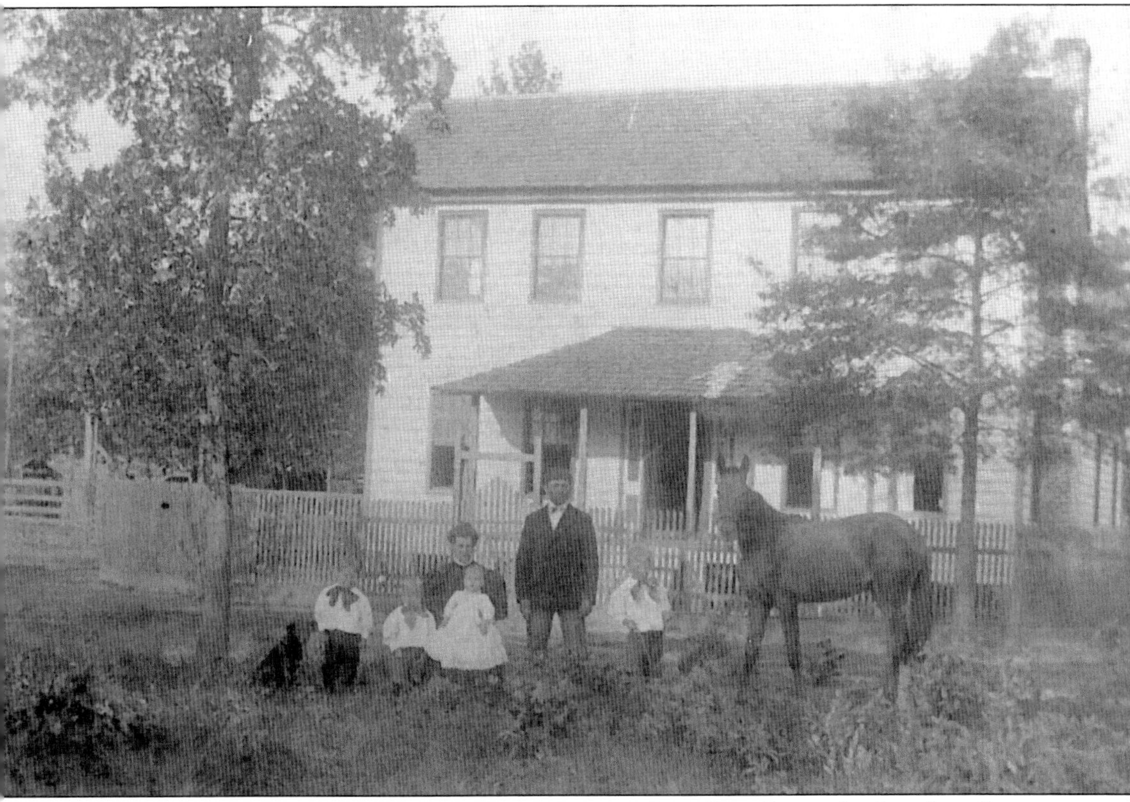

THE GEORGE Q. RAHN AND CORA EXLEY RAHN FAMILY. Artis, Roy, Kenneth, Grandma Cora, Grandpa George, and Merrill Rahn are shown here.

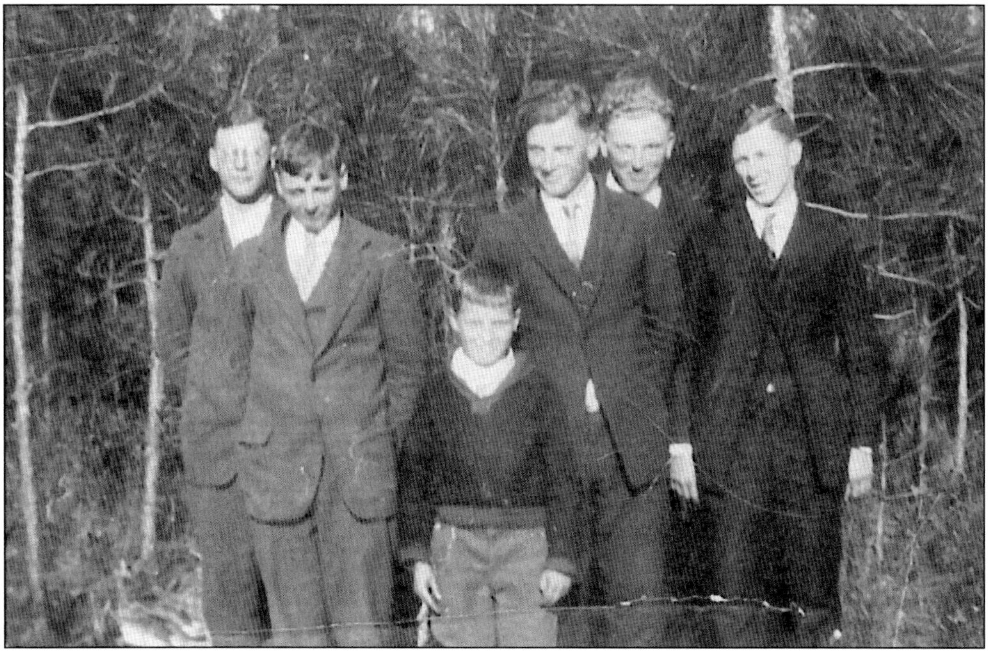

The Rahn Brothers. Kenneth, Harris, Corley, Roy, Merrill, and Artis Rahn pose for a photograph.

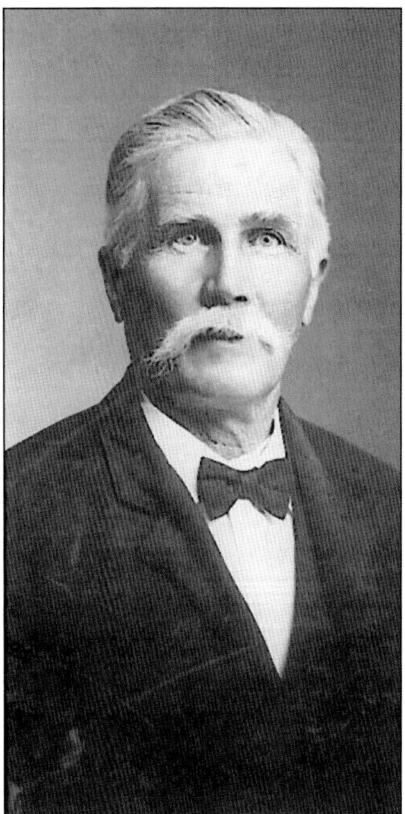

George Washington Fetzer. George was born in Ebenezer, Georgia on December 29, 1844, to Richard Isrel Fetzer and Salome Kieffer, both of whom were Salzburgers. When George was about 13 years old the family moved to the Zion community and lived in a house built by Richard about three miles south of Marlow. When George was 17 he joined the Confederate Army. When he returned at the end of the war, he and his father cut logs, made a raft, and floated logs to Savannah on the Ogeechee River. George and a friend, Glenn Dugger, eventually built and operated a sawmill. On December 1, 1870, George married Laura Heidt. The two had six boys and three girls: Adeline Eliza, William Richard, Evelina Salome, Bunyan George, Claudius Austin, Herbert Josiah, Emma Amelia, Robert Edward, and Laurice Elmore. South of his father's property, George bought land and started construction of a colonial-style home. The family remained here until the building was destroyed by fire on January 15, 1922. Eleven people were asleep at 1 a.m. when someone woke up and heard fire crackling. Screams ran through the house and everyone rushed out into the night dressed only in their night clothes, but no one was injured. George built another house and lived there until his death on May 17, 1930.

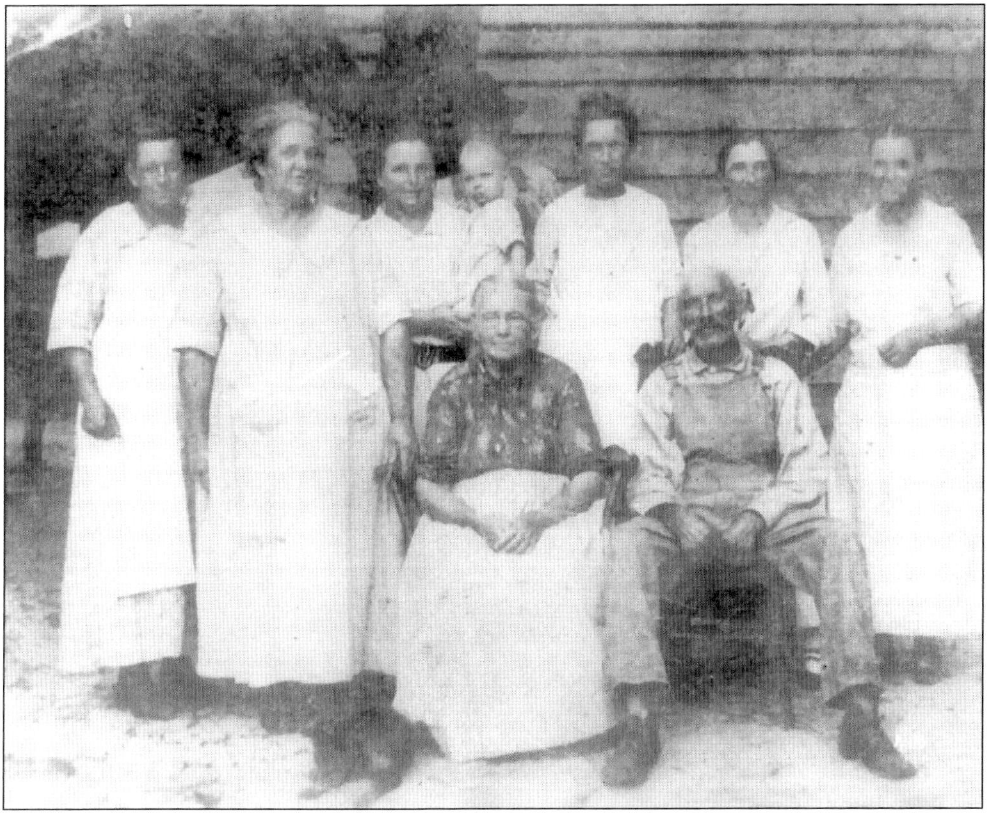

THE FREYERMUTH FAMILY.

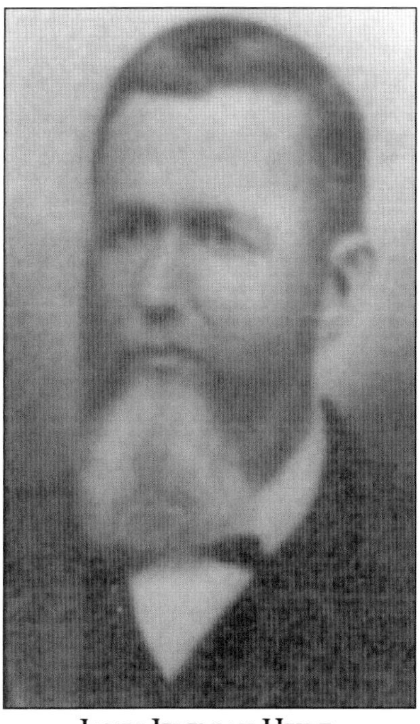

JAMES JEREMIAH HEIDT.

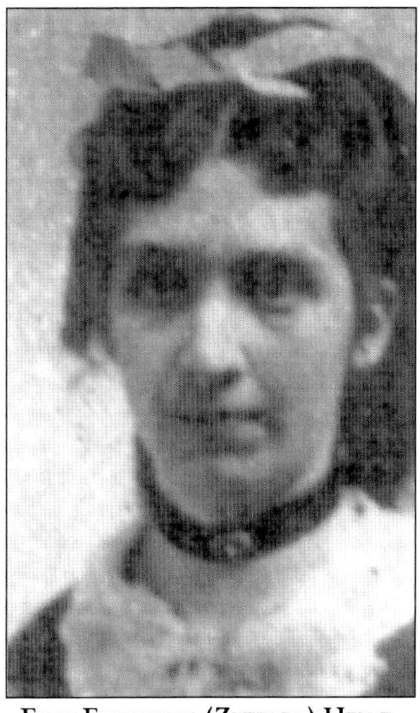

ELVY ELIZABETH (ZETTLER) HEIDT.

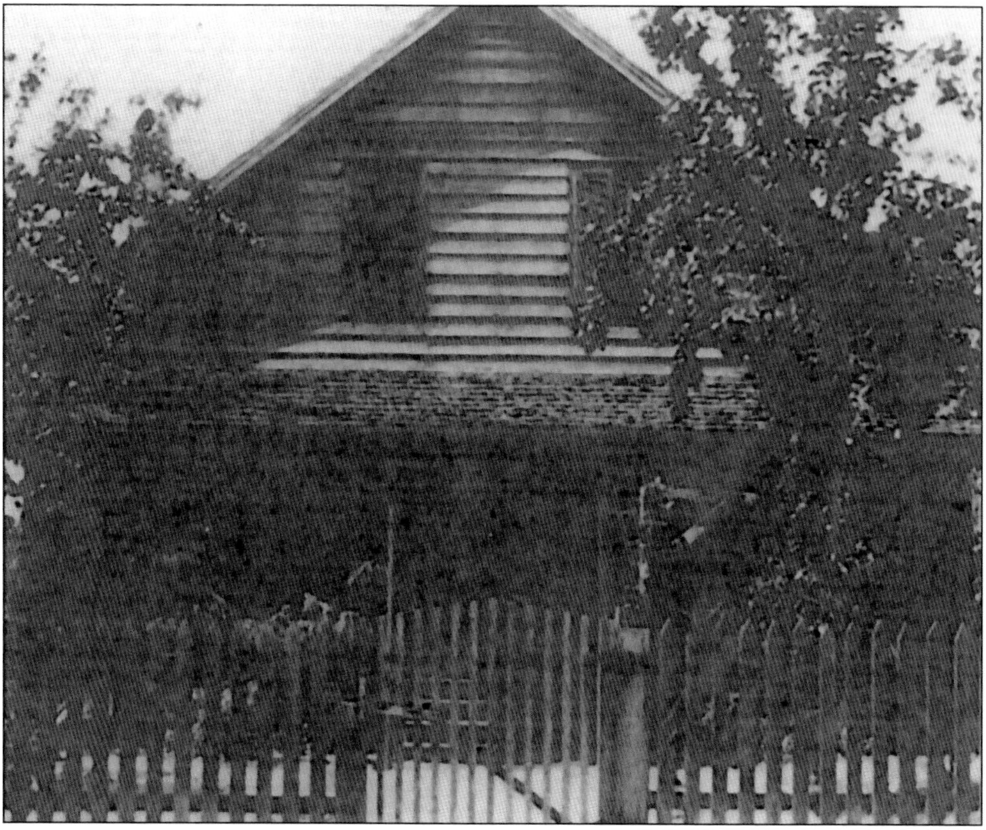

THE HEIDT FAMILY HOME, BUILT IN THE 1880S.

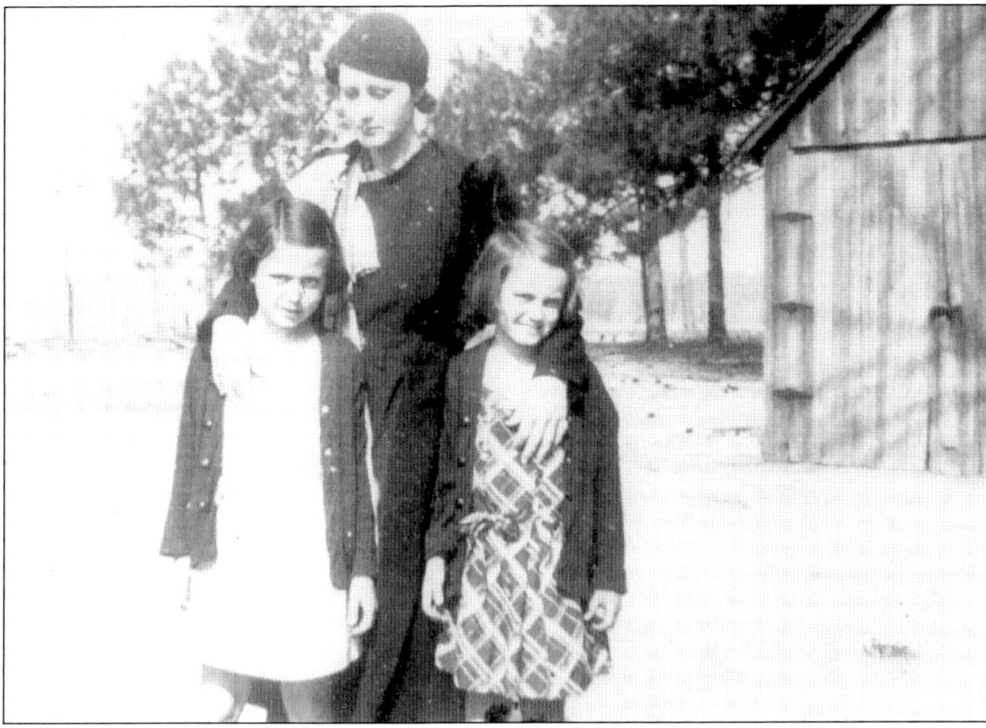

Georgia Burns Smith with Daughters Virginia and Mary.

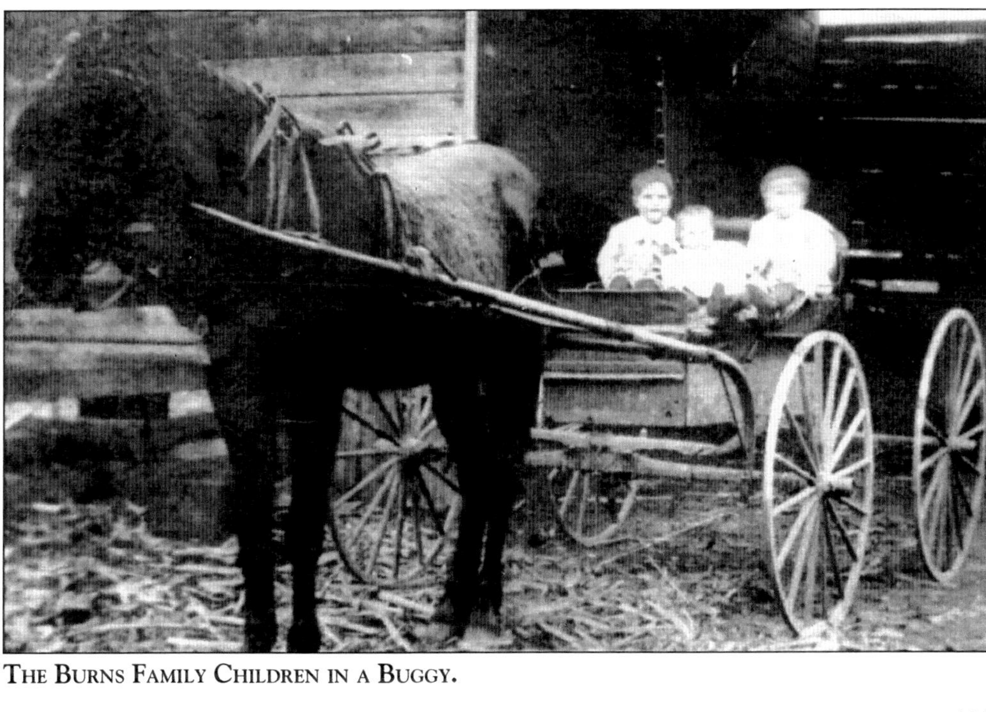

The Burns Family Children in a Buggy.

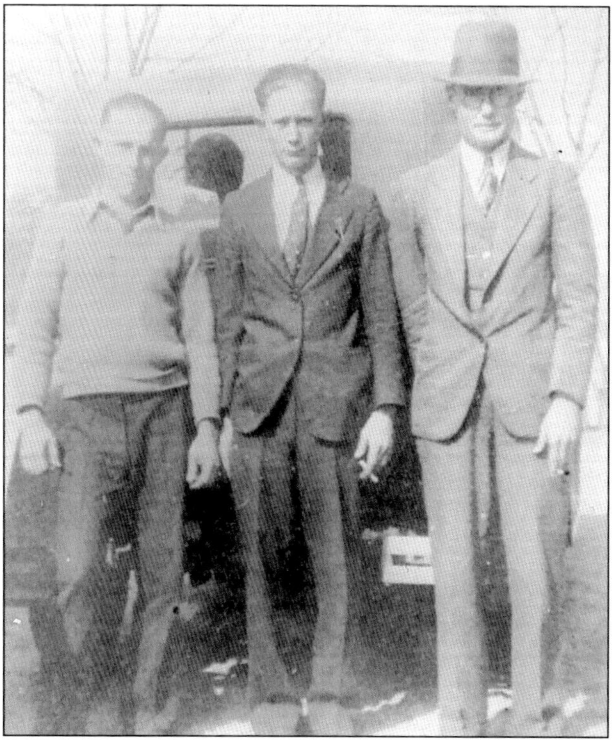

LESTER BURNS AND SONS LAMAR AND GUERRY.

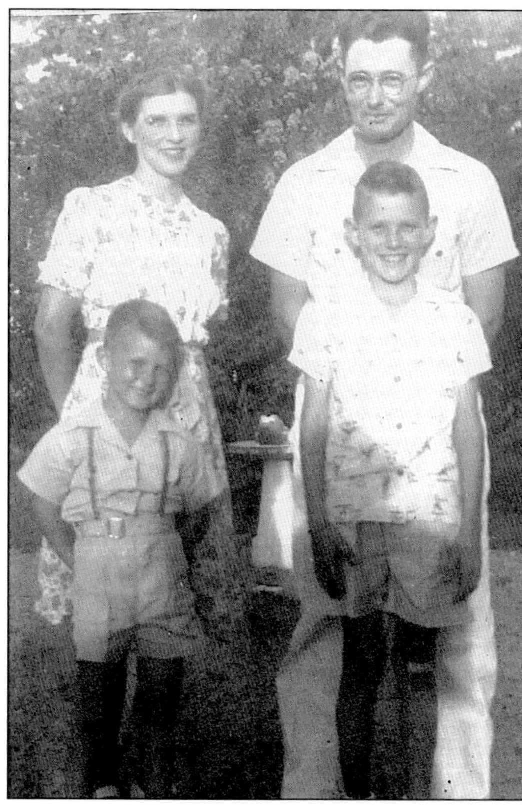

THE LAMAR BURNS FAMILY. Pictured here are Sherley and L.A. with their parents, Nadine and Lamar.

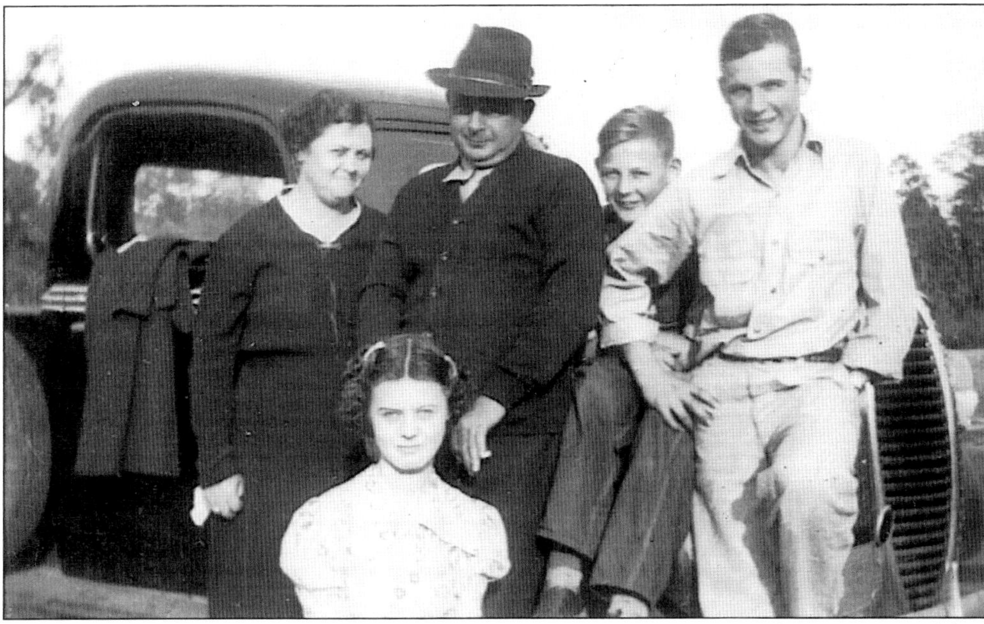

THE ZITTROUER FAMILY. From left to right are (front row) Matilda Talulah "Matra" Fulcher; (back row) Ruth Etheredge Exley Zittrouer, Franklin Zittrouer, George Robert Zittrouer, and Clinton Zittrouer.

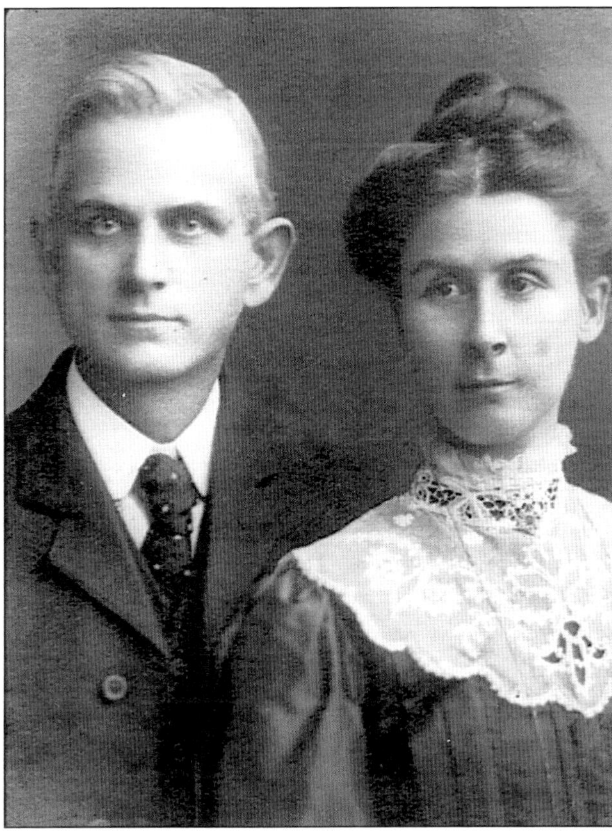

GEORGE E. USHER AND HATTIE USHER.

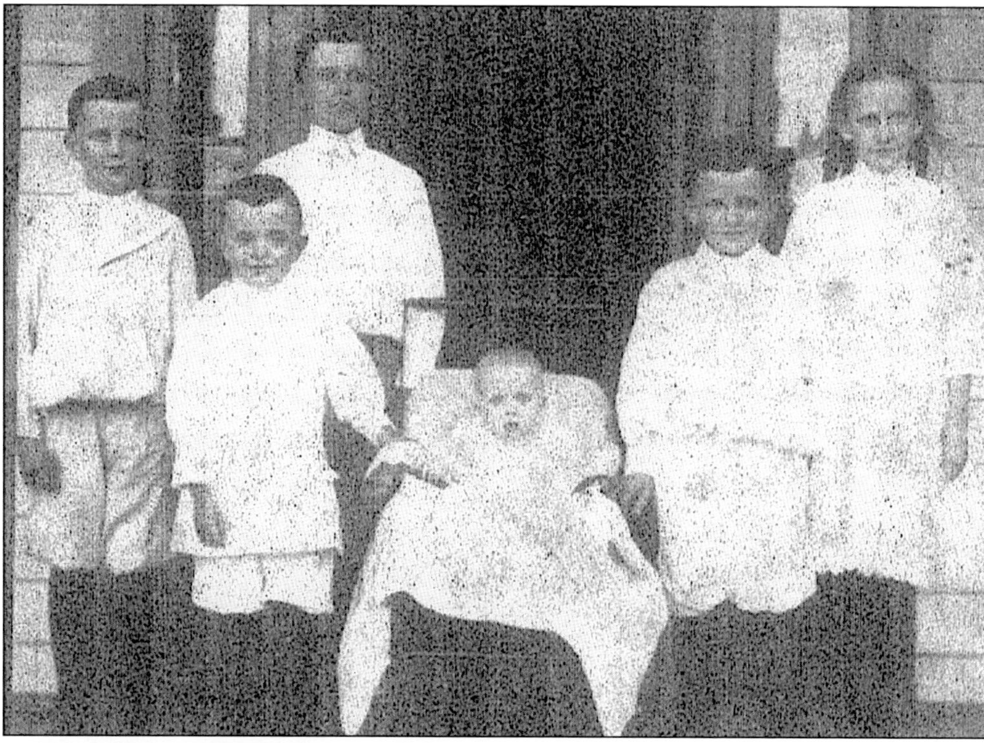

The Weitman Children. From left to right are George, Herman, Freddie, Estelle, Milton, and Nettie.

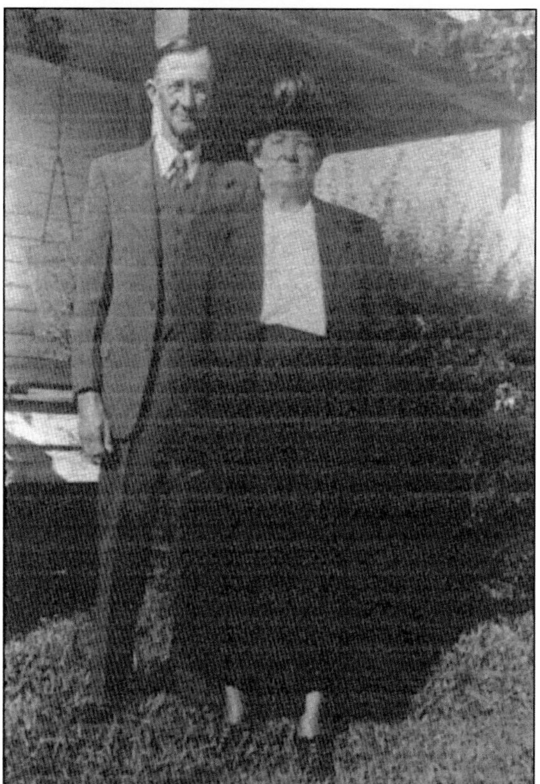

The Dugger Home in Blandford. Herman Bartow Dugger and Lucy Rosannah Dugger pose in front of the home.

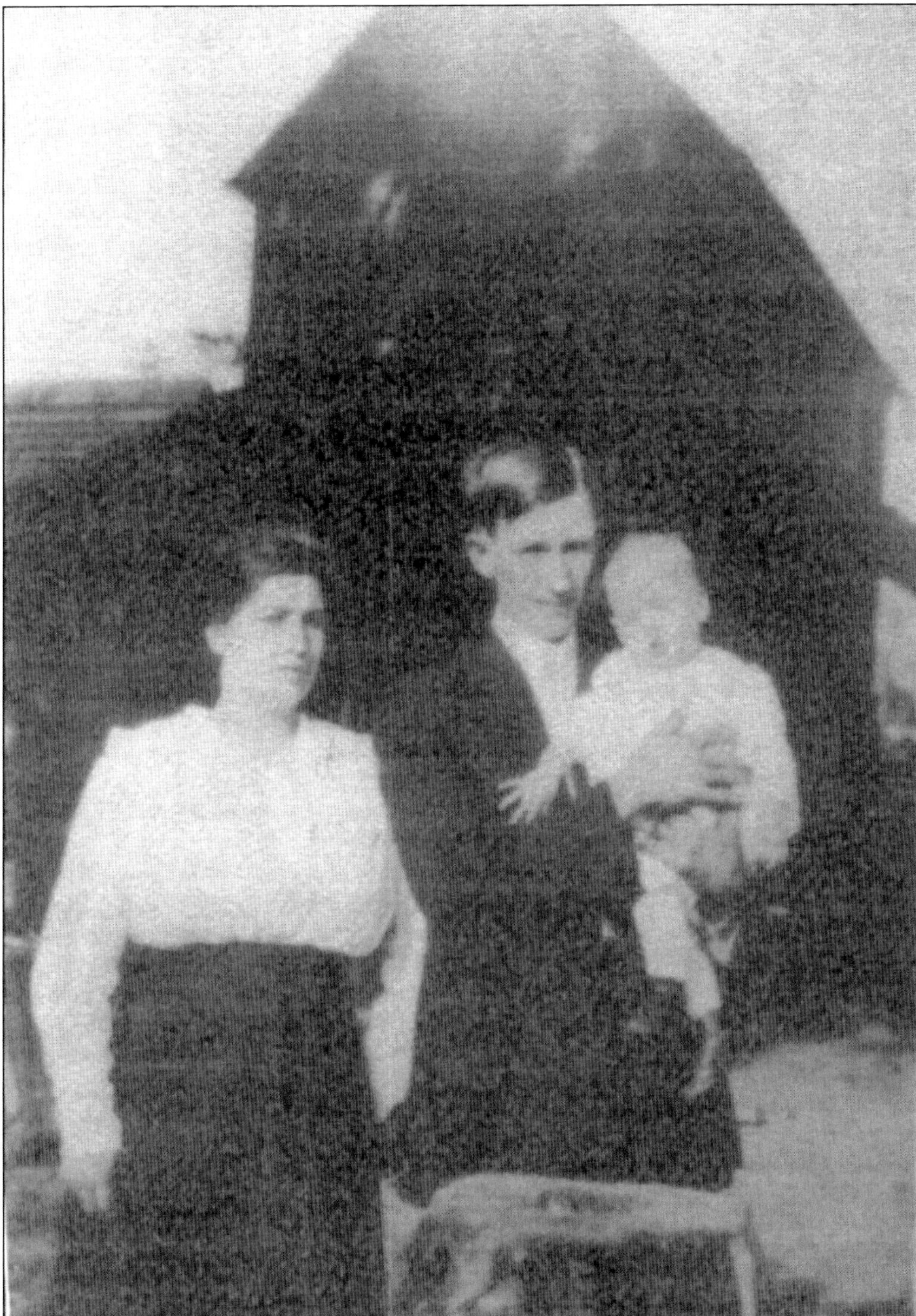

The Zipperer Homeplace. Shown here are Lucy Rosannah Dugger Zipperer, Herman Bartow Zipperer, and baby Mary Matilda Dugger.

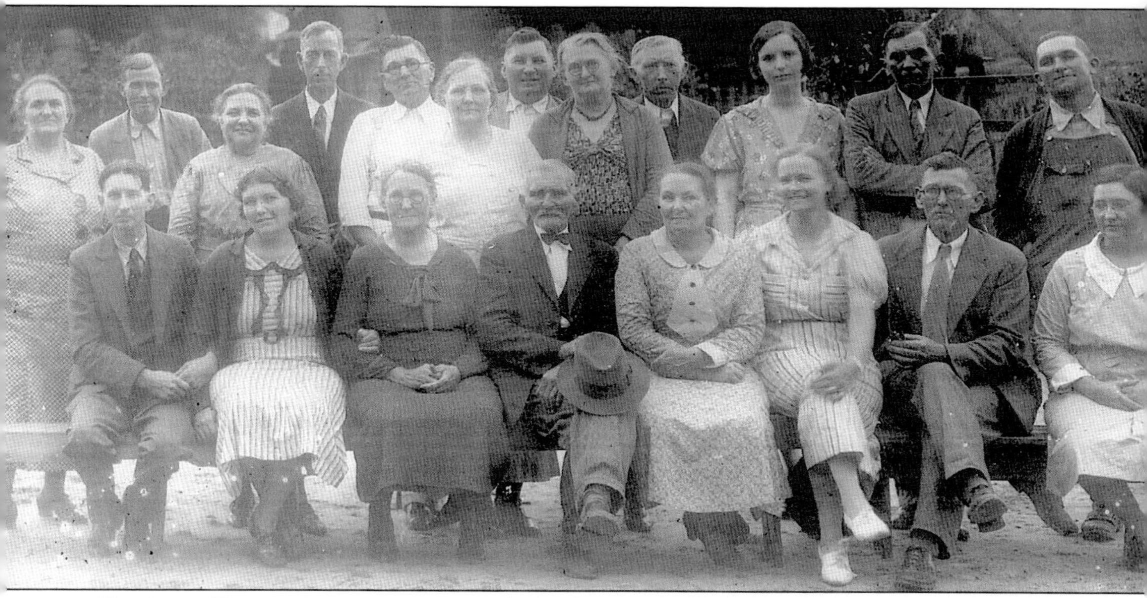

The John Wesley Edwards Family. Shown here are, from left to right, as follows: (front row) Earl Morgan, Pearl Morgan, Laura A. Morgan (step-mother), John Wesley Edwards (father), Lillie Arnsdorff, Susie Edwards, Brooks Edwards, and Helen Edwards; (back row) Fannie Wilson, Perry Wilson, Etta Nease, Alton Nease, Pierce Edward, Dessie Edwards, Christopher Edwards, Ora Edwards, Johnnie Arnsdorff, Winifred Edwards, Billy Edwards, and Marshall Edwards.

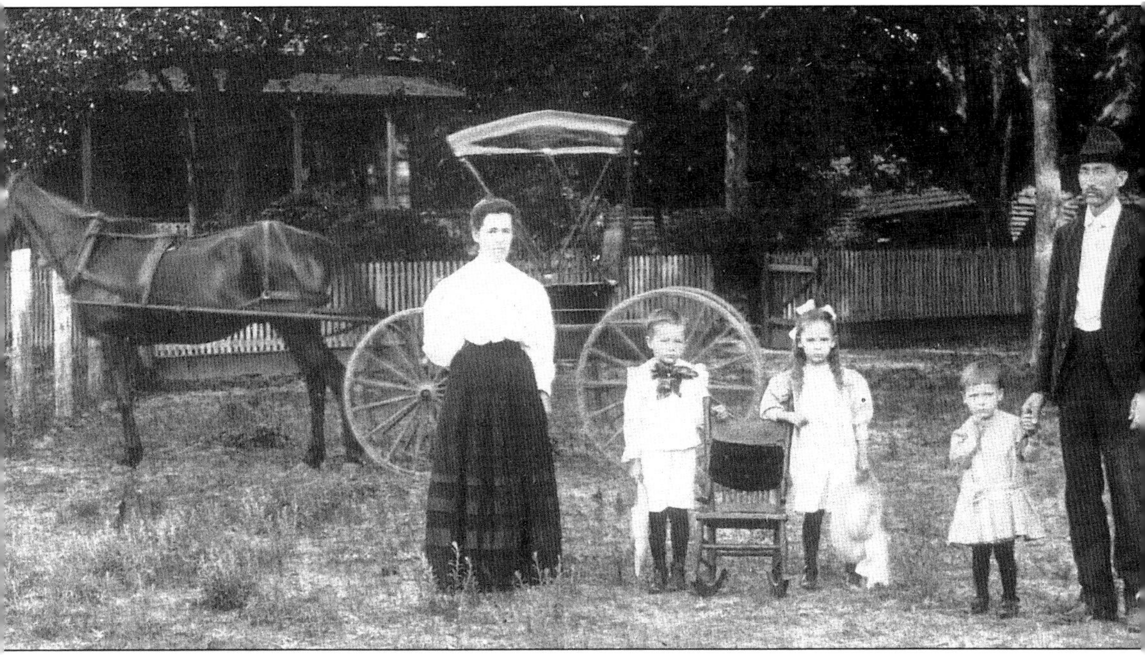

THE BENJAMIN LESTER MORGAN FAMILY. From left to right are Mary Catherine (Mamie) Hodges Morgan, Glenn W. Morgan, Lila Morgan Sykes, Lester H. Morgan, and Benjamin Lester Morgan.

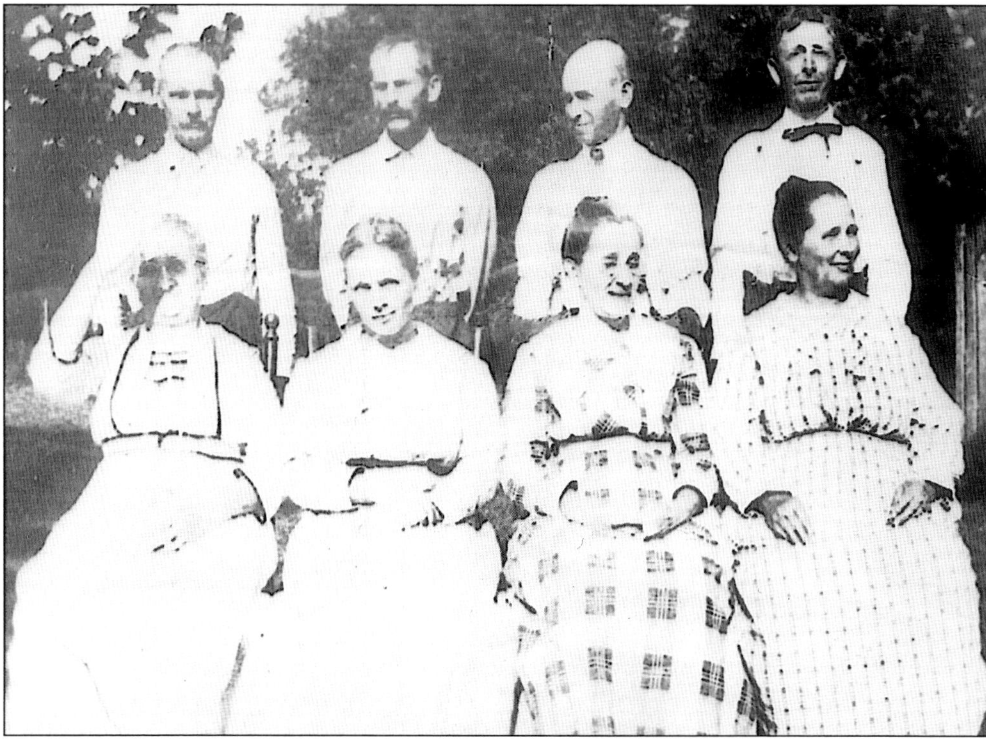

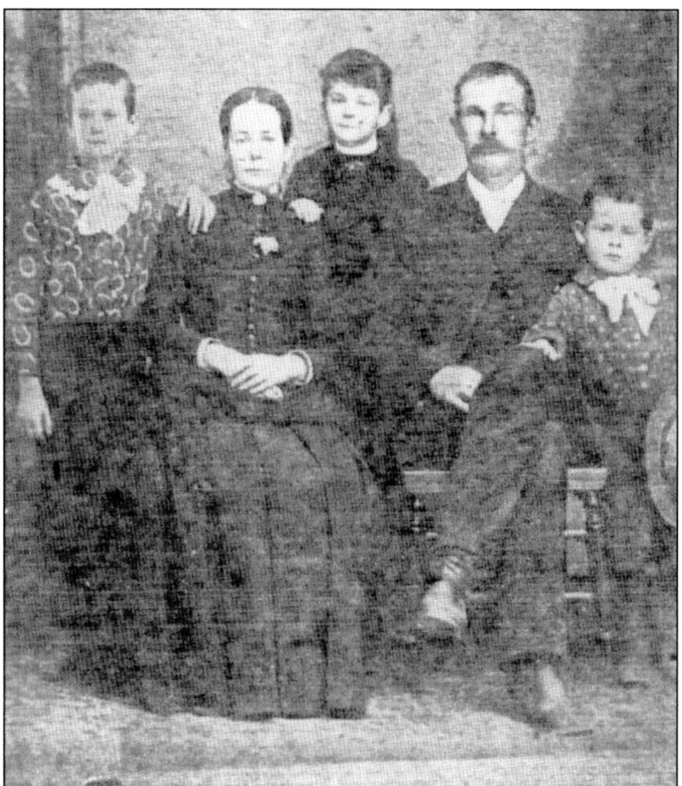

THE CHILDREN AND SPOUSES OF JOHN BUNYAN KIEFFER AND ISABEL ZETTLER KIEFFER. Shown above, from left to right, are (front row) Katie Kieffer Rahn, Gussie Arnsdorff Kieffer, Florence Kieffer Dasher, and Anna Kieffer Shearouse; (back row) Orville A. Rahn, Robert (Bobby) Kieffer, Robert (Bob) Dasher, and Barton K. Shearouse.

THE CORNELIUS GREEN ROUNTREE FAMILY. From left to right are Warren Preston Rountree, Roxie Ann Wolfe Rountree, Alverine Rountree, Cornelius C.G. Rountree, and Roy Rountree.

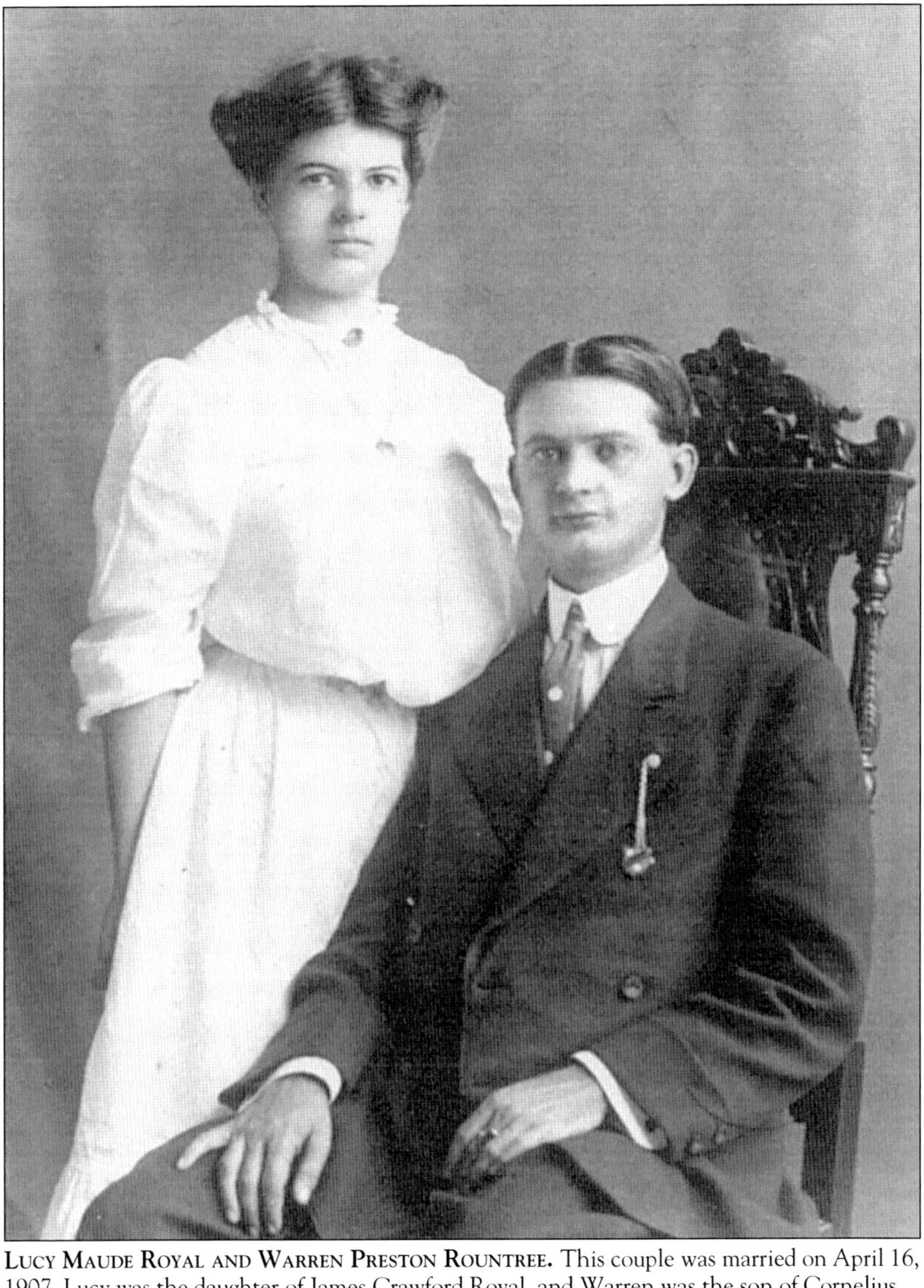

LUCY MAUDE ROYAL AND WARREN PRESTON ROUNTREE. This couple was married on April 16, 1907. Lucy was the daughter of James Crawford Royal, and Warren was the son of Cornelius Green Rountree and Roxie Ann Wolfe.

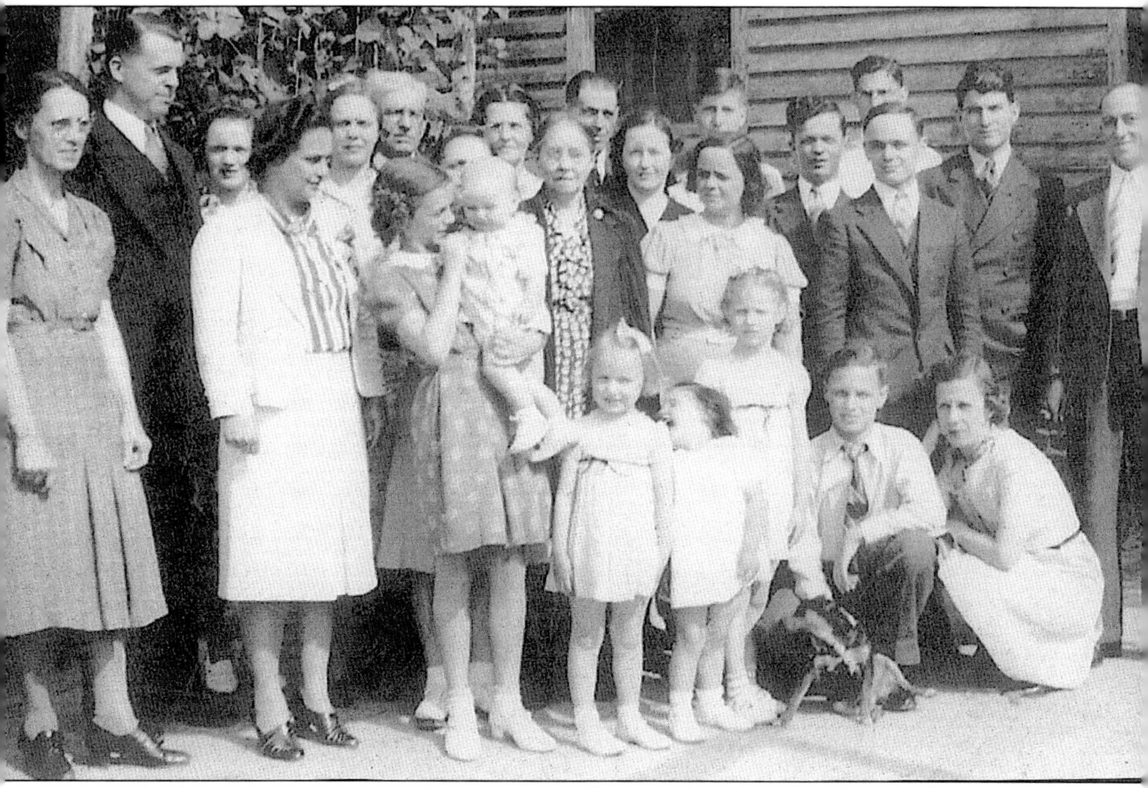

THE WALDHOUR FAMILY. Jacob Radley Waldhour and Frances Adeline Helmly Waldhour are surrounded by their descendants. The children are, from left to right, (front row) Jane Seckinger (holding baby Dianne Baxter), Sara Baxter, Marilyn Waldhour, Jocelyn Baxter, Calvin Seckinger, and Grace Waldhour. Others included in this picture are Effie Seckinger, Ben Waldhour, Evelyn Baxter Seckinger, Claudine (Peggy) Waldhour, Mary Seckinger, Hugh Seckinger, Lrona Seckinger, Ola W. Seckinger, Addie H. Waldhour, Sidney Waldhour, Bessie Z. Waldhour, Madge Seckinger, Sidney (Sid) Waldhour Jr., Muller Seckinger, G.W. Seckinger, Fulton Seckinger, H.D. Seckinger, and Bill Arnsdorff.

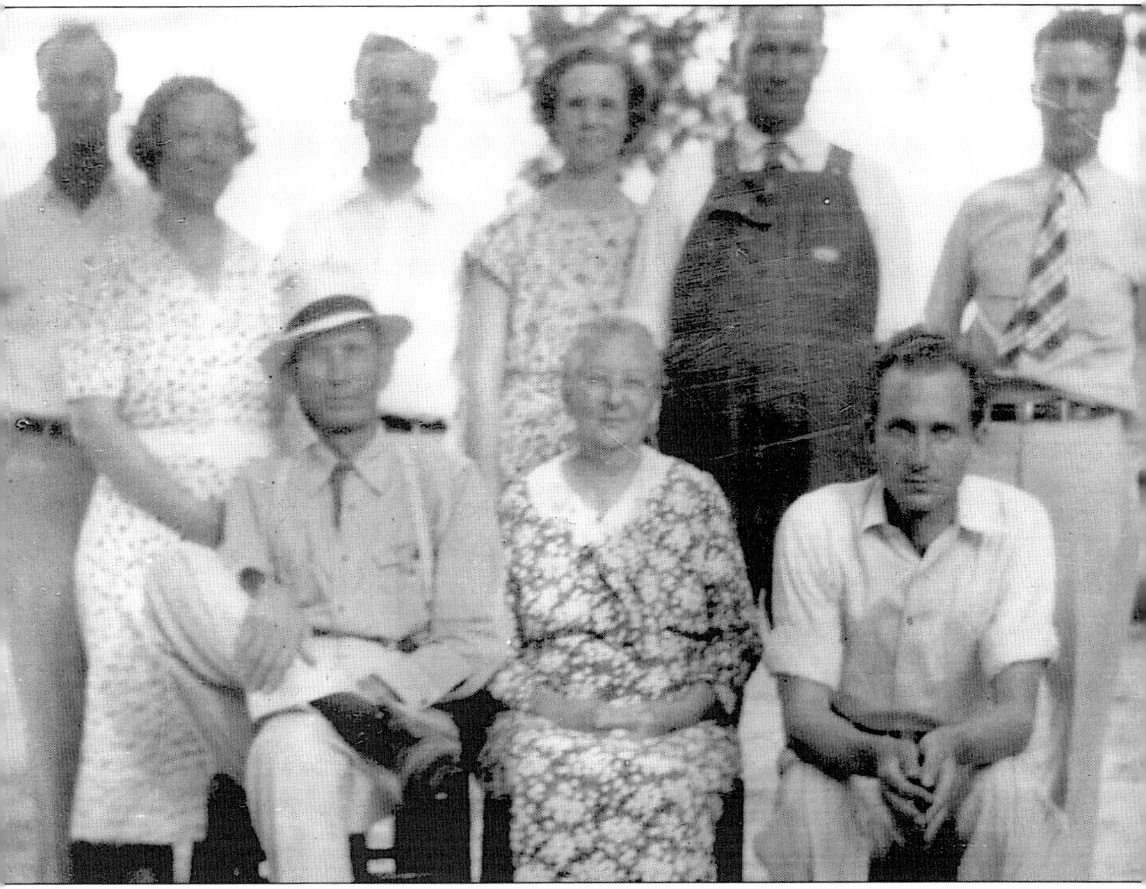

The Melton W. Bragg and Sivility (Scott) Bragg Family. From left to right are as follows: (front row) Melton Bragg, Sivility S. Bragg, and M.W. Bragg; (back row) Cliford L. Bragg, Corrine (Bragg) Hinely, Elmon C. Bragg, Lizie Mae (Bragg) Morgan, Willie J. Bragg, and Johnnie D. Bragg.

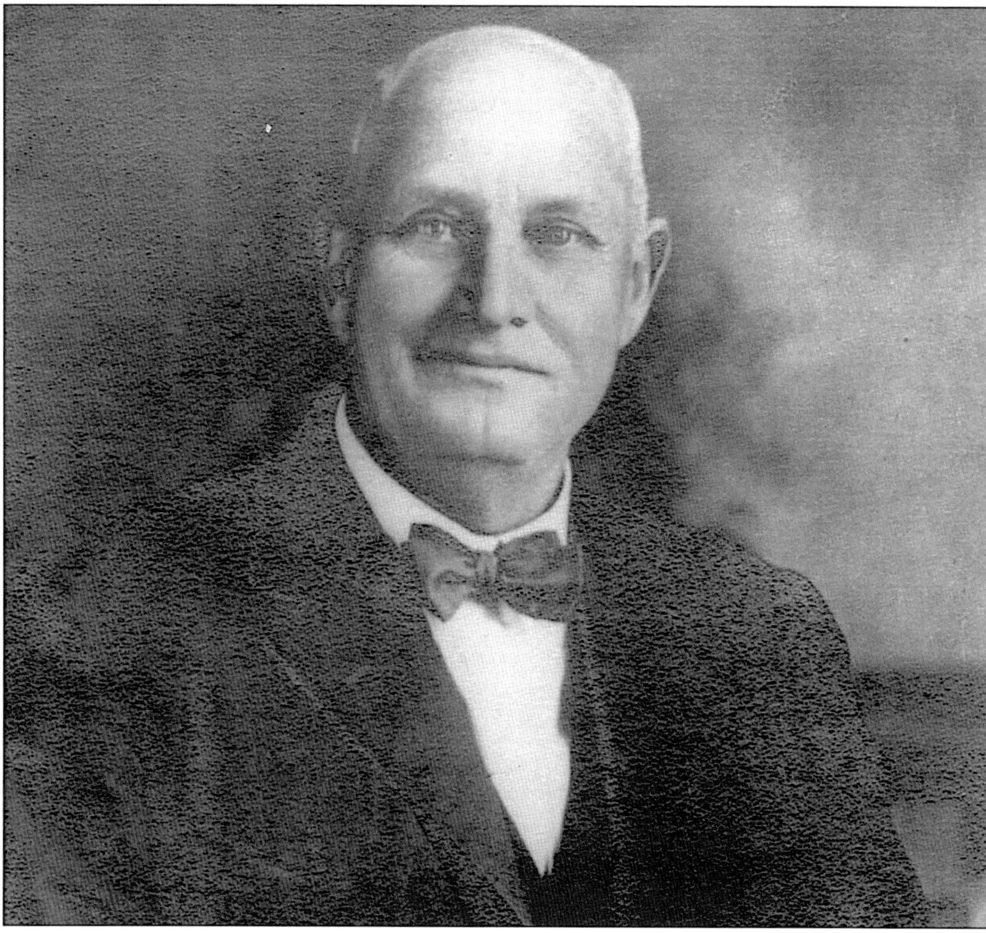

Leonorian Neidlinger. Leonorian Neidlinger was born to Frances Melissa Neidlinger in the county of Effingham on April 4, 1865. His father, Edwin Samuel Shadrack Neidlinger, died in the Civil War on March 12, 1865, less than a month before his birth. After Shadrack's death Leonorian's mother moved back to Effingham County from Savannah during the siege of war. She and her young son Eddie came to live with her parents, Emanuel and Elizabeth (Miller) Shearouse, in the house that still stands on Pleasant Acres Road. Leonorian was born in the front bedroom of this house. When he was four months old his brother Eddie died from the fever epidemic. Leonorian's uncle, Jonathan Shearouse, was among the seven interested citizens that came together in a board meeting to organize a public school system in Effingham County in 1871. We know that he was a learned man, and it is assumed that he took an interest in Leonorian's education. Leonorian became a highly esteemed citizen at a very early age. He taught in the community grammar school of Shiloh located on the Guyton Blanford Road (now Little McCall Road). It was there that he first saw Annessnetia (Annie) Shearouse. He was ten years her senior, but they were married on April 10, 1892 and had seven children: Langdon, Laurie, Preston, Corin, Hazel, Leonorian Jr. (Mosser), and Ellie Lou. Leonorian's mother and his unmarried uncle, Washington, lived with Leonorian and Annie until their deaths. Leonorian was a Georgia senator of one term (1917–1918), a member of the Guyton Masonic Lodge, and the superintendent of the Springfield Methodist Church Sunday School. He was involved with the Pineora Manufacturing Co. and was one of the founders of the first tobacco sales in Effingham. He was also county treasurer for nine years and served as clerk of the county commissioners until his death.

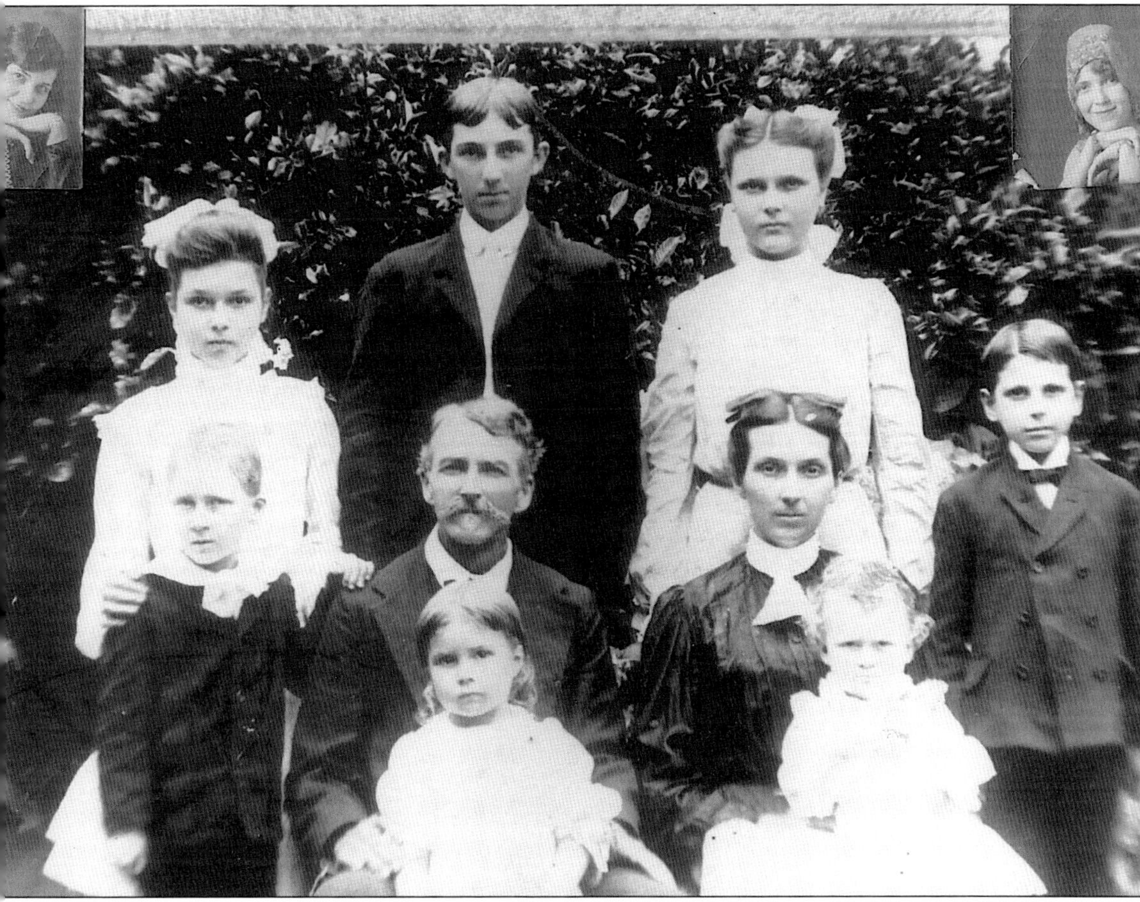

The Neidlinger Family. From left to right are as follows: (front row) Gladys Neidlinger Rowe (Mrs. Arlie Rowe) and baby Carlyle Matthew Neidlinger; (middle row) Elliott Jackson Neidlinger, father Elliott Bascomb Neidlinger, Temperance Zeigler Neidlinger, and Wardlaw Neidlinger; (back row) Florrie Neidlinger, Romie Neidlinger, and Annie Neidlinger Joudon (Mrs. Charles Joudon). Inset at top left is Evelyn Neidlinger Cone (Mrs. W. Cone), at top right is Lillian Neidlinger Beale (Mrs. Edward Beale).

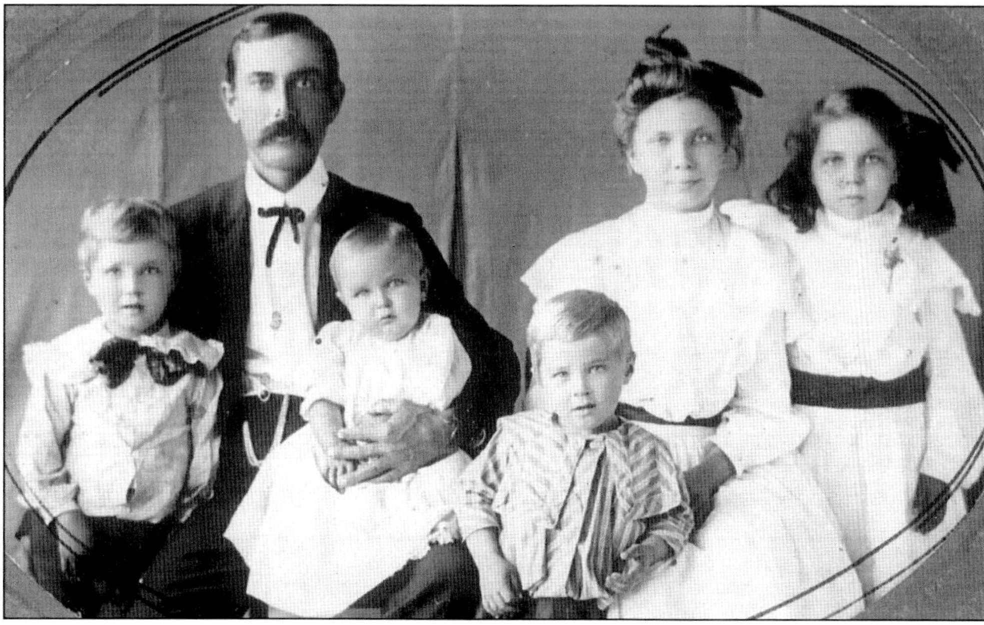

The Ulrich Jerome Neidlinger Family. Ulrich Jerome Neidlinger is shown here with his five children: Mellie Lee, Charles Virgil, Ulrich Madison, Bessie (Moise), and Sarah (Porter).

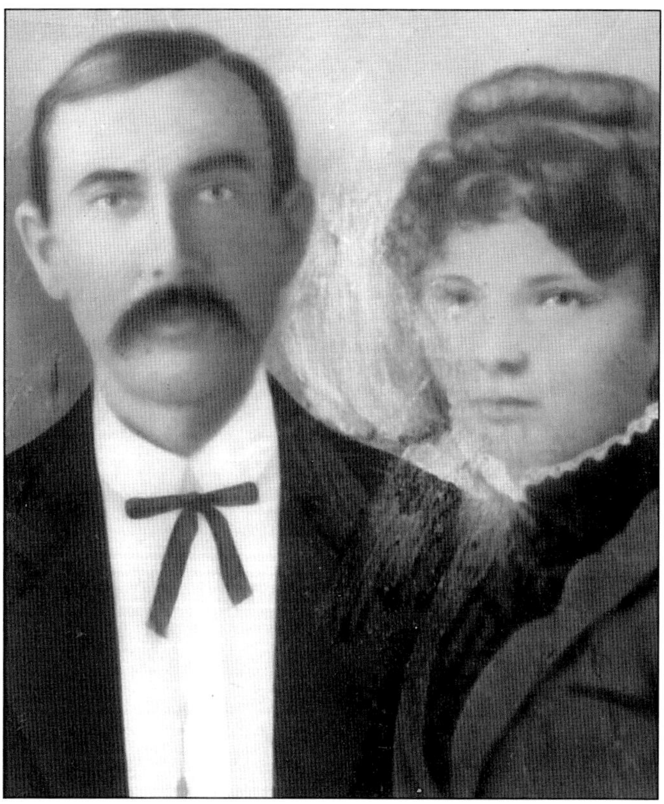

Ulrich Jerome and Laura Ann (Rahn) Neidlinger.

John Wilkins and His Wife, Mary Catherine Gnann. Born on March 26, 1808, John Wilkins married Mary Catherine Gnann (b. June 5, 1816) on September 16, 1839, and the couple had 11 children. It is not known exactly when John Wilkins arrived in Effingham, but the 1860 census described him as a farmer. In 1858, he bought a 600-acre farm located northwest of Guyton on the Ogeechee River. After the Civil War John moved to Savannah, where he opened a shop and manufactured furniture at a location between Abercorn and Lincoln Streets. His works are late expressions of the early 19th-century Federal style, and a few pieces are on display at the museum at Ebenezer. John Wilkins died on December 18, 1886; his wife died on October 2, 1905.

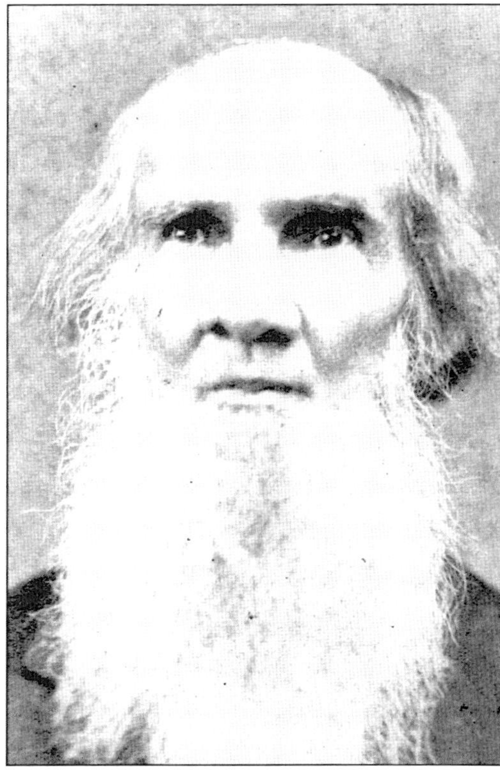

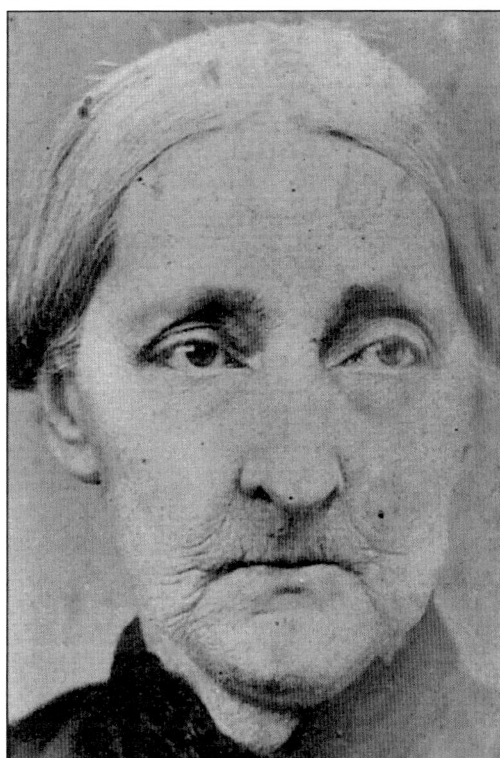

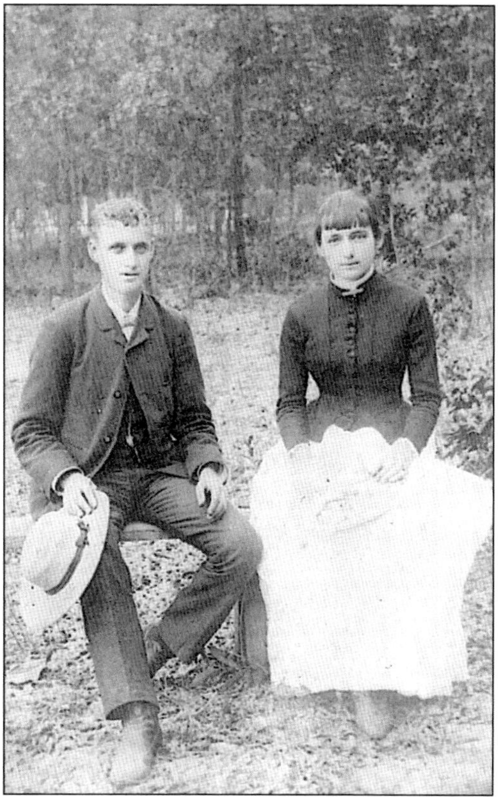

Clifton Etheridge Kessler and Arabella Salina Nease Kessler. The two are pictured here shortly after their marriage on August 22, 1888.

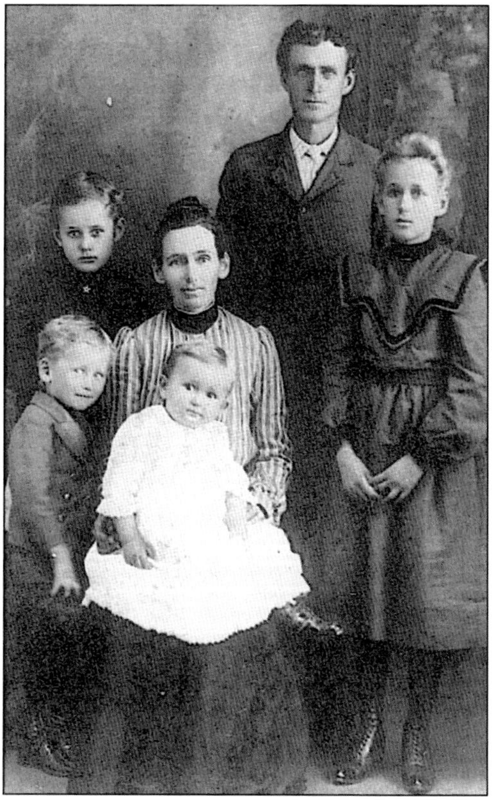

The Kessler Family. From left to right are (front row) Herbert Walter Kessler and Wiley Branch Kessler; (back) Clark Luellon, Arabella Salina Nease Kessler, Clifton Etheridge Kessler, and Gertie Estell.

FRANCES ADELINE HELMLY WALDHOUR AND JACOB RADLEY WALDHOUR.

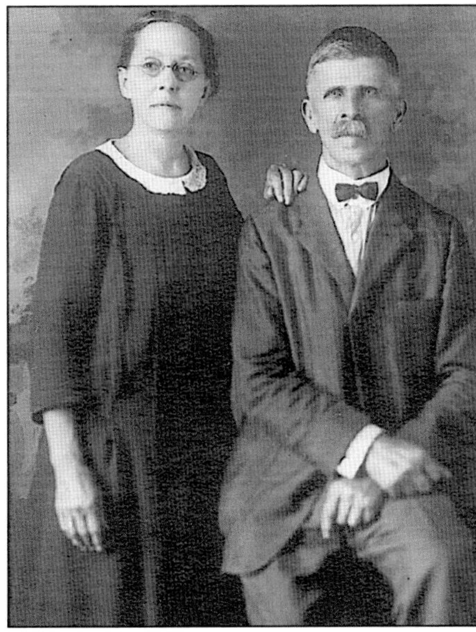

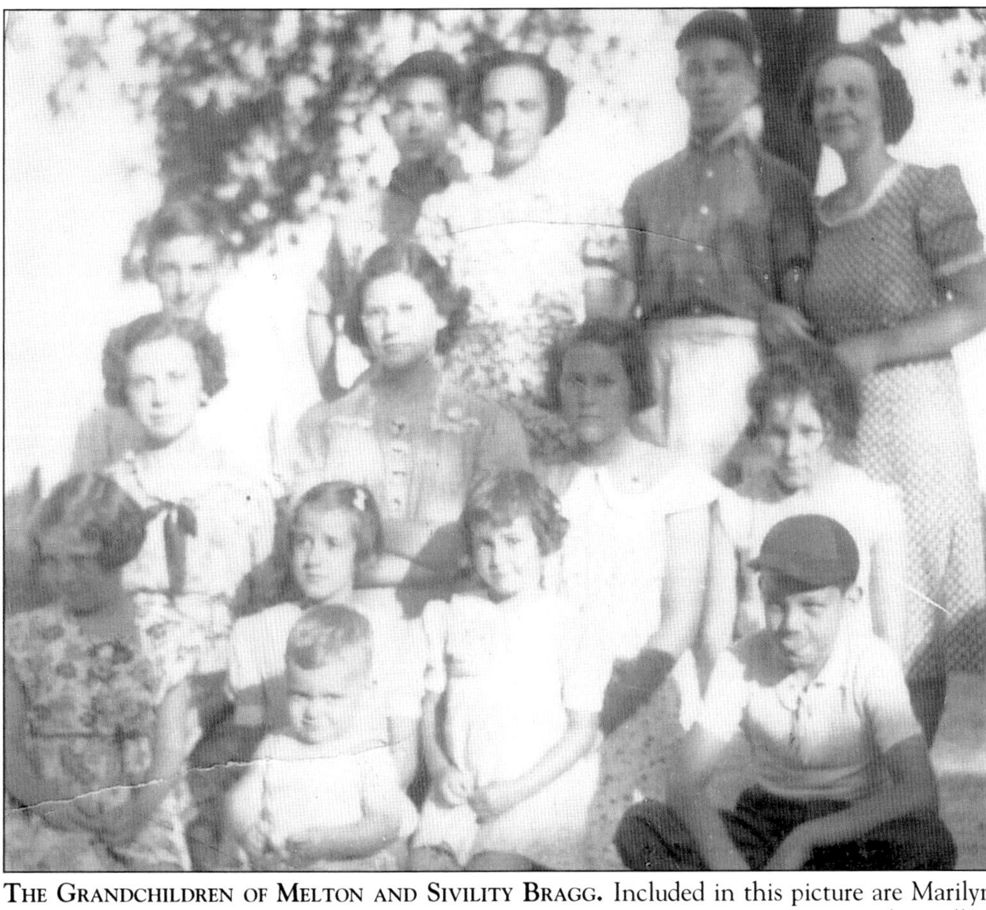

THE GRANDCHILDREN OF MELTON AND SIVILITY BRAGG. Included in this picture are Marilyn (Bragg) Odom, Ree Lee Bragg Exley, Glenda Ree Bragg Bailey, Margaret Bragg Doyle, Wilbur Bragg, Cauley Bragg, Madina Hinely Edenfield, Lester Bragg, and Margarite Hinely Dutton.

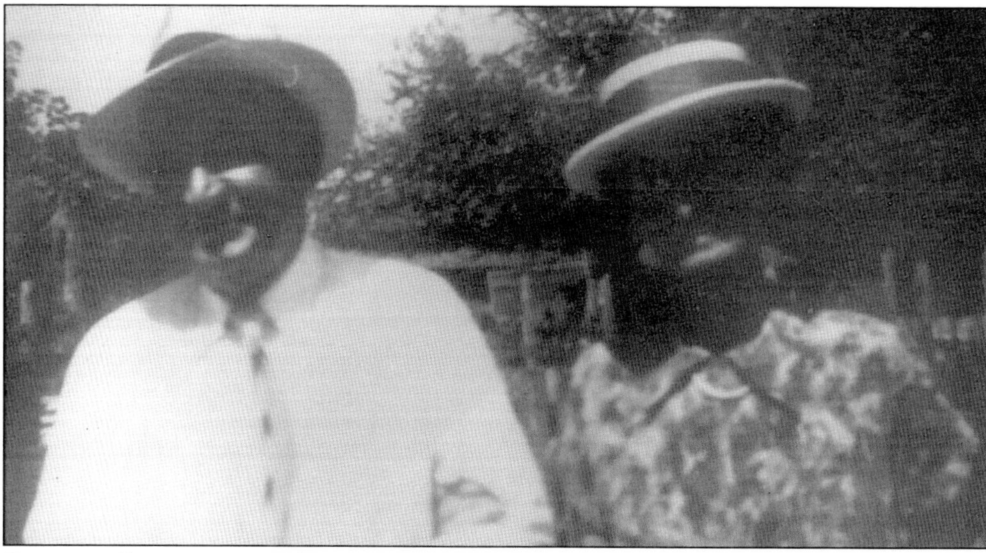

Carswell Shearouse and Camilla Zipperer Shearouse. The couple are dressed to attend a campmeeting at the Springfield Campground in the early 1900s.

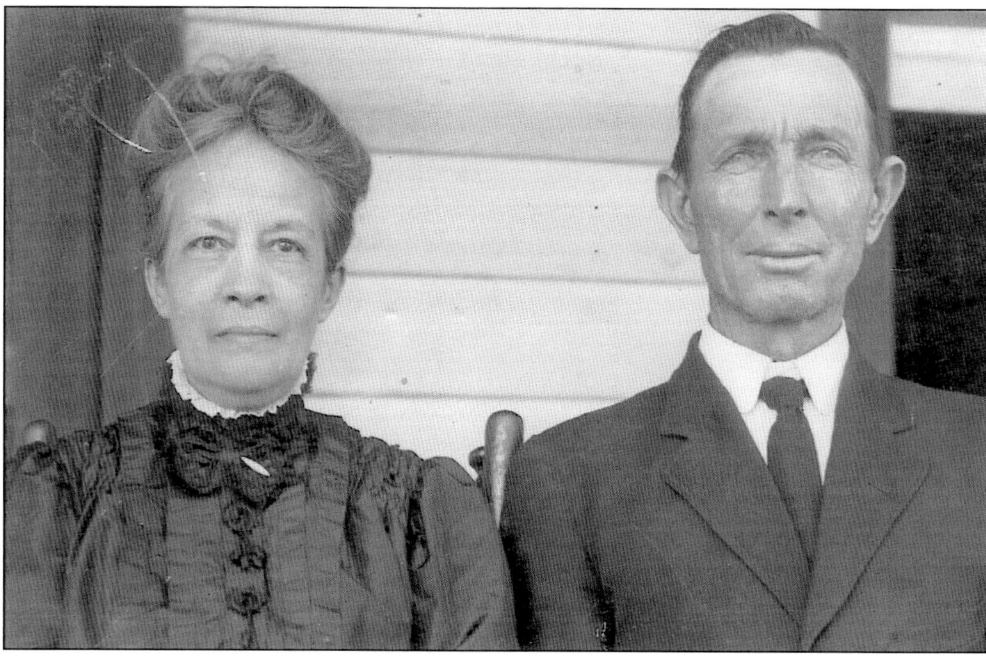

Reverend Thadeus Nease (1852–1935) and Emma Shearouse Nease (1851–1942). Reverend Nease served in the active ministry of the Methodist Church for 50 years, and he began his ministry as a circuit rider traveling on horseback. The couple parented three children who died at birth; son "Pate," who died as a young man; Ester (Mrs. W.W.) Bruner; Alma (Mrs. R.J.) Bird; Rev. Corley Nease; and Lily (Mrs. L.B.) Ackerman. Rev. Thadeus Nease's gravestone reads as follows: "Servant of God 'Well done'/Rest from thy loved employ/The battle fought, The victory won/Enter thy Master's joy."

LOTTIE MAY (SMITH) ALLEN AND JEFFERY ARTHUR ALLEN. The two were married in 1906.

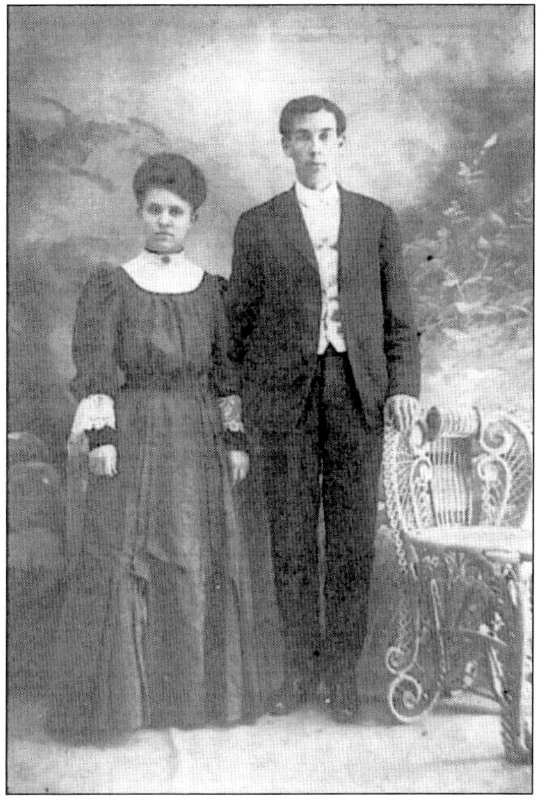

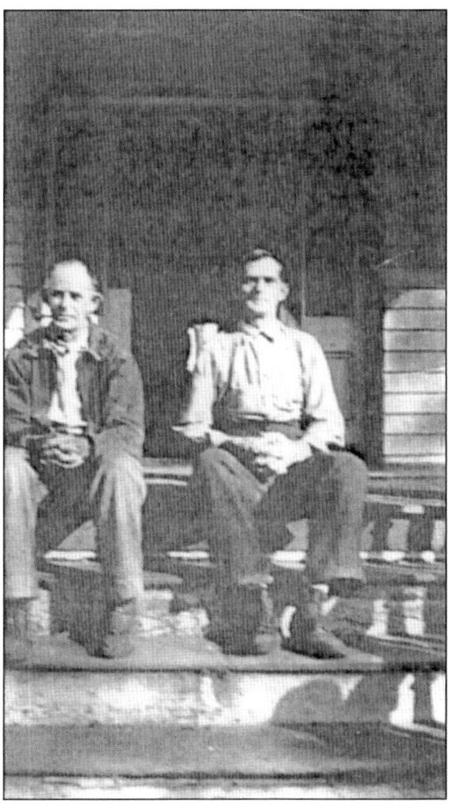

MARTIN LANIER SNOOKS AND CHARLES DAVID SNOOKS IN CLYO, GEORGIA, 1931.

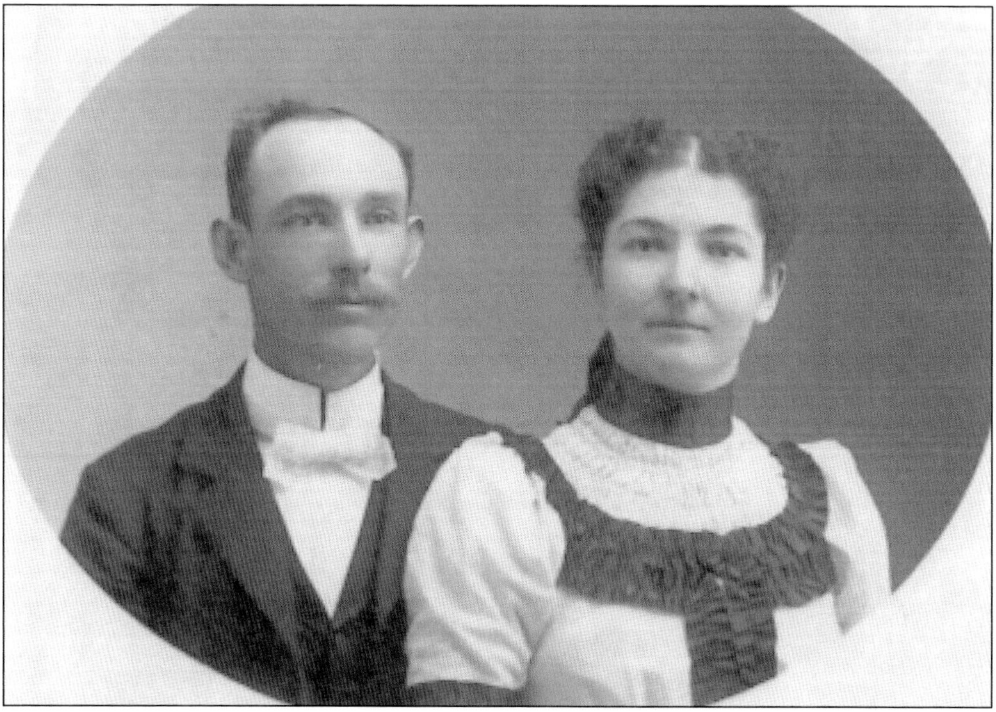

EFFINGHAM COUNTY EDUCATOR ALVIN OSGOOD GNANN AND HIS WIFE, LENA (EXLEY) GNANN. Alvin was born on December 12, 1866 and died on May 15, 1973.

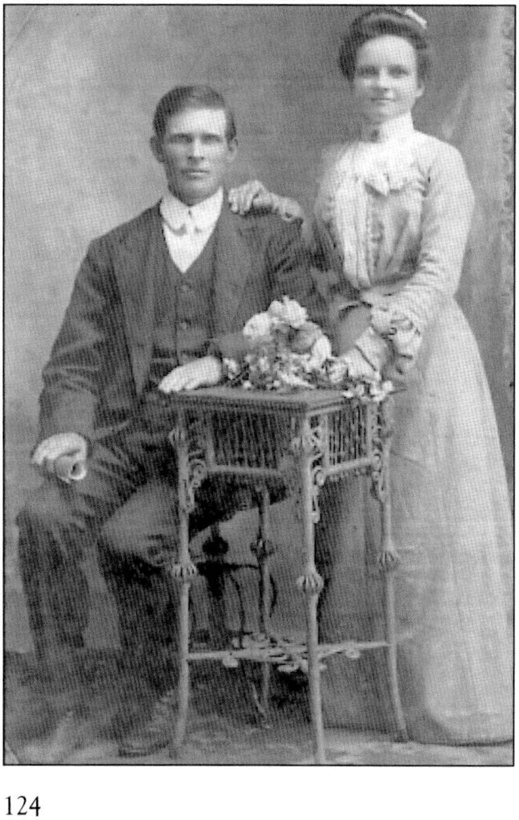

MR. AND MRS. GARRICK GNANN.

THE SECKINGER FAMILY. Charles Marion Seckinger (1855–1937) married Rebecca Exley Seckinger (1852–1931). The children, from left to right, are Essie (1890–1944), Angus (1888–1961), and Rosa (1885–1893).

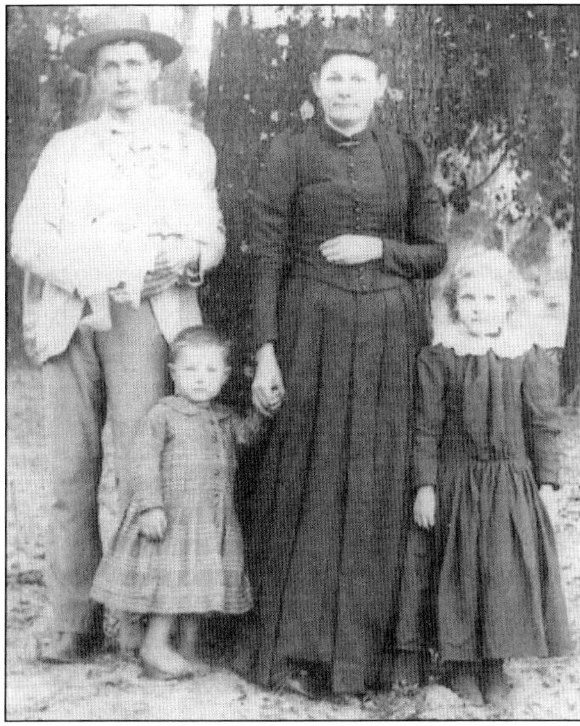

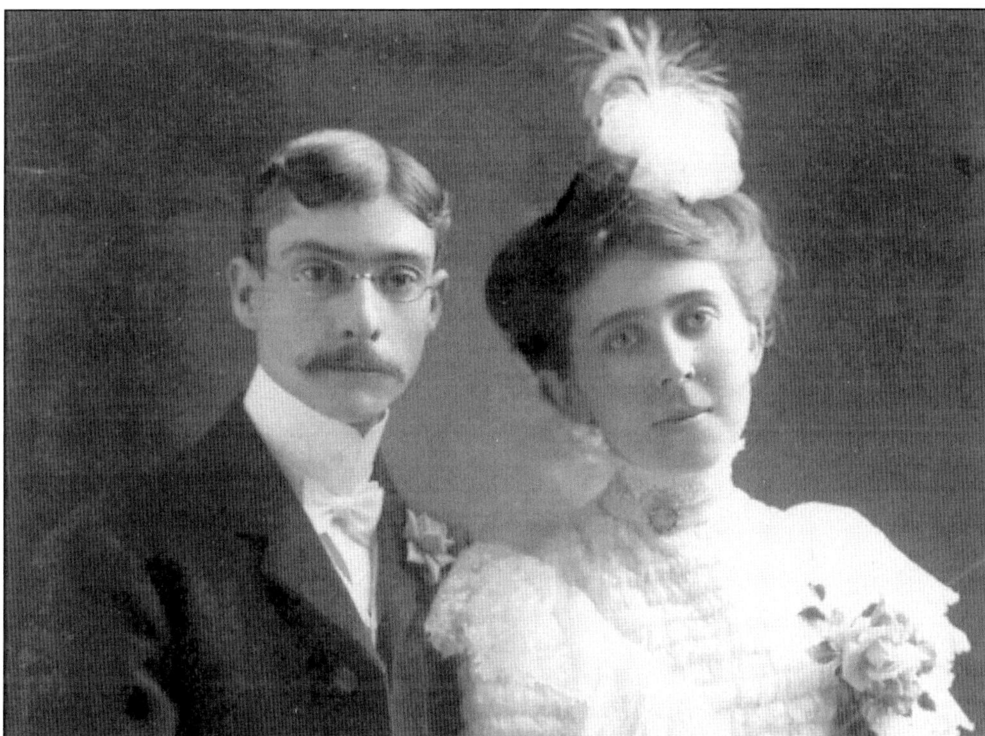

WILLIAM GEORGE GNANN AND PEARL HAVILLA (RAHN) GNANN ON THEIR WEDDING DAY, FEBRUARY 25, 1903. Pearl was the author of *Georgia Salzburger and Allied Families*.

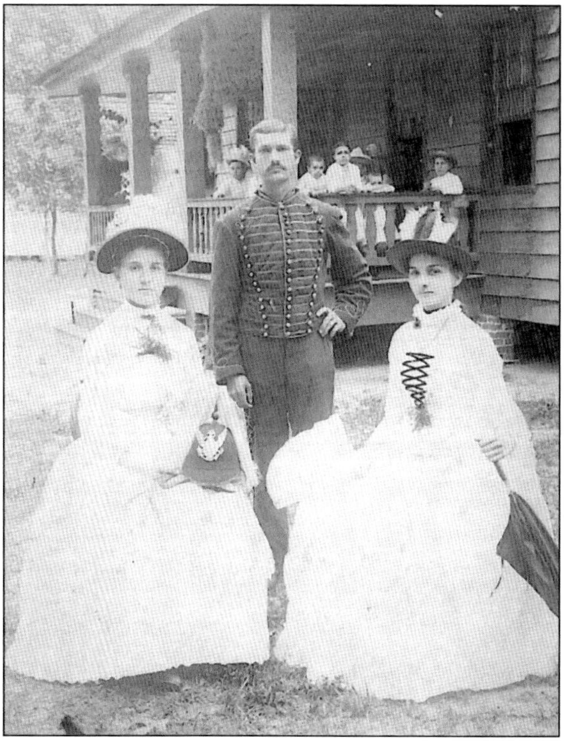

An Effingham Hussars Uniform. Shown here are Ida Hinely, Alfred Augustus Exley (in uniform), and Minnie Zittrouer.

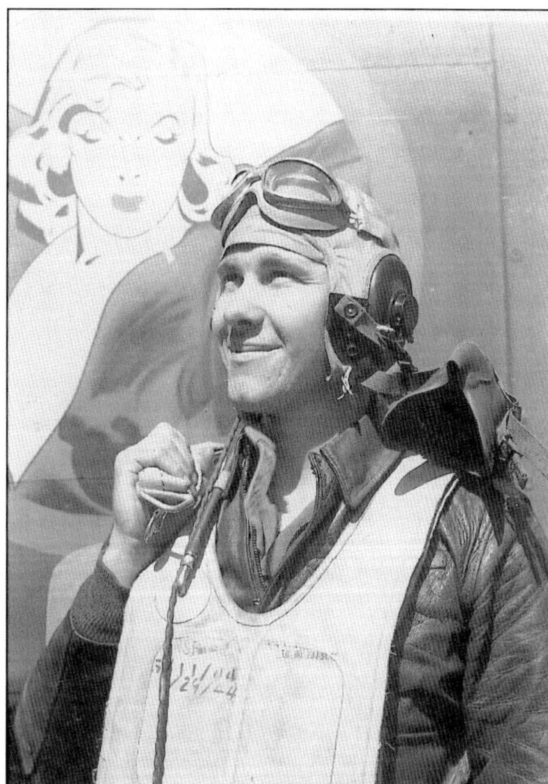

World War II Veteran Edwin Reiser Exley.

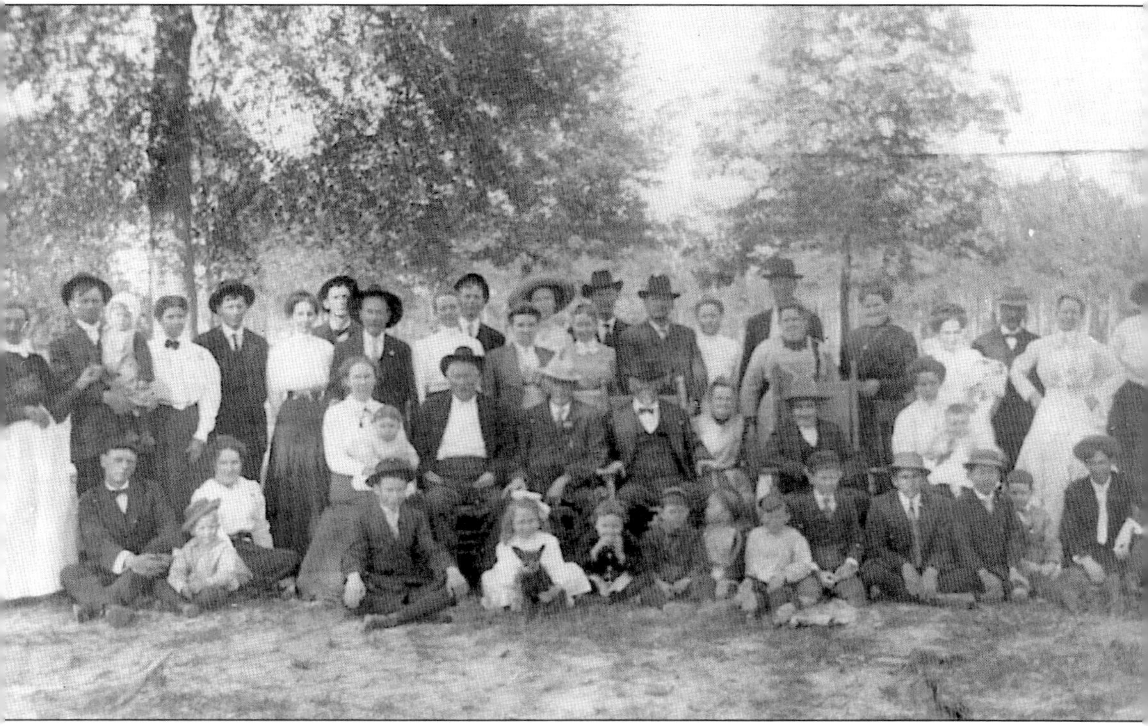

A Metzger Family Reunion. Shown here are the following, from left to right: (seated on ground) Walter Metzger, Tim Metzger (child), Ethel (wife of Walter Metzger), Curry Mingledorff, Inez Mingledorff, Ruth Jaudon, Jimmie (J.W.) Exley, Marion Exley, George Metzger, Perry Mingledorff, Marshall Edwards, Guy Exley, Deweese Bryant, and Elder Bryant (Deweese's father); (middle row) Margaret Ethel Metzger Exley (Aunt Maggie), Miller Exley (child in arms), Isadore Bartow Metzger (Dorie), Robert "Bob" Metzger Groover, William Washington Metzger, "Tampie" Snooks (Dasher), Lou Gnann (Louis), and an unidentified woman holding a baby; (back row) Sarah Reiser (Uncle Billy Reiser's sister), Henry Seckinger, Claud Seckinger (holding baby), Janie Metzger Seckinger, Caleb Metzger, Dozie Metzger (sister to Caleb), Nick Exley (back), Eddie Mingledorff (big hat), Nelia Metzger Mingledorff, Emmett Mingledorff (oldest son of Eddie and Nelia), Miss Florrie Spann, Maude Green Mingledorff (wife of Emmett Mingledorff), Alethia Metzger "Aunt Leach" Mallory, John Mallory, Ben Exley (man behind with hat), Ella Metzger Exley, Mr. Alec Metzger, Nollie Mae Snooks Metzger (in front), Laura Metzger Jaudon, Georgia Mingledorff Bryant, W.C. Reiser, Mary Susannah Metzger Reiser (Aunt Meddie), and Myrtice Snooks (Bryant).

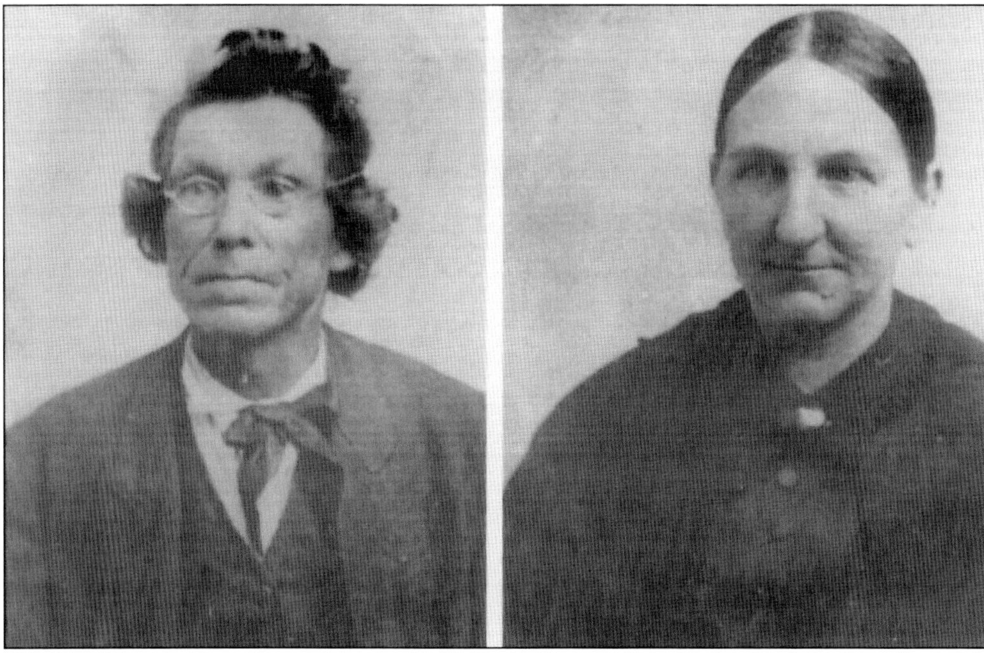

CHRISTOPHER FREDERICK AND CHARLOTTE C. RAHN REISER. Christopher (1813–1884) and Charlotte (1821–1899) was married on November 28, 1838 and had 17 children.

THE DESCENDANTS OF CHRISTOPHER FREDERICK AND CHARLOTTE RAHN REISER. 1] Hannah Caroline married Elbert Weitman. 2] Sarah Ann never married. 3] Frances Florence married John Helmly. 4] Susan Eveline married Allen Kieffer. 5] Margaret Winifred married Luther Groover. 6] Josephine Charlotte married Horace Everette. 7] Mary Felisha married Benjamin Metzger. 8] Jane Elizabeth married Louie Morgan. 9] Georgia Anna married John Wesley Edwards. 10] Virgil Herbert married Ella Gnann. 11] Adaline Althea married John Hinely. 12] John Walter married Mary Eliza Gnann originally. He later married Mrs. A. Mallory. 13] Matilda Victoria married John B. Gnann originally. She later married William C. Rahn. 14] William Christopher married Mary Metzger. 15] Bartow Bee never married. 16] Alice Naomi married Charles Gnann. 17] Ella Vanaesse never married.